IN A FEW HANDS

Monopoly Power in America

ESTES KEFAUVER

With the Assistance of Irene Till

PENGUIN BOOKS

BALTIMORE · MARYLAND

THIS EDITION PRINTED 1965
BY
PENGUIN BOOKS INC.
3300 CLIPPER MILL ROAD
BALTIMORE, MARYLAND 21211
BY ARRANGEMENT WITH PANTHEON BOOKS,
A DIVISION OF RANDOM HOUSE, INC.

PREFACE

*

About a year before his death, Senator Kefauver became deeply concerned with reaching a wider public on the problems of industrial concentration and monopoly. A vast amount of data had been presented in the administered price hearings of the Senate Subcommittee on Antitrust and Monopoly, over which he had presided as chairman from 1957 to 1963. But, unfortunately, public hearings often attain the status of "top-secret" documents by going unread, and the sheer bulk of the Subcommittee's twenty-nine volumes of hearings intimidated even the initiated.

During the course of the hearings on steel, automobiles, bread, and drugs, there was widespread coverage by the trade journals for these industries. Except for the drug hearings, however, the investigations were largely ignored by the news services and the general press.

In academic circles the Subcommittee's hearings and industry reports fared better. Considerable interest was aroused in the organization and pricing practices of the industries examined. The hearings on alternative public policies brought into striking contrast the views of many of the country's leading experts in the field. The result was to spark in our colleges and universities a fresh interest in and concern for problems of industrial concentration and monopoly.

But this was not enough. Senator Kefauver was particularly anxious to acquaint the general public with the fundamental changes occurring in our industrial system and the threat these pose to maintenance of a competitive order. By nature and training a Populist in his approach to these problems, he believed that an informed and aroused public opinion could achieve constructive results. He also believed that time was running out—that unless the problems were faced up to soon, the industrial landscape would be fundamentally altered and it would be too late.

At the time of his death in August 1963, a first draft of the book had been largely completed. A number of additions and minor changes had been indicated by the Senator, and these were in process of inclusion at the time of his death. The editor, who worked with him in the preparation and conduct of the administered price hearings, has sought faithfully to carry out his views in the preparation of the final draft.

Though a very complex human being, Estes Kefauver was also a man of great simplicity and human warmth. He was well aware that his road in the Congress, in the House and later in the Senate, would have been smoother had he let many economic issues go unraised. Often he appeared reluctant to be a dissident voice, but an inexorable conscience and an unremitting devotion to the public welfare could not be stilled. Some of his colleagues privately referred to him as "the conscience of the Senate," certainly a thankless role but a more influential one than is commonly supposed. The void created by his death has not been filled, and cannot easily be filled. For Estes Kefauver had unique gifts— combining a critical intelligence, a capacity for stripping down complex economic issues to their bare skeletal outlines, and a single-minded dedication to the public welfare. It was this combination which for decades made him a brilliant figure in public life and one of the country's most effective public servants.

Industrial inquiry—particularly when it is addressed to the country's largest and most respected corporations—is not embarked upon lightly. The political consequences can be searing. The corporate tentacles of the large firm reach out to embrace most, if not all, of the states in the Union. Although a company's central offices may be located in one state, within other states there may be regional offices, local branch plants and sales agencies, numerous wholesale and retail outlets for the sale of the company's products. Newspapers and periodicals and TV and radio stations within the state are often the recipients of cherished advertising contracts involving such products.

Thus the political pressures to cease and desist from a particular investigation can come from a wide variety of sources within the state or Congressional district. Some, perhaps many, carry great weight with an elected official who wishes to continue in office. Often gratuitous advice comes from close friends and associates. They may be speaking on behalf of others or merely expressing their own disinterested concern with activities that appear to jeopardize a promising political career. That Estes Kefauver persisted over the years with his administered price hearings, against this continuous barrage of pressures, gives some measure of the political courage of the man.

There are also real hazards in the device of the public hearing for airing problems of industrial concentration and control. In a sense, the amateur pits his knowledge and wits in open forum against the professional. The corporate executives who appear in defense of their industry's organization and trade practices are often seasoned veterans who have devoted most of their lives to mastering its intricacies. Not only are the technology and distribution arrangements highly complex; there is a web of trade practices which, over the years, has developed into an accepted code of behavior in the industry. All of these details constitute pitfalls for the uninitiated. Ordinarily, the small staff of the investigating committee assigned to the work have little familiarity with the industry under investigation, and must put together the basic economic data in a matter of a few months. Thus the danger is ever present that, somewhere along the line, an error in fact or in interpretation will be made. The presiding chairman is sensitive to the fact that, with a single misstep, he can be made to appear an inexperienced novice in the field; and, if the error is of real consequence, his whole inquiry may be discredited. To proceed under these circumstances takes not only personal hardihood but a deep conviction that the problems are of such public importance that great risks must be taken.

An investigating committee is also composed of members with widely varying views. Particularly where a large corporation is under investigation, it can be expected that some committee members will be present whose purpose is to insure that the corporation's point of view is fully elucidated in the public hearings. As a result, there may be no consistent and coherent line of questioning; a series of interruptions from several fronts often make progress difficult, if not almost impossible. And when, as often happened in the administered price hearings, these are accompanied by conflict and tension, the task of the presiding chairman is not easy.

In this milieu Senator Kefauver proved himself an accomplished master of his trade. As chairman, he exercised the unfailing Southern courtesy that characterized his personal relationships in private as well as in public life. Only at close range could one catch the physical evidences of strain that underlay the outward appearance of cool composure. Long prepared statements were allowed to be read in full at a measured pace; often they consumed an entire morning of the Subcommittee's hearing time, while the audience patiently followed the script from the ample store of copies stacked on the tables. Often this period furnished the Senator with the necessary time for careful study of the material presented by the witness and for working out his line of questioning. Once this was determined upon, there was no turning back. Patiently, methodically, persistently—but always giving the witness an opportunity for as full an answer as he wished—the inquiry went forward. Sometimes the Chairman set forth a variety of formulations of the same question, intermixed with interruptions from various quarters, before he shifted to another point. Referring to this procedure, a Senatorial colleague—long a member of the Antitrust Subcommittee—remarked that as presiding chairman Senator Kefauver combined the gracious manner of a Victorian with the relentlessness of an Apache.

The administered price hearings were often tedious; they were also frequently sparked with drama and excitement. In part, this may have stemmed from the fact that the corporate executives on the stand had become so accustomed to the industrial environment in which they functioned that it was difficult for them to appraise objectively their industry's practices. Thus, at times, there was an undercurrent of feeling that the questions posed were, if not unfair, at least improper. Certainly another factor involved was that the questions asked, though familiar in detail, were framed in an unfamiliar setting. Business executives are accustomed to make responses to problems in terms of the acquisitive urge and corporate strategy. It is a different matter when the particular solutions arrived at are examined in terms of their service to the general welfare and the needs of society. To Estes Kefauver, there was a real purpose to be served by shifting the focus of corporate policy-makers to this front.

ACKNOWLEDGMENTS

This book has been made possible by the efforts of all those on the Subcommittee staff who worked on the preparation of the administered price hearings and the subsequent economic reports. The list may be found in the Note on page 240. Appreciation is expressed to Dr. John M. Blair, Chief Economist of the Subcommittee, for his assistance in the conception and planning of the work and for his editorial suggestions and contributions. Thanks must be extended to Dr. Walter S. Measday of the Subcommittee's economic staff, who made substantial contributions to the bakery chapter. They and Dr. E. Wayles Browne, Jr., statistical expert for the Subcommittee, were generous with their time and suggestions in critical scrutiny of the final manuscript.

CONTENTS

CONTENTS

IN A FEW HANDS

Monopoly Power in America

INTRODUCTION

*

Every day in our lives monopoly takes its toll. Stealthily it reaches down into our pockets and takes a part of our earnings. For many, what is left must be spread more thinly over the necessities of life; for others, some of the amenities must be sacrificed. In either event the deed is done so smoothly, so deftly, that we are not even conscious of it. For in these days monopoly is seldom, if ever, a blatant affair; it lies behind the lines, unobtrusive and unseen. Sheer familiarity with the level of prices for a commodity, and the fact that there is no spectacular increase, blunts our senses to the presence of monopoly.

Excessive prices constitute one important consequence of monopoly. They appear to be the inevitable result of an economy wherein private control has superseded the forces of the market. In addition, monopoly permeates the society and affects us in other diverse ways. For all of us are more than consumers, shoppers of commodities, in the market-place.

Those who hold jobs are affected by monopoly. A rigid, high price structure in an industry curtails the volume of sales; some buyers do without or, where it is possible, seek an acceptable substitute from another industry. This means that productive capacity in the monopolized industry lies idle, and workers face periods of layoff and chronic unemployment. Even if capacity is severely controlled, as happens in some industries, a potential source of employment for our constantly expanding work force is lost. Workers are denied opportunity for jobs in the industrial expansion that would have occurred in the industry if competitive conditions existed. In an industrial climate such as that prevailing in the steel industry, where "prices are raised to meet competition," there is not only atrophy on the domestic scene, but the U.S. producers cannot effectively enter the struggle for business in world markets.

Small business is also deeply affected by monopoly. Everyone, at one time or another in his life, has seen economic power throw its weight around. Any small manufacturer can cite, though he seldom dares to, examples of the exercise of economic power by the corporate giants in his own industry. The continued increase in industrial concentration in this country has resulted in a diminishing role for small business; this is given dramatic expression in the rising number of failures and bankruptcies in recent years. Even when they survive, many of the smaller producers are beset with an intense feeling of insecurity, arising in part from the realization that they exist only at the sufferance of their larger competitors. Many small businessmen admit frankly that they could be snuffed out by their bigger rivals at will.

In addition to being consumers and workers, we are also citizens of the community. We have a vital stake in a society which provides, insofar as possible, the good life for all of us. One of the most obvious consequences of monopoly is the emphasis that is placed in such industries on non-price forms of competition. Whether by agreement or an accustomed set of trade practices, firms act as one insofar as prices are concerned. But the competitive urge still exists, and it finds outward expression in practices that are basically antisocial in character. By antisocial I mean practices involving unnecessary costs and economic waste insofar as the public is concerned. To a considerable extent the rise of the discount house is a direct expression of the public's resentment at paying for the superfluous. Indignation over packaging practices, as revealed in the hearings of our Subcommittee, is another manifestation of public displeasure at non-price forms of competition.

Each of us is also a taxpayer. The best protection monopoly can find is government sanction for its practices. Indeed, if its grip is tight on an essential group of products, an important technology, or an indispensable set of services, private monopoly can, with audacity, dip its hand deeply into the public coffers. The very business executives who seize the opportunities monopoly offers to wrest favors from the government are often among the first to attack social measures, such as medical care for the aged, as inflationary. Apparently, to some minds government aid to private monopoly is one thing; government aid to improve the living standards of the deprived segments of our population is quite another.

As members of the body politic, we are also deeply interested in our communities and their advancement. In the days when coal was our major source of fuel, the "company town," with its exploitation of coal miners through company housing, company stores, and the like, was a public scandal. There has been virtually no examination of the consequences of big business upon the life of modern communities; what little has been made suggests that levels of civic welfare are higher in predominantly small-business locales. This is only to be expected, of course, for the large corporation often means absentee ownership. Thus control lies elsewhere than in the local community, and over-all policy-making is more concerned with general industry strategy than with the consequences of actions to particular areas where branch operations occur. Local small business is an integral part of the life of the community; owners expect to spend their lives there; they are interested in its cultural and social advance. Thus the whole level of community life is affected by corporate size and industrial concentration.

The cases that follow are designed to give a glimpse by specific illustration of some of the costs of monopoly. Examples from other industries, similarly characterized by competitive inertia, could easily stand in their place. In each case the strategy of monopoly is to dig in at the most vulnerable spots and gradually to extend its control into other parts of the industrial structure. Only on occasion does the public catch a clear view of the pecuniary profits that are reaped by a few from these ventures. We cannot really measure the larger social costs, in terms of the denial of the good life to many of our citizens.

The illustrations of industrial practices that are discussed in the following pages were not specifically designed to serve the purpose of this book. In each case their selection was the result of a number of factors operating at a particular point in time. The first set of administered price hearings —those on steel in 1957—resulted from the industry's announcement of price increases which were bound to have inflationary effects upon the entire economy. The next group—the automobile hearings in 1958—reflected widespread concern with the costly styling competition that currently dominates the industry. To a considerable extent the bread hearings in 1959 were the consequence of a flood of complaints from small bakers whose numbers were being decimated rapidly.

The drug hearings, though treated first in this book, were the last in the series. The investigation was prolonged, extending from December 1959 almost until the passage of the Kefauver-Harris legislation in October 1962. The need for an examination of prescription drug pricing had long been apparent; widespread complaints of high prices had been made for many years. A real problem was the extraordinary industrial complexity arising out of the multiplicity of products and confusing array of brand and generic names. Indeed, when the investigation was initially announced, a number of experts—both in and outside the industry— expressed grave doubts that a Congressional committee could ever "figger it out."

For whatever success was achieved, the public itself must be thanked. The thousands of letters which inundated the Subcommittee and which came from all over the country provided valuable information and opened up lines of inquiry that had not been contemplated in the Subcommittee's original plan. In addition, the Subcommittee was aided by substantial numbers of experts in the health field who, in letters and telegrams, voiced their concern with abuses that had crept into the manufacture and marketing of drugs. The hearings themselves abound with the testimony of many of these experts who not only manifested great courage in fearlessly expressing their views, but who also proved to be amazingly articulate in expressing themselves in language that laymen could understand. Because of the importance of these hearings and their eventual culmination in corrective legislation, this book begins with an examination of the drug industry.

Chapter 1

*

MONOPOLY AND PRICES

The Case of Drugs

Perhaps no more dramatic illustration of the effect of monopoly on the consumer can be found than in the drug industry. Because of the importance to public health of ethical drugs—those that can be obtained only with a doctor's prescription—the Subcommittee's hearings were limited exclusively to that field. This group includes drugs vital in the treatment and cure of acute diseases as well as in the amelioration of chronic disorders. Thus all of us, young and old, have an abiding interest in the price of drugs. The family with young children inevitably will use antibiotics for the treatment of temporary but potentially serious infections; and apparently one of the inescapable hazards of living longer is a variety of chronic health problems that can be made more tolerable by the regular use of steroids, antihypertensives, and other types of drugs.

The drug industry is particularly susceptible to monopoly control because of its peculiar market structure. As was pointed out often during the hearings, the ultimate consumer—the patient—is captive. The doctor, in writing the prescription, places the order for the merchandise; the consumer foots the bill. Thus the man who orders does not pay, and the man who pays does not order.

This simple fact dictates the present practices of the

ethical drug industry. Clearly, the physician is pivotal in the scheme of things; he is the person who determines whether a drug will or will not be sold. To this end a mighty sales machinery has been set up, deluging the physician with promotional advertising on the superiority of individual companies' products. Much of this work is in the hands of professional advertising agencies; they have become adept in the art of the eye-catching photograph, the neat slogan, the persuasive phrase that snares the customer. To be sure, doctors are highly trained professionals, but they are also human beings. As testament of drug advertisers' belief in this fact, one has only to pick up a medical journal—any periodical designed for the physician's eye—and briefly scan the advertisements.

Officials of the drug companies argued that this flood of advertising to physicians indicates the intensity of competition. More correctly, it indicates the intensity of *non-price* forms of competition. In the various categories of drugs examined by the Subcommittee, prices of the major companies were identical, often to the last decimal. Since many of the newer drugs are accorded monopoly protection under patents, only a small handful of the big companies are engaged in their manufacture and sale. Curiously enough, even where drugs lack patent protection and are marketed by the smaller drug companies, there are frequently two levels of prices quite far apart. On the one hand, there is the high level maintained by the large drug companies for their brand-name products; here again prices are, more often than not, identical. On the other hand, there is the considerably lower level of prices of the smaller companies. Here, almost invariably, there are marked differences in price from one company to another.

Does this fact indicate a difference in the quality of the product? Actually, all companies must maintain the standards of quality and purity established by the United States Pharmacopeia or be subject to action by the Food and Drug Administration. If this sanction is not enough, there is also the fact that most drugs are actually manufactured and sold in bulk form by two or three producers—sometimes only one. All companies, large or small, that market the product buy the drug in bulk form from these sources. Thus identity of the product, both in quality and in purity, is assured by identity of source. There remains for the drug companies the task of tableting and bottling; as numerous experts testified before the Subcommittee, this art is in the public domain. Small companies can and do perform these operations with the same skill, experience, and equipment as the large companies.

But if the products are identical, how can their prices be different? It is an elementary principle in economics that the product selling at a lower price will capture the market; other sellers must reduce their prices to meet the competition if they wish to make sales. In drugs the process works differently, precisely because of the important factor of advertising. Since the prescribing physician is pivotal in the whole structure, he is the one to be persuaded. If he can be made to prescribe by a company's particular brand name, only that company's product can by law be sold to fill the prescription. Thus there ensues an intense struggle among the major companies to out-advertise each other. This is a fight in which the small companies cannot participate; they lack the essential financial sinews that are required for such economic warfare. The success of the major companies in their effort to persuade physicians to prescribe by private brand names cannot be denied; the dual price structure currently in existence is mute evidence of the accomplishment.

This is the reason why such emphasis was placed in the hearings on the importance of physicians' prescribing by generic names rather than by companies' brand names. At least for those drugs without patent monopoly, a physician can usually save his patient a sizable sum by prescribing the common name for the drug. The cause is obvious. The druggist who fills the prescription is then free to use the product of a small drug company which sells at a lower price. If the particular druggist carries only major companies' brand-name products, the patient may try another drugstore to get the lower-priced product sold under generic name. Particularly in large communities this effort will prove successful; even in smaller communities if generic-name prescriptions are frequently presented, druggists will stock what the public calls for.

Price Saving under Generic-Name Prescriptions

A few examples will illustrate the size of the saving for the public by generic-name prescribing. Prednisone and prednisolone, derivatives of cortisone, are widely used in the treatment of arthritis. This ailment is common among the older members of our population; at present it falls within the category of chronic disorders, those that can be ameliorated but not cured. Ordinarily the drug must be taken regularly each day, often at the rate of about three tablets per day. Unlike the treatment for acute diseases, where use of the drug ends with the patient's recovery, the arthritic patient must often take cortical steroids constantly throughout his life.

Indeed, during the Subcommittee's drug hearings, a number of letters were received from elderly citizens suffering from arthritis. Their social security payments, they stated, were in the neighborhood of $60 a month. Their doctor's prescription called for Meticorten or Meticortelone, the largest-selling brand names marketed in the United States. The cost to them was 30 cents for each tablet; taking three a day, their daily outlay for the drug was nearly $1.00. This meant that half of their total monthly income went for the treatment of arthritis. But, as everyone knows, it is impossible to live on $30 a month even under the most meager standards. The result, they said, was that regularly toward the end of each month they were faced with the stark alternative of choosing between food or medical treatment. Their budget could not cover both; they could eat and be physically miserable, or they could buy the drug and go hungry.

Yet these drugs, under their generic names, are available at a fraction of the brand-name price. This situation has been true for years. They were first placed on the market in 1955; by 1957 small companies were actively competing for sales with significant price reductions. Over the years their prices have steadily been falling; but those of the large drug companies, including Schering, the marketer of Meticorten and Meticortelone, have remained at 30 cents per tablet. Since only three companies in the United States manufacture this drug, both the large and small drug companies secure their finished bulk material from the same sources.

In 1961 McKesson & Robbins inaugurated the practice of selling, on a nation-wide basis, ethical drugs under generic names. One of the first drugs selected was prednisone. The company reported to the Subcommittee that their prednisone can be sold profitably to the public at about 3 cents per tablet. Briefly, their situation is as follows: purchasing the finished bulk from the same sources as the large companies, and doing their own tableting and bottling, actual cost to them is less than one cent per tablet. Their price to the retail druggist, in bottles of 1000, is $20.95— roughly, 2 cents a tablet. For exactly the same volume, Schering and the other major drug companies charge the retailer $170.00—more than eight times the price charged by McKesson & Robbins. At the consumer level, the price is $30 as compared with $298.

Obviously, this is a tremendous price disparity by any standard. For the arthritic patient living on $60 a month, generic-name prescribing means an expenditure of around 10 cents a day as against 90 cents, $3 a month as against $30. Instead of spending half of his monthly income on prednisone, the patient can secure the identical drug for one-twentieth of his monthly budget.

In his prepared statement which opened the Subcommittee's hearings on cortical steroids, Francis Brown, president of Schering Corporation, stated:

The best indication that Schering's prices were not excessive and that its products were good is found in the ready acceptance given them by the medical profession. Unlike consumer marketing, Schering cannot expand its markets by lowering prices. Cortisone proved this. After all, we cannot put two bottles of Schering medicine in every medicine chest where only one is needed, or two people in every hospital bed when only one is sick. Marketing medicine is a far cry from marketing soft drinks or automobiles.[1]

Yet Schering was purchasing finished bulk prednisolone from Upjohn and doing its own tableting and bottling of this material, at a cost of around 1½ cents per pill. The Syntex Corporation, a pioneer in the steroid field, was selling bulk prednisone to all comers at a price equivalent to one cent per tablet; and if the tableting and bottling charge was added, the cost of the finished product was 1½ cents per pill.

The president of Schering did not feel that its markup from 1½ cents to 17.9 cents per tablet to the druggist was excessive, nor that its price of 30 cents to the consumer was too high. He explained to the Subcommittee:

Undoubtedly some people find it difficult to pay for needed medication. They will also have difficulty in meeting their rent and food bills as well. It seems to me that this problem must be viewed in its true light—it is a matter of inadequate income rather than excessive prices or even "administered prices," whatever this may mean. It is not limited to aged people. It is just plain inability to pay for the necessities of life, where income has not kept in step with today's cost of living. I suggest that a

---

[1] U. S. Senate, Committee on the Judiciary, Subcommittee on Antitrust and Monopoly, 86th Cong., 1st Sess., *Hearings on Administered Prices,* Part 14, p. 7854. (Referred to hereafter as *Hearings.*)

citizen's advisory committee be created to work with welfare
representatives and your congressional staffs—Senator McNa-
mara's committee comes to mind as well as this subcommittee—
so that businessmen from the so-called basic necessity industries
like food, housing, and drugs, can offer their assistance in re-
solving their social problem. We are doing this for the under-
privileged or underdeveloped countries—why not help our own
underdeveloped people?

Needless to say if I personally could be of any help in this way,
I would be only too happy to do so.[2]

The Subcommittee was particularly interested in the fact
that other major cortical steroid companies—Merck, Upjohn, and Pfizer—were selling prednisone and prednisolone
under brand names at exactly Schering's high price. In a
genuinely competitive situation, would not one of these
companies be tempted to narrow its wide margin to increase
its business? In this connection the following exchange
occurred:

Senator Kefauver: . . . How is it, if you want to be really competitive, you don't lower your price to get more of the business?
You are the originator of prednisolone and you are setting the
price.
Mr. Brown: You mean to get more from a competitor?
Senator Kefauver: I mean to get more business for yourself.
Mr. Brown: Senator, we can't, as I pointed out this morning,
we can't put two sick people in every bed when there is only one
person sick.[3]

When Mr. Brown was asked what Schering would have done
if Merck had reduced its price, he replied, "Senator, in this
industry you don't sell your product if a company of equal
standing has a lower price, so you have to meet their price."
Yet this particular situation never materialized from 1955
to the time of Mr. Brown's appearance before the Sub-

[2] *Hearings,* Part 14, p. 7855.
[3] *Hearings,* Part 14, p. 7888.

committee in December 1959, nor indeed has there been any price change up to the present time. It was then suggested to Mr. Brown that, since Schering was the largest U. S. producer and the dominant seller of prednisone, it was the price leader in this field and set the level of prices:

Mr. Brown: I don't know what you mean by price leader, Senator.

Senator Kefauver: I mean you fix the price and keep the price.

Mr. Brown: We determine our price within our company only.

Senator Kefauver: You were the first company to announce it and the others have followed your price, and you never changed yours.

Mr. Brown: I beg your pardon?

Senator Kefauver: I say you were the first one to announce it, you set your price. The others followed you and you have never changed your price.

Mr. Brown: We originated the product. We priced our product. We announced our price. These prices become generally available to anyone after they have once been announced, and presumably the other people decided to price theirs on the same basis.

Senator Kefauver: With your company doing 89 per cent of the business in prednisone, would you be able to sell at a lower price than another company which is doing only 2 per cent of the business?

Mr. Brown: We wouldn't be able to do any more, I don't think, at a lower price, Senator.[4]

The Subcommittee hearings on the cost-price relationship in cortical steroids created an indignant furor in the drug industry. It was argued that Schering's costs shown for prednisolone covered only the price it paid Upjohn for the finished bulk material, plus tableting and bottling; that they did not take into account Schering's research expenses. But as Dr. Upjohn acknowledged in his testimony, each sale of

[4] *Hearings,* Part 14, p. 7889.

a product—including Upjohn's bulk sales to Schering—bore its proportionate share of the company's total research expenses. Moreover, Schering's research expenses, as reported by it to the Subcommittee, amounted to about 8 cents on every sales dollar, and if this were directly taken into account, the effect on Schering's margin would be negligible. Instead of a ratio of 1½ cents to 18 cents on prices to druggists, it would amount to 1½ cents as against 16½ cents.

The argument that high prices are necessary to carry on research was reiterated time and again throughout the Subcommittee's hearings. The benefits to the public, it was said, more than balanced the high price structure that was shown to exist. Yet an official of a small drug company stated that often these benefits did not reach the public. As an example, he cited the case of dexamethasone, a derivative of prednisone, which is sold under the trade name of Decadron by Merck and Deronil by Schering. This drug has the same physiological activity as prednisone and the same side effects, with only one-seventh of the drug content. A .75 mg. tablet of Decadron or Deronil sells at a similar price to the druggist and the public as does a 5 mg. tablet of Meticorten. In this connection Seymour Blackman, executive secretary of Premo Pharmaceutical Laboratories, told the Subcommittee:

From this, it is obvious that the public does not benefit by the applied research of the pharmaceutical industry. It is also obvious that the selling price for a particular ethical specialty product is not predicated on the cost of the materials but, rather, predicated on what the traffic will bear.

In other words, if we, in the field, introduce a new product that is ten times as effective, and which costs us one-tenth the amount per dose, and if we reduce our selling price to one-tenth of the price for the product already on the market, we have just reduced our market and cut it to one-tenth of its previous volume.

This is not a businesslike way of doing things, when you have a natural monopoly going, now, in a captive market. It can only occur when true competition sets in.[5]

So far as selling costs were concerned, the point was well taken. Schering's selling costs were among the highest of any reported by the major drug companies to the Subcommittee. For every dollar of sales, Schering spent 32½ cents for advertising and promotion. This is, of course, an expense incurred by the company, but it is of a very different order from the costs necessitated to produce the article. Advertising costs of this magnitude tend to be a reflection of the prices charged; they are both a result of monopoly and a causative influence in prolonging monopoly. Thus Schering was in the enviable position of being able to spend lavish sums on promotion because of its high profits, and then to perpetuate these high profits because its heavy promotional campaigns to physicians increased prescriptions of Schering's brand-name products.

This interesting interrelation was noted by Mr. Blackman in his testimony to the Subcommittee:

Spending three-quarters of a billion dollars in advertising, to produce 2½ billion dollars in sales, seems to me to be excessive, especially since the products being propagandized are absolutely necessary and an artificial demand need not be created. It is my personal opinion that at least one-half of the sum spent on advertising and promotion is totally wasted.

Likewise, I feel that the three-quarters of a billion dollars in net profits, before Federal corporate taxes, is excessive by at least 50 per cent.

This brings us to the figure of three-quarters of a billion dollars which the public pays unnecessarily. The trend shows, in the pharmaceutical field, even before the Second World War and especially now for the last ten years, that the industry is spending more and more money, proportionately, on advertising to the physician and, in addition, taking a larger and larger percentage of net profits in a market which is expanding nor-

[5] *Hearings*, Part 14, p. 8217.

mally due to normal population growth and a larger proportion of aged people.

This has made the drug industry Wall Street's "fair-haired boy."[6]

In Mr. Blackman's opinion it arose out of the unique circumstance that "He who orders does not buy; and he who buys does not order."

Now, how can this condition exist when other vital industries, such as food and clothing, must be satisfied with net profits much lower in relation to sales? The basic and only reason for this continuous spiral of heavy advertising and profit taking, in the pharmaceutical industry, is the fact that the consumer, in this field, cannot exercise his normal, economic prerogative of shopping or pricing before he purchases. The normal laws of supply and demand have no application here. The prescription customer can only purchase the brand that the physician prescribes.[7]

Great differences in price between the large and smaller drug companies exist in almost every area of drugs unprotected by patent monopoly. In the case of Penicillin G tablets, for example, the public may pay anywhere from 3½ cents per tablet to as much as 20 cents, depending upon the way the prescription is written. At the present time dextroamphetamine is being widely promoted for the "control of appetite" as well as for "chronic fatigue." If the prescription calls for Dexedrine, the most widely sold of the private brand names, Smith, Kline & French charges the druggist $22.60 for 1000 tablets, and the public must pay almost $40. Many of the smaller companies sell this product under its generic name for around $1 for 1000 tablets and the consumer pays about $2. The same is true of secobarbital, a widely used sedative. Here the principal brand-name supplier is Eli Lilly, selling under the trade name Seconal. For this product Lilly charges the druggist $18.30 for 1000

[6] *Hearings*, Part 14, p. 8205.
[7] *Idem*.

capsules, and the consumer is charged around $30. Yet secobarbital can be purchased in the same amounts by the druggist for $6.50, and the cost to the public would then be in the neighborhood of $10.

Or take the case of reserpine, widely used in the treatment of hypertension. This particular drug is a derivative of Rauwolfia, which, in its untreated root form, has been used for centuries in the Far East for various physical and mental disorders. Reserpine is the generic name for a more purified version of this ancient drug. Largest sales under a private brand are made by CIBA, the Swiss company, using the name Serpasil. CIBA's price to the druggist for 1000 tablets is $39.50; the consumer pays $65.83. Now it is an interesting fact that CIBA and S. B. Penick have been the sole producers of reserpine in the United States; all of the other drug companies selling this product must purchase in finished bulk form from one of them. McKesson & Robbins, which now sells this drug, informed the Subcommittee that its factory cost—the price to it of the finished bulk material plus the costs of tableting and bottling—was 63 cents per 1000 tablets. Its price to the druggists is $2.75; the price to the patient is less than $5.00. Thus the same product can be purchased by the public for as low as $5 or as high as $65. It all depends upon whether the doctor prescribes by generic name or by a highly advertised brand name.

Needless to say, these sizable price differences have not escaped the attention of experienced buyers of drugs. For decades the larger hospitals of the country have purchased under generic rather than trade names. Indeed, the associate director of the New York Hospital informed the Subcommittee that his hospital introduced the formulary system as early as 1816. Under this system, hospitals make their purchases in terms of generic names, and all physicians making use of their facilities signify their willingness to have such drugs employed on their patients even if their prescriptions actually specify trade names. By requiring bids on the basis of generic names, the hospitals insure a competitive struggle for their orders. Large drug companies must vie with their smaller rivals for hospital business, and the bigger manufacturers have learned that if they are not to lose out, they must set prices at the lower level maintained by the small companies. An official of the New York Hospital estimated that, on total annual purchases of $500,000, another $250,000 would be added to the hospital's cost if purchases were made on the basis of trade names.

Other large purchasers include state and local governments, as well as the Veterans Administration and other agencies of the Federal Government. Probably the largest single purchaser in the world is the Defense Medical Supply Center. This agency acts as a unified central purchasing agent for all hospitals and dispensaries operated by each of the armed services; it also purchases on request for the Office of Civil and Defense Mobilization, the U.S. Public Health Service, and, under the military assistance program, for allied nations. For the fiscal year 1961 this agency bought 58.6 million dollars worth of medical supplies, over half of which represented drugs and biologicals.

The prices charged these large buyers indicate what happens when there is active competition in the market. Again, let us take the case of prednisone. It will be recalled that Schering, one of the largest sellers, has from the beginning charged the retail druggist $170 for 1000 tablets. Yet in March 1958 Schering was offering to sell to the Military Medical Supply Agency (the predecessor of the Defense Medical Supply Center) this same quantity for $79.74, and actually lost out to a smaller company, Chase Chemical Company, who secured the bid at a price of around $41.50. By March 1960 competition had become so intense that Schering was offering to sell to MMSA for $17.97 and the winning bidder was down to about $11.79. It is significant that the small company involved, Premo Pharmaceutical Laboratories, was offering prednisone in these quantities to the retail druggist for $31.47 while Schering's commercial price of $170 was 9½ times higher than its MMSA bid of around $18. Since then, of course, prices to large buyers have been reduced still further by competition; at the same time the price of Schering and other major drug companies to retailers has remained fixed at $170.

Among the bidders on prednisone to the military was the Panray Corporation. At the hearings, Myron Pantzer, vice-president, stated that almost 80 per cent of his company's business came from institutional or hospital sources, of which a substantial portion represented the "competitive bidding market." He had bid as low as $20 or less on 1000 tablets of prednisone, and in several cases had been awarded the contracts. When asked if this had been remunerative business, he replied, "We made a profit." When asked to clarify this remark, he said:

We have a plant, sir, that is capable of turning out tremendous quantities of finished tablets, and we like to see our machines rolling at all times, because we like to see people gainfully employed. And the only way to do it is to try to get production on which we can make a fair and reasonable profit, but we make their situation in our picture as part of the whole, not single them out as an individual entity, and this has been an area of reward for us in many instances.[8]

An equally startling comparison exists in the case of reserpine. As mentioned earlier, CIBA's price to the druggist for 1000 tablets is $39.50. Yet CIBA's first reported bid (in February 1956) to the MMSA for this quantity was $2.04, and the company actually lost out to another large drug manufacturer, Eli Lilly, which won with a bid of $1.39. By February 1959 CIBA was fighting competitively and won the contract with a price of 60 cents—98.5 per cent below its price to the retail druggists. But time passed them by; by April 1960 a small company emerged as the victor with a winning price of 51 cents. Thus MMSA was buying 1000 tablets at about the price the druggist pays CIBA for 15 tablets. The situation is the more ironic because all of the

[8] *Hearings,* Part 16, p. 9365.

IN A FEW HANDS

dozen or more bidders were securing their finished bulk
supplies from CIBA itself or Penick, the only manufacturers
in this country. CIBA could profitably sell to other drug
companies at a price which allowed them to bid to MMSA
about 50 cents, inclusive of profit; yet CIBA itself charges
the druggist $39.50, and the public must pay at the rate of
$65.83.

The explanation for this state of affairs offered by T. F.
Davies Haines, president of CIBA Pharmaceutical Products,
Inc., the U.S. subsidiary of the Swiss parent company, was
somewhat different from that of Mr. Pantzer. When asked
about the great disparity between 60 cents and $39.50 for
the same quantity of tablets, he replied:

When we bid 60 cents for bottles of 1000 here, we didn't
anything like recover our out-of-pocket cost, we were poorer when
we got through with this than we were before we started. I am
not talking about overhead, I am talking about the direct labor
and material that went into those pills.

In retrospect, it was perhaps a mistake that we did that.
I only hope for the sake of my stockholders that we got some
benefit out of it, that we got prestige in having our material
used by the armed services, that the doctors who used it in the
military hospitals saw our name on it, and when they go out
and practice in civilian life will remember it so that we get some
institutional advertising out of it. I think in retrospect, perhaps,
it is a mistake. It hasn't come forcefully to my attention until
I prepared myself to come down here, I don't think I would do it
any more.[9]

All of this raised the interesting question of how it could
happen that Panray could enjoy profits on its primarily in
stitutional business when CIBA could not even recover its
direct labor and material costs, without taking into account
its overhead expenses. Mr. Haines steadfastly clung to his
position that CIBA's sales of reserpine to the military were
at a loss and that these losses were offset or "cushioned"

[9] *Hearings,* Part 16, pp. 9430–9431.

by their profits on sales to retail druggists. When asked how a small company without this "cushioning" of retail sales could stay in business, he replied, "I think Mr. Pantzer is doing all right. He said he was."[10]

Patents and Drug Prices

Where a product is protected by a patent monopoly, the situation is, of course, quite different. One of the large drug companies—Smith, Kline & French—has an exclusive license from Rhone Poulenc, the French company which holds the patents, to sell Thorazine and Compazine, potent tranquilizers used primarily in mental hospitals. Since Smith, Kline & French has not sublicensed any other company and permits no foreign imports, competition has been impossible in the United States. The same situation holds for Orinase, the most important of the oral antidiabetic drugs now on the market. In this case Upjohn is the exclusive U.S. licensee of Hoechst, the German firm which originated the drug.

Where a patent monopoly is effective, use of the generic name for price savings on drugs is, of course, futile. Even the large buyers are confronted with a stone wall of resistance to any price reductions on these products; in the absence of competition, there is no incentive for prices to be forced down. Thus, in the case of Thorazine and Compazine, MMSA was able to secure reductions of only 25 to 35 per cent below the prices charged retail druggists. A similar price rigidity has confronted the state and county agencies buying these potent tranquilizers for their mental hospitals. Since these hospitals are supported by the taxpayers, the brunt of these monopoly charges are, of necessity, borne by the public.

Unfortunately, monopoly pricing under patents is widespread in the drug industry. An official of Nationwide Insurance informed the Subcommittee that a study by his company indicated that between one half and two thirds of all prescriptions written in the United States were for brand-name

[10] *Ibid.*, p. 9432.

products protected by patent. Thus, for a substantial proportion of all ethical drugs prescribed, there is little escape from
high prices. The single possibility is that, whenever possible,
the physician prescribe by generic name an older drug that is
not covered by patent. Actually, this escape from high prices
is more feasible than is generally recognized; the difficulty
is that physicians are so deluged with advertising for brand
names of newer modifications of established drugs that most
prescriptions are written in those terms. It was for this
reason that the first draft of the Kefauver-Celler drug bill, as
originally introduced, required compulsory licensing under
patents, after three years, upon payment of a royalty up to
8 per cent of sales in finished form.

Such a requirement was incorporated in the consent decree
entered into by Carter Products on meprobamate, widely sold
in this country under the trade names Miltown and Equanil.
Following the Subcommittee's hearings, a suit was instituted
by the Department of Justice for violation of the antitrust
laws.[11] In November 1962 Carter signed a consent settlement
agreeing to license every qualified pharmaceutical company
that wished to sell the drug.[12] A number of companies immediately applied for licenses, and their entrance into the
market has resulted in lower prices for the drug sold under
its generic name.

The hearings on meprobamate also had the effect of
strengthening the Subcommittee's position with respect to its
cost-price presentations. Carter did not manufacure meprobamate, but was the sole buyer of the finished bulk powder
from several chemical manufacturers. Under their contracts
with Carter, they agreed they would make no sales of bulk
meprobamate to any other company. The cost to Carter of
the finished bulk material for Miltown, plus tableting and
bottling, was calculated by the Subcommittee to be seven-

[11] *U. S.* v. *Carter Products and Amer. Home Products Corp.* U. S. Dist.
Court, So. Dist. of N.Y. Civil Action filed Jan. 27, 1960.
[12] 1962 Trade Cases ¢ 70, 473.

tenths of a cent per tablet. When Henry H. Hoyt, president of Carter, appeared before the Subcommittee, he presented a breakdown of Miltown price and costs per tablet which paralleled those of the Subcommittee. As Mr. Hoyt remarked, his figures were "practically what you have on your table."[13] Carter had licensed only one other company to sell meprobamate tablets in the United States. This was Wyeth Laboratories, subsidiary of American Home Products, marketing the product under the trade name Equanil. Carter's price to American Home for the bulk material was roughly double that of Carter's own purchase price. As a result, the production cost for Equanil, after tableting and bottling, was 1½ cents per tablet as compared with Carter's cost of seven-tenths of a cent for Miltown. When this figure was presented to Alvin G. Brush, chairman of the board of American Home Products, he concurred in its accuracy and informed the Subcommittee, "I think you have done an excellent job on Equanil."[14]

The Special Case of Tetracycline

Another vivid illustration concerns tetracycline, one of the newer broad-spectrum antibiotics. This important development in the treatment of bacterial infections stems from the observations of Sir Alexander Fleming in 1929. The English physician made no attempt to secure a patent on his basic discovery, and thus today the older forms of penicillin are marketed widely, the small companies supplying intense price competition. The situation is quite otherwise with the newer antibiotics produced by slightly different microorganisms found in nature. All of these newer products have been subjected to rigid patent and price control by the major drug companies; their smaller competitors have not been allowed to get into this business. The most important of these

[14] *Ibid.*, p. 9301.
[13] *Hearings*, Part 16, p. 9162.

IN A FEW HANDS

products, both in terms of sales volume and significance to the public health, is tetracycline. The product patent on this antibiotic is held by Pfizer.

Until recently all tetracycline sold in the United States has been manufactured by three firms—Pfizer, the Lederle Division of American Cyanamid, and Bristol. Two other companies—Squibb and Upjohn—have been licensed to sell the product in final packaged form from bulk material purchased from Bristol. All five of these companies sell under private brand names—Tetracyn, Achromycin, Polycycline, Steclin, and Panmycin—and all have sold at substantially identical prices. This situation has existed since 1954 when the drug was first introduced on the market. For years the druggist paid about 30 cents a capsule; the price to the public was 50 cents. Immediately before the Subcommittee's hearings on antibiotics in the fall of 1960, a 15 per cent reduction was made in the price.

In view of the monopoly hold on this product, the large buyers, such as hospitals, were faced with a united front on the price of tetracycline. The Military Medical Supply Agency, spending substantial sums each year in the procurement of this important drug, had particular cause for concern. In the beginning things seemed auspicious enough. The first purchase of tetracycline by MMSA in 1956 was at the rate of 11 cents per capsule—the same price as was charged for Aureomycin, an earlier broad-spectrum antibiotic sold exclusively by American Cyanamid. Apparently this had been a mistake. Within a few months the price was raised to 17 cents a capsule. The price remained impregnable at this level for two years; irrespective of the volume ordered, all five sellers maintained a united front. Suddenly, in June 1959, there was a brief thaw when the price declined to 14 cents per capsule, but two months later the price was again restored to 17 cents. When this occurred, MMSA informed the Subcommittee, it felt "it had no alternative but to cancel the procurement because of the unreasonably high price."[15]

[15] *Hearings*, Part 24, p. 13780.

Admiral William L. Knickerbocker, executive director of the MMSA, informed the Subcommittee of other characteristics in the "peculiar pattern of cost to the Government" in the procurement of tetracycline. On occasion the Agency bunched its orders into a single request for bids on 150,000 bottles; at other times only small quantities were asked for. According to Admiral Knickerbocker, "all price quotations to the Government bore no relation to the quantities ordered."[16]

There was also a remarkable uniformity in price, even when price changes occurred. Admiral Knickerbocker remarked:

On a number of procurements, more than one supplier initially offered the identical low price. Furthermore, even when one supplier was low, others came in at higher but identical prices (i.e., either the specific prices offered were the same, or they became identical when the prompt payment discount was applied).[17]

Plans were instituted to secure bids from outside the United States. Under our law the U. S. Government, irrespective of the existence of a product patent, may import from abroad; the patent holder, if he feels injured, may sue in the Court of Claims for damages. This litigation, however, has its hazards: to show damages, the patent owner must divulge his costs of production. This cost-showing is a routine procedure in Government negotiations for procurement, and is frequently presented by private contractees when the Government questions the fairness of the price. Throughout the MMSA negotiations with the tetracycline manufacturers between 1956 and 1959, the companies had steadfastly refused to supply any information on costs as a justification for the prices they were charging the Government. Thus the move to secure bids from abroad had the added advantage that, if the companies brought suit in the Court of Claims, the procurement agency would have the benefit of some information on costs to determine the reasonableness of price.

Plant inspection is a necessary prerequisite to the sale of

[16] *Idem.*
[17] *Idem.*

antibiotics in this country, and this cost is borne by the company whose plant is inspected. With this formality completed for foreign plants, bids were again called for. Again the U. S. companies bid 17 cents per capsule. The award went to an Italian company whose bid was less than half that of the U. S. companies—about 8 cents per capsule. This was in December 1959. In conformance with regular MMSA policy, this material was checked upon arrival and found wholly satisfactory in terms of quality and purity. Subsequently, additional bids have been called for by the procurement agency, and there have been further declines in prices.

The situation by mid-1961 was particularly interesting. The infusion of real price competition was having its effect upon the American companies. Pfizer had reduced its bid to MMSA from 17 cents to 6 cents a capsule.[18] However, it lost to an Italian firm with a winning bid of less than 5 cents, including the added costs of customs duty, freight, and the like. Again in November 1961, in another bid, Pfizer lost with a bid of 6 cents to a foreign source which offered tetracycline at less than 4 cents a capsule. By July 1962 Pfizer was still bidding 6 cents, but by that time foreign sources had reduced their prices to the neighborhood of 2½ cents, and by 1963 were bidding around 1½ cents per capsule.

Viewed in the aggregate, the savings attained through effective price competition were substantial. Between December 1959 and July 1962, the MMSA imported from abroad 4.8 million dollars worth of tetracycline.[19] Had these supplies been secured from noncompetitive U. S. sources, it would have spent almost double that figure—9 million dollars—for the same quantity.[20] In the meantime, of course, the retail druggist and the general public were paying prices vastly higher. Even with the reductions following the Subcommittee's hearings on drugs, the retailer in 1962 was charged

[18] *Hearings*, Part 24, p. 13793.
[19] House Committee on Government Operations, Military Operations Subcommittee, 87th Cong., 2d Sess., "Defense Procurement of Foreign-Made Drugs," Oct. 1962, p. 5.
[20] *Ibid.*, p. 34.

about 26 cents per capsule and the patient paid about 40 cents.

Does this mean that European companies can produce tetracycline more cheaply than American manufacturers? On this point the Subcommittee secured evidence in the form of cost data subpoenaed from the files of Bristol. In late 1957 when Bristol, along with the other tetracycline manufacturers, was standing adamant on a 17-cent price to MMSA, its costs were about 1⅔ cents per capsule.[21] The fabulous profits that can be reaped from a monopoly grip on an essential drug are indicated in an intra-office memorandum prepared for top Bristol officials. For the single month of December 1956, this memorandum discloses, sales of Bristol's brand of tetracycline were 2 million dollars. The actual cost of manufacture amounted to less than $350,000, about one-sixth of the receipts. A heavy advertising and promotion campaign to physicians was undertaken; on this item the company spent about $400,000, a sum exceeding the actual cost of making the product. Even so, Bristol was able to report a profit on the business, before taxes, of about 1.3 million dollars for that month alone.[22] How many firms can show a pre-tax profit of 1.3 million dollars and an after-tax profit of about half that amount, on sales of 2 million dollars?

Obviously, with its costs for manufacturing tetracycline, Bristol could have bid below the foreign producers and still have made a comfortable profit. Had it wished, it could have done so from the very outset of MMSA's call for bids. Undoubtedly this is equally true of Pfizer and American Cyanamid, companies considerably larger than Bristol and fully experienced in the art of antibiotics manufacture. It is not true, however, of Upjohn and Squibb. Under their licensing agreements, they were permitted to sell but not to manufacture, and they could purchase only from Bristol. Upjohn, for

[21] U. S. Senate, Committee on the Judiciary, Subcommittee on Antitrust and Monopoly, 87th Cong., 1st Sess., *Hearings on S. 1552*, Part 4, p. 2408.
[22] *Ibid.*, p. 2404.

example, in 1958 was buying the bulk powder for around 8 cents a capsule; packaging, royalty, and other costs brought its expenses to around 9 cents a capsule. Squibb was in a similar position. Thus Bristol, with costs of around 1⅔ cents, was making sizable profits on its bulk sales to Squibb and Upjohn. However, in the light of the 30-cent price all three companies were then charging druggists, presumably everyone was satisfied.

A single dark cloud hovered on the horizon. In the summer of 1958 the Federal Trade Commission issued a complaint charging the five companies with unfair methods of competition under the Federal Trade Commission Act. Five years later, in 1963, after building up one of the largest records of public hearings in FTC history, the Commission reached a decision. It found that the five tetracycline companies had, since 1954, been unlawfully fixing prices under a patent that had been obtained by misrepresentation in the U. S. Patent Office.

In consequence of this decision, other drug companies have entered the market, selling tetracyline under its generic name. This material, whether imported from abroad or manufactured in the United States, must have each batch tested and certified by the Food and Drug Administration that it meets the requirements of strength, quality and purity. It can be purchased by druggists for as low as 6 cents; and consumers with a prescription written in terms of the generic name can, by shopping around, buy at roughly double this amount. Of course, if the prescription calls for a particular brand name—Achromycin, Tetracyn or Polycline, for example—the situation is different. Though competition is having some effect, the retail price is around 35 cents per capsule.

The Determination of Price

How does a company determine its prices when it has a monopoly? In the case of Miltown and Equanil, both companies have maintained an identical price of about 6 cents per tablet to druggists since 1955 when the drug was first introduced. The consumer has paid—and still pays today—about 10 cents per tablet for the brand-name product. It is of interest that in Mr. Hoyt's explanation of how the price was arrived at, the cost of production was an irrelevant factor. The president of Carter stated:

> Considerable thought was given by Carter to the price of Miltown. Our objective was to set a price that would enable Carter to make a fair profit; and that would enable the wholesaler and retail druggist to obtain their usual markups; and that, above all, would produce for the ultimate patient a price that, considering the value of the drug, its anticipated dosage and other factors, would be a reasonable price—within his means.
> Before determining the price to the wholesalers, Carter made a survey of the prices at which competitive products were generally sold. It then established a price for Miltown in line with competition.[23]

Mr. Hoyt made some interesting comparisons to justify the reasonableness of the price charged. He explained to the Subcommittee:

> A survey of the use of Miltown shows that the average dose is three tablets a day. The price to the patient is 10.6 cents a tablet, about the price of a cup of coffee or a candy bar. The average dose of three tablets a day, or a total cost of 31.8 cents a day, is comparable to the price of a pack of cigarettes or a gallon of gasoline. Of the 10.6 cents per tablet the patient pays, I have estimated Carter's profit to be about 1.2 cents per tablet.
> Considerable stress has been placed on the fact that many drugs are required by elderly persons living on pensions or limited incomes, unable to afford them. The principal use of Miltown is by active, productive people in the age groups which normally work under pressure.[24]

Carter's selling costs, as reported by it to the Subcommittee,

[23] *Hearings*, Part 16, p. 9110.
[24] *Idem.*

are a substantial element in costs—roughly about 28 cents in every sales dollar.

It was pointed out to Mr. Hoyt that, when his company first began purchasing meprobamate in 1955, it was paying around $25 per pound. By 1958 the bulk price had fallen to around $4.50 and, indeed, continued to fall to as low as $3 in 1961. Under these circumstances, it was asked, why had Carter not reduced its price to druggists and consumers? Mr. Hoyt replied in no uncertain terms:

. . . I think that our price is a fair price. We sell it. The consumer gets the product at 10 cents a tablet. The average is three tablets a day, that is 30 cents a day. We had had no complaints about our price to the druggist, from consumers, or druggists, so I didn't change the price whatsoever.[25]

The reality of price reductions arising from use of the generic name is strikingly illustrated in meprobamate. Under the consent decree negotiated with Carter in November 1962, the Government did not disturb the company's ownership of the patent nor the arrangement under which chemical manufacturers of meprobamate sold exclusively to Carter. Apparently in an effort to supply some price protection to Carter's licensees under the compulsory licensing requirement, a maximum price was set on Carter's sales of bulk meprobamate to them. This maximum price, established under the decree, is $20 per pound.

Instantly, as might be expected in a monopoly structure, the maximum price became Carter's minimum price. In consequence, Carter has been enjoying a profit of $17 or more per pound on all bulk meprobamate sold to its licensees under the terms of the consent decree. Yet, despite this high price, Carter's licensees have made extensive sales of the drug under its generic name. Their prices to druggists have been around 3 or 4 cents per tablet. Carter has steadfastly adhered to its long-established price of 6½ cents per tablet to the retailer. And the 10-cent price to consumers is, as Mr.

[25] *Hearings*, Part 16, p. 9153.

Hoyt remarked, no more than the cost of a cup of coffee or a candy bar.

The way in which prices of patented drugs are set is also illustrated in the case of Upjohn's pricing of Orinase, the oral antidiabetic drug. At the time of the Subcommittee's hearings Upjohn was purchasing the drug in bulk form from its licensor's U.S. subsidiary, Hoechst Chemical Corporation in Rhode Island. Taking into account the price paid by Upjohn for this material, royalty charges, and the costs of tableting and bottling, total costs for Upjohn were about 1 cent per tablet. It charged the retailer about 8 cents per tablet; the diabetic patient paid 14 cents. For 1000 tablets, maximum cost to Upjohn was $13.11; the druggist paid $83.40; the public was charged $139.00.

The validity of these figures was not contested by Dr. E. Gifford Upjohn, president of the company, who insisted that the price for the diabetic patient was "just a matter of pennies a day." It was suggested to Dr. Upjohn that diabetes is a chronic, not an acute, disorder; that pennies a day for a life-time constitute a sizable expenditure. Upjohn officials had pointed out that over half a million diabetic patients were on daily maintenance dosages of Orinase, with an average of three tablets per day. On this basis, at 90 tablets a month, the patient paid around $12.50 a month for a drug that cost Upjohn no more than $1.18. An expenditure of "pennies a day" added up to $150 a year, as contrasted with a manu-facturing cost of less than $14.

But how did Upjohn happen to settle upon 14 cents as the price to the diabetic patient? On this point there was some enlightening evidence. Dr. Upjohn explained that the price "was arrived at on the basis of competition, of course. Diabetic patients can be treated by diet or by insulin." He con-tinued:

. . . and insulin had been on the market for many years, during which time its price had come down very markedly, and even though the price of insulin was at quite a low level, it was neces-sary for us to consider that as our competition. So in arriving at any price you consider what the competitive situation is going to be.

Now the competition does not necessarily fix the point at which the pricing will be made, because there are other things to be considered, such as competitive advantages that one might have.[26]

Until the discovery of the oral treatment, diabetic patients using drugs had recourse only to insulin injection. For years the cost of an average injection of insulin to the patient has been 14 cents. Thus the price for the pill was set at the same level as the price for an injection of insulin. It was pointed out that the production of insulin, involving the use of animal pancreas, is a complex and relatively high-cost process; that, in contrast, Orinase is a chemical combination, both simpler and cheaper to manufacture. Dr. Upjohn merely replied, "That was our competition, Senator."[27]

Why Are Foreign Prices Lower?

Very early in the Subcommittee's work on drugs, a request was made to our State Department to secure, through American embassies abroad, price information on some of the more important drugs. The data provided showed, in general, much lower prices in foreign countries than in the United States.

In the case of meprobamate, marketed in this country under the brand names of Miltown and Equanil, a bottle of 50 tablets sells to druggists for 75 cents in Argentina, $1.38 in Germany, and $1.48 in England. In the United States the price is $3.25. For Penicillin V, one of the newer penicillins, the price to druggists is $6.50 in England and $8.67 in Brazil; in this country, for an equivalent quantity, Eli Lilly charges $18.00. Even in Australia, where the drug is supplied from

[26] *Hearings,* Part 20, p. 11037.
[27] *Ibid.,* p. 11039.

the Indianapolis plant of Lilly, the druggist pays $10.75—
40 per cent less than the druggist in the United States.

In both of these cases the drug was developed by American
companies. The Subcommittee was puzzled by the fact that
these same price differences existed even when the drug was
invented abroad. Take, for example, Orinase, the antidiabetic
drug discovered by Hoechst, a German firm. Hoechst sells
this drug in its own country for $1.85 to druggists, but Up-
john, the exclusive licensee in this country, charges $4.17
for the same amount. Reserpine, the hypertensive drug, was
developed by CIBA in its Swiss research laboratories. It is
marketed the world over by this company under the brand
name Serpasil. Throughout most of Europe the parent company sells Serpasil to druggists for around $1, but the com-
pany's U.S. subsidiary sells the same quantity for $4.50.
Similarly, in the case of Thorazine, the price in France asked
by Rhone Poulenc, the originator of the drug, is 51 cents to
the retailer; the United States licensee charges $3.03 for this
potent tranquilizer. The same disparity exists for Compazine;
the French licensor charges druggists in its country 80 cents
as against Smith, Kline & French's $3.93.

The contention that drug prices are high because of the
cost of research would certainly not apply to the cases just
mentioned. The European companies must also make expenditures for research; the large number of important drugs
that have emerged from foreign laboratories over the years is
proof of this fact. So far as prices in this country are concerned, it appears irrelevant whether the drugs originated in
Europe or not. Even where all of the pioneering work was
done abroad and the American company is simply licensed
to manufacture and sell in the United States, it charges significantly higher prices than the European firm which supplied
the funds for the research work.

Some effort was also made by drug officials at the hearings
to explain their higher prices in terms of higher labor costs
in this country. However, the available evidence suggests

that American companies have, if anything, lower unit costs than their European confreres because the chemical industry, of which drug operations are a part, is highly mechanized. One of the documents placed in the record was a Chemical Fund *Newsletter* reporting that "it takes only 833,000 American workers to produce $25 billion of chemicals a year; while in Europe, by comparison, it takes more than 1,400,000 employees to produce only 10 billion of chemicals a year."[28] Thus, despite lower wage rates in Europe, European labor costs per unit of output are higher than those in the United States.

One factor of considerable importance, the Subcommittee found, was the patent situation. European countries generally have taken the position that drugs are so important to the public health that private monopoly cannot be permitted. To this end, product patents on drugs are not obtainable. In Germany and Switzerland, two countries which historically have been leaders in chemical and drug research, only process patents may be secured on drugs. Thus, other companies are free to develop new processes of production, and where they are successful, they may market the product. In consequence, there is greater freedom and more price competition in the marketplace abroad.

The situation is quite different in the United States. Drugs are accorded the same treatment as ordinary commercial products; a company may secure a patent on the product and insulate itself from competition on that product for a period of seventeen years, the term of the patent grant. Even if other companies develop superior processes for making the product, they are unable to make use of them and enter the market, for without a license from the holder of the patent, they would be subject to suits for infringement. Their only opportunity then is to develop a "me, too" product—that is, one that is therapeutically similar but slightly different in chemical structure. The defensive strategy of the patent holder, of course, is to attempt to wall himself against attack

[28] *Hearings*, Part 17, p. 9483.

by securing patents on a variety of compounds closely related to the successful product.

In his appearance before the Subcommittee, John T. Connor, president of Merck and Company, grouped American drug firms in three categories. First, there were the firms actually engaged in research programs and developing new and useful products. Connor continued:

The second category I call the molecule manipulators, those who also have research programs but aren't too successful in hitting the home run first, but are quick to observe the competitive situations, and when they find out about them, get their pharmacological and chemistry work going so that they are in on the race. They have to spend quite a bit of money as well as the creators.

The third firms I call the coattail riders, like in the story in the Bible, they neither sow nor do they reap, but the Lord seems to take care of them. They wait until the market is established, and then they offer their products to the physician.[20]

Particularly among the major companies, the practice of molecule manipulation is a tried and true way of breaking into an assured market. It is a device for circumventing the pioneer's patent by making a slight chemical change in the compound and then securing a patent on the modification. This is, of course, a competitive activity but it is expressed almost wholly in non-price terms. The Subcommittee's hearings are replete with instances in which the "me-too" products appear on the market and are priced to the last decimal like their predecessors. Thus the public pays for whatever research costs are involved but derives no benefits of price reductions.

For the most part this kind of activity is confined to the major firms. Generally speaking, the difficulties faced by a small company in promoting a new product or engaging in a patent fight with a major company discourage such action. Often patent rights are disposed of outright by the small

[29] *Hearings*, Part 14, pp. 8049–8050.

firms on a "paid-up royalty, one lump sum" basis. As Mr. Blackman of the Premo Pharmaceutical Laboratories told the Subcommittee:

We have sold them, chiefly, because we know that a patent is little more than a piece of paper and a license to fight your competitors in court. I would much rather take a small return, if you would call it a gratuity, than to go into court and battle my larger competitors. If they are willing to take a license, under the patent, at a nominal fee, and we have received, for example, on this drain-away feature, some $70,000 in royalties, paid-up patents, both here and abroad, we are happy.[30]

When Mr. Pantzer was asked what his company, Panray, would do if its small laboratory made an important drug discovery, he replied, "We as a company would, frankly, be stuck; we couldn't get the product off the ground."[31]

In the light of this weak bargaining position, it is not surprising that small firms are conspicuous in their absence from participation in patent licensing agreements on important products. Early in the hearings this exchange occurred:

Senator Kefauver: What is the policy followed by some of these large companies on licensing?

Mr. Blackman: I cannot tell you of any significant patent in the pharmaceutical field that we, and several of the smaller drug firms, have been licensed under.

Senator Kefauver: Have you tried to get licenses?

Mr. Blackman: On a few occasions. Mostly, we knew it was futile, but we tried here and there.[32]

It is to the smaller units in the industry, presumably, that the term "coattail rider" is applied. However, the existence of a product patent is a powerful barrier to entry into the market; only where the patent has expired, or where an interference fight in the Patent Office has held up the issuance of

[30] *Ibid.*, p. 8254.
[31] *Hearings*, Part 16, p. 9373.
[32] *Hearings*, Part 14, p. 8230.

a patent, is coattail riding possible. Even then, if the product falls within the "New Drug" definition of the Food and Drug Law, there must be clearance of each company's New Drug Application by the Government agency prior to marketing. The regulatory requirements are of such character that FDA clearance of a new drug for sale has frequently been described as a "super-patent," infinitely more powerful in the economic protection it accords than the grant from the Patent Office. But if, to use Mr. Connor's lexicon, the small companies neither sow nor reap the monopoly from new products, they do provide a vital service to the public. They are the single source of price competition in an otherwise closed industry.

The High Rate of Profits

In addition to research costs, another justification was presented for high drug prices. This related to the industry's service to the public. As Dr. Austin Smith, president of the Pharmaceutical Manufacturers Association, pointed out to the Subcommittee, the cost of drugs is lower than the cost of dying: "Death costs about $900, and that does not include legal fees or doctor's fees, only the funeral director and the embalming service and the coffins and the monuments and the tombstones and the cemetery services.[33] On the other hand, he suggested, drugs can save a trip to the hospital; and if hospital costs are stacked against drug costs, any drug— whatever its price—is a bargain. Thus, Dr. Smith remarked, for years he has been "speaking of the low cost of drugs."

If this is the standard for judgment, clearly this view has merit. No one wishes to minimize the medical advances that have been made even in our own lifetime, and all of us hope that this is just the beginning. But is service to the public the proper standard for a judgment of the reasonableness of price? Wherever an essential commodity is concerned,

[33] *Hearings,* Part 19, p. 10615.

should price be determined by its importance to the public welfare?

Indeed, the rejection of this doctrine brought about the establishment of regulatory agencies in the public utility field. Electric power, natural gas, telephonic communication, and the railroads, it was argued, are "natural monopolies"; because of the absence of competition, the market cannot be depended upon to set a fair price. Yet the products are so important to the public welfare that some substitute for the automatic checks of the market had to be found. It was in this historical context that Government regulation of rates for public utilities was instituted.

The justification of high price in terms of value of the service to the public is the ideology of monopoly. Implicit in this defense is the concept that costs and profits are irrelevant in the whole price equation; that the ordinary standards used for the judgment of business enterprise cannot be applied. It is all very well for business firms subject to the vicissitudes of competition to have their prices determined by the forces of the market; but where competition is absent, then the test is the uncertain standard of service to the public. In plain language, this is a defense for pricing on the basis of what the traffic will bear. Under such circumstances the sole check upon the seller is the possibility that he may go so high that he prices himself out of the market. But for an essential commodity like drugs, even this check has a limited function, as was indicated in the letters to the Subcommittee from aged persons living on retirement pensions.

The ethical drug industry, by any standard, has been remarkably profitable. Its rate of return on investment, after taxes, is higher than that of any other industry in the country. Since 1957 it has averaged around 20 per cent, as compared with 10 per cent for all manufacturing. In dramatic fashion it outranks other noted moneymaking industries, such as industrial chemicals, office machines, automobiles, glass, and electrical machinery, all of whom enjoy in the neighborhood of a 15 per cent return after taxes.

Even as individual firms, the large drug companies lead corporations in all other industries in terms of profitability. In the 1958 *Fortune* magazine ranking of major industrial corporations by net profit, after taxes, on invested capital, three drug companies headed the parade. These were Carter Products, with earnings of 38 per cent; American Home Products, with 33.5 per cent; and Smith, Kline & French, with 33 per cent. Altogether, thirteen of the major drug companies fell within the fifty most profitable companies listed by *Fortune* for the entire country. Each of these companies had net profits exceeding 17 per cent.[34] For *Fortune*'s complete list of 500 largest corporations, the average rate of return was 9.5 per cent in 1958. Nineteen of the country's largest drug companies exceed this rate, with net profits ranging from 11 per cent to 38 per cent.

Because of the essential nature of its product, the drug industry also appears to be insulated against the ups and downs of the business cycle. For example, Upjohn presented a chart showing that, during the depths of the business depression in the early 1930's, it was enjoying a return on its net worth, after taxes, of about 30 per cent.[35] A similar chart offered by Carter Products showed that, in the economic dip that occurred in 1938–39, it was earning over 50 per cent net profit on net worth after taxes.[36] Both companies showed some variations in returns over the decades spanned, but in each case net profits almost invariably exceeded 20 per cent each year.

[34] U.S. Senate, Committee on the Judiciary, Subcommittee on Antitrust and Monopoly, 87th Cong., 1st Sess., S. Rept. No. 448 "Administered Prices: Drugs," p. 5a. In addition to the three listed above were Norwich Pharmacal Co. 23.7 percent; G. D. Searle 23 percent; Sterling Drug 22.7 percent; Schering 21.8 percent; Parke, Davis 21.6 percent; U.S. Vitamin 20.9 percent; Warner-Lambert 20 percent; Upjohn 18 percent; Pfizer 17.3 percent and Merck 17.1 percent. The companies, too small to attain *Fortune* ranking, had their profit rates computed by the same method used by *Fortune* and were inserted in their proper places.

[35] *Hearings*, Part 20, p. 11082.

[36] *Hearings*, Part 16, p. 9170.

SCHERING AND PREDNISONE

Of particular interest was the relation of net profit to a company's introduction of an important new drug under monopoly control. For example, Schering placed Meticorten on the market in 1955, and for a brief time it was alone in the field with this important cortical steroid. That company's profits on net worth after taxes jumped from 12 per cent in 1953 and 11 per cent in 1954 to 46.9 per cent in 1955. Though Schering did not hold the patent on prednisone, it licensed five of the large drug companies under its pending patent application. Four of these companies—Merck; Pfizer; Parke, Davis; and CIBA—were licensed to sell in final packaged form only; they were not permitted to make bulk sales to smaller companies who usually engage in price competition. The fifth company, Upjohn, did not have this restrictive provision written in its contract, but under questioning during the hearings the president of Upjohn stated that his company sold in bulk only to Schering, its licensor.

Despite the absence of a patent, all of the companies agreed to pay an interim royalty on sales under the pending patent application. However, there was something less than total accord among the large firms on Schering's insistence on an interim royalty. John T. Connor, president of Merck, informed the Subcommittee that these were contract provisions "that we objected to violently in the negotiations with Schering." He stated:

... We have never ourselves entered into an agreement where as patentee or prospective patentee we have asked for a royalty or agreed to a royalty during this period, before the issuance of the patent with any other commercial organization.

Now I heard Mr. Brown's testimony on that, and I might say that he and I don't see eye to eye on this as a business management matter.

... As a matter of principle I am opposed to that, because I think until the patent issues, it is hard to say who is going to win the interference, and therefore I don't think it is sound business judgment to try to figure out who pays what to whom during this period.[37]

This structure of monopoly control over prednisone failed by sheer accident. Two events contributed to its collapse. Schering's patent application became involved in a patent interference in the U. S. Patent Office; one of the contestants for the patent was a small Mexican company, Syntex Corporation, then independent. As the patent fight dragged on, Syntex began to ship bulk prednisone into the U. S. market in 1957. This was possible because prednisone was at that time removed from the Food and Drug Administration's "New Drug" category; companies no longer had to submit detailed clinical testing data in support of their applications to market the product. Large amounts of finished bulk prednisone were sold by Syntex to small American drug companies who engaged in price competition, particularly on sales to large buyers. In consequence, by 1958, Schering's net profits of 23 per cent were still high by normal standards, but they were roughly half those which prevailed in 1955.

The recent issuance of a patent on prednisone may alter the competitive picture. In March 1959 Schering and Syntex entered into an agreement providing for the settlement of their patent interference. Briefly, it provided that if Schering secured the patent, Syntex would sell the finished bulk only to licensees of Schering, and Syntex itself would market in final packaged form only.[38] On May 26, 1964 Schering received a patent on prednisone. Immediately it sent letters to drug companies informing them that, unless a license were secured, sales of this drug would constitute infringement of Schering's newly acquired patent rights.

The likelihood of Syntex's serving a similar competitive role on the newer cortical steroids now under development in its laboratories has virtually been eliminated. In 1958 Syntex was acquired by Allen & Company, an American investment firm, and a radical change in corporate policy has gradually

[37] *Hearings*, Part 14, pp. 8095–8096.
[38] *Hearings*, Part 15, p. 8878.

occurred under the new ownership. In mid-1959 Syntex entered into an agreement with Eli Lilly similar to the earlier Syntex-Schering agreement on the prednisone patent interference. It provides that Lilly has the right of first refusal on all new drug developments from the Syntex laboratories; if Lilly elects to take up the option, its right to exploit the product shall be exclusive, save for the right reserved to Syntex to sell in final packaged form only.[39] Thus, it appears to be unlikely that finished bulk supplies of new products will become available to the smaller, competitively oriented drug companies.

THE MAJOR TRANQUILIZERS

A more typical situation is illustrated by the important potent tranquilizers, Thorazine and Compazine. In 1952 Smith, Kline & French entered into a patent agreement with the French firm of Rhone Poulenc, under which it secured an exclusive license to manufacture and market Thorazine in the United States.[40] At this time SKF was enjoying a net profit, after taxes, of 23 per cent; by 1955, one year after the new drug had been introduced, its net profits had more than doubled, reaching 50 per cent. Its introduction of Compazine, a derivative of the former drug, occurred in 1956, under a similar agreement with the French firm.[41] Net profits for SKF have continued to remain extraordinarily high— usually 35 per cent or more on investment after taxes. Since these potent tranquilizers are primarily used in mental hospitals supported by state and local governments, these monopoly profits have been made directly at the expense of the taxpayer. At the Subcommittee's hearings, the president of SKF stated that approximately 40 per cent of the company's total business derives from these two products.[42]

Some idea of the gold-mine character of Smith, Kline & French stock is indicated in an article entitled "Smith, Kline

[39] S. Rept. No. 448, "Administered Prices: Drugs," op. cit., p. 76.
[40] *Hearings*, Part 17, p. 9474.
[41] *Ibid.*, p. 9484.
[42] *Hearings*, Part 16, p. 8929–8930.

& French Bonanza" published by an investment periodical, *Investors Reader*, for February 18, 1959. Under the subtitle "Philadelphia Druggist Thrives on Tranquilizers and Stimulants," one paragraph reads as follows:

A little over two decades ago Atlantic City druggist Harry B. Leeds carefully stowed away his 40 shares of Smith Kline & French common. His original purchase of 10 shares for less than $1,000 early in 1929 had been multiplied by a 4-for-1 split later that bullish year and was already worth $4,800 by 1938. Chances are investor Leeds never realized what a much bigger bonanza lay ahead. At any rate, the stock was still in the safe when his widow Harriet died last year. However, thanks to stock splits in 1947, 1950 and 1954, the holdings had by then expanded into 4,800 shares worth $477,000. After the usual tax deductions and fees the Atlantic City Court which reviewed the estate approved $390,773.73 for distribution to the Leeds heirs.[43]

Carter Products' exploitation of meprobamate, a widely sold mild tranquilizer, follows a similar pattern. During the hearings, Carter presented a chart showing its net profit after taxes on net worth. This chart discloses that from 1951 through 1954 Carter was earning net profits of about 15 per cent per year. Immediately after the introduction of Miltown, net profits rose steadily until they exceeded 55 per cent by 1957. Up to the time of the hearings in 1960, they fell somewhat, but never below 43 per cent.

American Home Products also did well with the introduction of Equanil. In 1954 its net profits, after taxes, amounted to 21 per cent; by 1956 they had jumped to 34 per cent and reached 36.4 per cent by 1957. Since that time they have remained in excess of 30 per cent.

THE PLOW-BACK OF PROFITS

During the appearance before the Subcommittee of economic experts on the general problem of administered prices, some attention was given to the business practice of plowing back

[43] This article is reprinted in *Hearings*, Part 17, p. 9481.

profits into the corporate enterprise. The effect, of course, is constantly to swell the financial base; profits must be quantitatively increased in order to maintain the same rate of return on an enlarging base. Financing from retained earnings transfers from investors to consumers the function of providing capital for corporate expansion. However, the consumer receives no share in the ownership of the corporation for his contributions, but merely enhances the value of the equity held by the existing stockholders.

As Senator John A. Carroll remarked, the consumer is not only "purchasing the commodity, but he is also paying for the expansion of an industry." Dr. Gardiner C. Means agreed, and pointed out that public utility commissions usually allow utilities to earn around 6 per cent on their capital. At this rate, he stated, the public utilities have had no difficulty in raising funds in the open market. On that basis, ordinary corporations should follow the same practice; if they withhold earnings for expansion purposes, he suggested, "justice would be done" if corporations issued shares of stock to each purchaser of their products in proportion to the contribution he made to capital.[44]

This view was shared by Professor Walter Adams, who thought the existence of the prevailing practice was indicative of the absence of competition in the drug industry. Only a monopolistic firm, he said, can force the consumer to subsidize its expansion; in a genuinely competitive market, the level of prices bars the practice. In a sense this is "taxation without representation," for the public is defenseless against the power of giant corporations to tax them for expansion of the private corporate enterprise. If such companies wish to expand their facilities, he remarked, "They should go into the capital market and raise their money and then pay a return to the investor for the money that he has risked."[45]

During the course of the drug hearings, a number of

[44] *Hearings,* Part 9, p. 4776.
[45] *Ibid.,* p. 4789.

charts were placed in the record to illustrate the rapid recovery of investment through profits. For this purpose no
differentiation was made between the share of profits re-
invested in the company and the share paid out in dividends,
since the latter varies with individual company policy. The
purpose was to compare the volume of profits with the
company's total investment of a few years earlier. The result
was illuminating in terms of the profitability of the large
units in the drug industry.

Consider, for example, the case of Schering. This corporation had been seized as enemy-owned by the Alien Property Custodian at the outbreak of World War II. In March
1952 it was sold to a U. S. syndicate for 29.1 million dollars.
Between the time of its sale and mid-1957 the corporation
earned net profits, after taxes, of 32 million dollars, a sum
in excess of the cost of the entire investment five years
earlier.

Growth of profits was even faster for American Home
Products. At the beginning of 1949 American Home had a
net worth of 54 million dollars. In the next five years it
earned 54.8 million dollars, a sum slightly in excess of its
entire net worth in 1949. By the end of 1959, its net profits
reached 127.7 million dollars.

For Smith, Kline & French the relationship of profits to
net worth was even more astonishing. In 1949 its net worth
was 10.8 million dollars; in the next two years its profits
of 10.3 million dollars nearly equaled that figure. By the
end of 1959, total net profits amounted to 134.2 million
dollars, twelve times the entire net worth of eleven years
earlier.

The public record for Carter is shorter but the pattern is
similar. Until 1957, Carter's stock was not sold on the ex-
changes; it was an unregistered corporation with its stock
closely held. In mid-1957, when the company determined
to "go public" and sell its stock generally to investors, its net
worth was only only 9.5 million dollars. Within three years its
net profit aggregated 21.5 million dollars.

Is it any wonder, then, that the drug stocks of the major companies became favorites on Wall Street?

The Problem of Advertising

Selling expenses for the major drug companies constitute the largest single item in expenditures, next to the cost of goods sold. For the twenty-two largest companies reporting to the Subcommittee, cost of goods constituted on the average 32 per cent of drug receipts, 25 per cent was spent on advertising, and research and development accounted for 6 per cent. For eight of the companies reporting, advertising costs actually exceeded the cost of goods sold.

This situation is all the more remarkable in that prescription drugs are marketed in an entirely different manner from proprietaries, which are sold directly to the consumer. For the latter, of course, the public is exposed to a barrage of brand-name promotion through newspapers, magazines, radio and, above all, television. But so-called ethical drugs can be prescribed only by the physician, and it is he who is the recipient of drug company advertising which the Subcommittee estimated costs the industry in excess of 750 million dollars annually.

The amount of drug promotional material reaching the doctor is truly staggering. Dr. James E. Bowes, a physician in private practice in Salt Lake City, dismayed by the amount of direct mail advertising reaching him, decided to make a study. For two months he weighed each piece that arrived at his office and calculated the wholesale cost of the samples. His own circular and sample pile averaged over a pound daily; he calculated that the total for all physicians in the country amounted to nearly 80 tons per day. On an annual basis, this came to well over 24,000 tons. He remarked:

It would take two railroad mail cars, 110 large mail trucks, and 800 postmen to deliver the daily load of drug circulars and samples to doctors if mailed to one single city. Then after being delivered, it would take over 25 trash trucks to haul it away, to be burned on a dump pile whose blaze would be seen for 50 miles around.[46]

What happens to all this material? Dr. Bowes decided to find out. In phone contacts with 100 doctors' offices, he found that 54 per cent immediately dumped most circulars into the wastebasket, except those dealing with new drugs. He reported:

Doctors in two of the large medical clinics in town had an equally drastic policy. Their mailroom clerk was instructed to throw out all circulars and store the samples in a separate room for the doctors' leisured perusal. One clinic tried to have the post office burn all their circulars before delivery to save wear and tear on the postmen. This idea had to be shelved because "the mail must go through."

Hospital physicians often instruct their mail clerks to discard all circulars that are delivered. At one university hospital there are several huge wastebaskets at the foot of the mail slots for quick disposal of all third-class mail.[47]

In addition to direct-mail advertising, the drug industry reaches the medical profession in a number of other ways. Dr. William Bean, professor in the School of Medicine of Iowa State University, described them briefly:

What are the ways of promoting the sales of drugs, new and old? Four major avenues are (1) visits by detail men, (2) mailing of brochures and samples, (3) advertising in medical journals, and "throw away" journals which have no subscription costs, and (4) the exhibits at medical meetings. None of these is bad in and of itself, but certain abuses and corruptions may occur. Some of the dangers and damages are self-evident.[48]

Dr. A. Dale Console, who was medical director of Squibb and is now in private practice, referred caustically to

46 *Hearings,* Part 18, p. 10453.
47 *Ibid.,* pp. 10454–10455.
48 *Ibid.,* p. 10336.

. . . the trip-hammer effect of weekly mailings, the regular visits of the detail man, the two-page spreads, and the ads which appear six times in the same journal, not to mention the added inducement of the free cocktail party and the golf outing complete with three golf balls stamped with the name of the doctor and the company in contrasting colors.[49]

Obviously, the cost of this mountainous mass of advertising is included in the price charged the patient. It means that prices will be far higher than they need be—another striking instance of a non-price form of competition that yields no benefit to the consumer.

But is this the only cost attached to this saturation advertising? Dr. Bowes raised some trenchant questions:

. . . What purpose does it accomplish for the drug manufacturer or for the doctor? Does a doctor, who has a professional education, require so much repetition to get across to him the idea of a new drug, or push an old one? And do the drug firms have the right to take up so much of a doctor's time or his tax money—and that of other taxpayers—by burdening the post office to deliver circulars at a reduced rate?[50]

A number of the country's leading medical experts appearing before the Subcommittee expressed grave doubt as to the reliability of much of the printed advertising material sent to physicians. Here, clearly, is a potential for harm to the public, which sets the drug industry apart from most others, for what is involved is the health of the patients treated by the physician. Professor Harry F. Dowling, head of the department of medicine in the University of Illinois College of Medicine, stated:

One especial source of confusion for the practicing physician is printed advertising that comes to him by direct mail or in medical journals. In this present era when truly new drugs are appearing with rapidity and causing revolutionary changes in the practice of medicine, the physician needs facts most of all.

[49] *Hearings*, Part 18, p. 10375.
[50] *Ibid.*, p. 10454.

Because misinformation and mistakes about drugs can affect health and life, advertising of drugs cannot be allowed to fall to the level of other advertising.[51]

Dr. Maxwell Finland, associate professor of medicine at the Harvard Medical School, informed the Subcommittee:

There can be no doubt that the representatives of the pharmaceutical companies have a great deal of influence on the prescription of drugs. And I think also that there cannot be any doubt that the quality of information that is given by different drug houses varies with the quality of the personnel in that drug house, and also with the integrity of the individuals in these drug houses.[52]

Several of the physicians expressed the view that some of the more responsible drug companies had been reluctantly driven into advertising excesses by the practices of their less scrupulous competitors. As Dr. Bean remarked, the real problem is with the companies "whose sole concern is business." Real conflicts may emerge between the natural business urge for profits and the commanding necessity for protecting the public health.

. . . The stockholders' appropriate interest is in income. The richest earnings occur when a new variety or variation of a drug is marketed before competing drugs can be discovered, improvised, named, and released. This bonanza time may last only a few months. Unless there are large earnings, the quick kill with the quick pill, the investment does not pay off. Commercial secrets must be kept dark, lest a competitor get the jump.[53]

In this competitive climate it is impracticable to make the time-consuming tests necessary to establish the drug's range of usefulness and potential dangers from toxicity. This has meant that, for some drugs prematurely marketed, the sick patient has been the subject in clinical testing; and the pre-

[51] *Hearings*, Part 24, p. 14172.
[52] *Ibid.*, p. 13944.
[53] *Hearings*, Part 18, p. 10335.

scribing physician has, on occasion, discovered that the toxic side effects of the drug were more serious than the malady it was intended to cure.

Another consequence is that, if new discoveries do not materialize from the corporation's laboratories, they are artificially created by the advertiser's art. Dr. Louis Lasagna, head of the division of clinical pharmacology at Johns Hopkins, remarked:

The advertising agencies are being asked to sell to the medical profession a whole bushel basketful of sows' ears for silk purses each year. It is no wonder that there are advertising excesses, and that there are so-called product failures and that obsolescence sets in. This plethora of poor compounds and of new mixtures of old agents that appears each year confuses physicians.[54]

He added that the effect of this practice is not merely to raise the cost of drugs to the patient; but also to bar him from access to adequate therapy through the use of drugs with proved usefulness.

Basic to this whole problem of misleading drug advertising has been the difficult task placed on physicians to keep abreast of the flood of medical literature. The specialists informed the Subcommittee that, even in their own areas of interest, the problem was almost insurmountable; for the busy general practitioner it must be a virtual impossibility. Yet many of the new potent compounds are widely prescribed by the general practicing physician. Speaking of drugs for mental illness, Dr. Fritz Freyhan, then director of research at Delaware State Hospital, stated:

While it may, even for psychiatrists, be difficult to keep up with the literature, psychiatric drugs are now prescribed for many reasons by every doctor; the family physician, the obstetrician, the pediatrician, and so on. The physician who is not a psychiatrist depends that much more on the accuracy of information which comes from the promotional literature.[55]

[54] *Hearings,* Part 14, p. 8140.
[55] *Hearings,* Part 16, p. 9037.

SOME ILLUSTRATIVE CASES
MEDROL

A few cases may illustrate the point. In 1960 Upjohn sent physicians a series of nine advertisements on Medrol, its exclusive cortical steroid with the imposing generic name of methylprednisolone. Each of the folders was addressed to a particular illness—acute rheumatic fever, asthma, rheumatoid arthritis, refractory edema—for which the doctor was urged to prescribe Medrol. Each ended with the same advertising flourish in large print: "The best therapeutic ratio in the steroid field makes MEDROL the corticosteroid that hits the *disease*, but spares the *patient*."

Number 5 in this series was concerned with the use of Medrol in the treatment of ulcerative colitis. It contained two X rays, one headed "Barium enema in ulcerative colitis demonstrating loss of haustrations, narrowing of colon and development of polypoid changes"; the other, "Barium enema following successful therapy for ulcerative colitis." This particular set of X rays aroused the curiosity of Dr. Loren T. DeWind, a specialist in endocrinology practicing in Los Angeles. On March 29, 1960 he wrote to the medical director of Upjohn, asking three questions:

"1. Are these X-ray pictures of the same patient?
2. What is the time interval?
3. What was the treatment given?"

A reply to this inquiry came from Upjohn's Manager of Professional Advertising:

The X-rays enclosed in this brochure were not of the same patient, and were not so labeled. They were enclosed simply to demonstrate a typical case of ulcerative colitis, and a typical result of steroid therapy in this condition. We can, in retrospect, appreciate the fact that their very juxtaposition could lead to the impression that they represent before-and-after X-rays. We did not specifically indicate this in the data printed on each X-ray, because it was our feeling that the X-rays were so obviously of different patients that the physician was unlikely to make this assumption. But the fact that other physicians have asked the same question that you ask indicates that this assumption constituted an error in judgment on our part, and care will be taken, in any future use of photographs or X-rays of this type, to differentiate very clearly between typical shots and the usual before-and-after shots.[56]

Dr. DeWind was still less than satisfied. On April 21, 1960 he wrote Upjohn again, stating that their answer was "interesting and illuminating so far as current pharmaceutical promotion practice is concerned" but he still wished for a fuller response to his questions. He added:

I have shown these X-ray pictures to a number of physicians, including a competent radiologist. In all instances it took more than casual inspection to convince each one that these were not pictures of the same patient. I feel that as a matter of simple justice to the medical profession, whose respect I am sure your company wishes to retain, that a mailing calling attention to this error in judgment on your part, would be highly desirable and an indication of your sincerity in providing the high type of medical promotion.

In some despair at this persistence, Upjohn's representative replied that "the X-rays under discussion were secured by the medical director of our advertising agency in New York" and the matter was being referred to them for answer.

On May 9, 1960 Dr. A. S. Jacobson, medical director of William Douglas McAdams, Inc., the country's largest medical advertising agency, replied to Dr. DeWind. One of the X rays, he stated, was of a thirty-four-year-old female who "responded symptomatically to sedation and superficial office psychotherapy." The other was of a twenty-seven-year-old woman who "responded symptomatically to sulfidine, rest, phenobarbital, reassurance, and dietotherapy." Thus it turned out that not only were the X rays of different patients, but neither had taken Medrol. Dr. Jacobson's letter

[56] *Hearings on S. 1552*, Part 7, p. 3307.

ended with expressions of regret that there had been any misinterpretation; there was no intention "to mislead the reader in any way"; and personally he had felt when the final copy passed over his desk that "it all represented a remarkable achievement of accurate review of a very difficult subject in a concise and readable form."

Dr. DeWind felt quite differently. In a letter forwarding this correspondence to the Medical Letter, a non-profit organization established by physicians to distribute accurate information on drugs to member-doctors, he stated:

My conclusion after reading this material was that it was subtly designed to lead busy physicians to the belief that it is possible to reverse the advanced changes of ulcerative colitis by corticosteroid therapy.

As you will note from the enclosed correspondence, there is no relation whatever between the X-rays pictured, nor was there any use of Medrol in the treatment of either patient. The advertising agency in a devious way explains all this after my two letters to the Upjohn Company.

The cost of drugs is high enough without being raised by senseless promotion such as this. I think it is high time steps are taken to curb this sort of thing. Perhaps a project could be started to ferret out and expose to the medical public the techniques used in drug promotion. If in this way the amount of drug promotion material could be reduced, it would be a great saving of money for drug consumers and time for busy physicians.[57]

During the appearance before the Subcommittee of Dr. Arthur M. Sackler, chairman of the board of William Douglas McAdams, Inc., and himself a physician, this episode was discussed at some length. When Dr. Sackler was asked why, in an advertisement extolling Medrol, X-ray pictures were used of two different patients, neither of whom had taken the drug, he replied:

The purpose of this series is to do precisely what you would like to see ethical promotion do, to be useful to the doctor, to be

[57] *Ibid.*, p. 3310.

helpful, to be informative. It does not relate to one patient—the bulk of the whole mailing relates to the total disease entity, and the smallest section of the mailing relates to a drug product. Now, this is constructive service.[58]

When it was pointed out that the purpose of Upjohn's ad was to persuade the physician to prescribe Medrol, this exchange occurred:

Dr. Sackler: Senator, I would like to get one thing very clear. In our statement we said that we favor the proper use of drugs. We favor it medically, and let me say it is also sound business practice. The administration of a drug in an irreversible condition is the most damaging thing to the drug product, to the trademark, and to the company, and the last thing in the world we would want any physician to do is to give a drug where he would get no result and it would end up by negating our own promotion.

Senator Kefauver: For instance, if you had a picture of a man weighing 300 pounds before therapy, and you had a picture of a man weighing 150 pounds after therapy, and all through it you had the name of a drug that is described as helpful in weight reducing, the impression, I think, would be that the drug you were advertising had something to do with it.

DIABINESE

During the hearings the pharmaceutical manufacturers stressed the educational value of their advertising. Dr. Austin Smith, president of PMA, the trade association, remarked:

Indeed, the word "advertising" is perhaps something of a misnomer when it applies to prescription drugs. Our so-called advertising is far different from the customary sales promotion message American consumers normally associate with the word. For the most part, our advertisements are more like scientific treatises, which differ from learned editorial comment in medical journals to the extent that we ourselves write these treatises and pay for the space where they are printed.

[58] *Hearings on S. 1552*, Part 6, p. 3091.

Ours are about the only ads in America that tell not merely the good things about our product, but deal exhaustively with the bad ones as well. Toxicity, side effects—all must be exposed in full detail.[59]

Diabinese is a striking example in which essential information on side effects was not adequately disclosed. In August 1958 Pfizer filed with the Food and Drug Administration its new drug application on this oral antidiabetic drug; two months later the compound was cleared for sale. The drug entered the market amid a fanfare of advertising. In December 1958, physicians were being informed that Diabinese represented "the latest word in diabetes control. . . . A major advance in oral therapy." During the ensuing months, the advertising pressures were intensified. Pfizer announced that Diabinese "provides the potency essential for predictable, precise response"; that it "provides constant activity preventing wide fluctuations of blood sugar and insuring optimum safety"; and that it represented "More effective control of more diabetics more economically." The product was urged for "smoother, lower cost oral antidiabetic control," for "more efficient oral control in maturity-onset diabetes." It was described as "The oral antidiabetic most likely to succeed" and a new compound "extending the frontiers of oral antidiabetic therapy."

With respect to side effects, an ingenious device was employed. Statements asserting the absence of side effects were usually placed in quotation marks. Such claims as "well tolerated with minimal side effects," "almost complete absence of unfavorable side effects," "appears to be safe, effective, and well tolerated, with minimal side reactions" were excerpted from published reports of investigators whose critical comments in the same article were ignored. Many of the studies represented early clinical work in the field; and the authors often were careful to point out the limited character of their findings from the few cases studied.

A number of medical experts appearing before the Sub-

[59] *Hearings*, Part 19, p. 10702.

committee in April 1960 expressed their concern about the drug's toxicity. Advertising claims were making much of the fact that Diabinese was more potent than Orinase, a similar compound, because only half the essential ingredient was required for equivalent dosage. Dr. Henry Dolger of New York City, an eminent authority on diabetes, stated:

In publications of 1959 and 1960 I stated that "this increase in potency is associated with an increase in serious side effects and toxicity, especially in liver damage. There is no decrease in side effects despite the advertisements."

It seemed to me that potency manipulation was comparable to the horsepower race in the automotive industry. In a chronic disease like diabetes where a therapeutic treatment must be administrated for nearly a lifetime, safety becomes paramount in medical treatment.[60]

Dr. Hans Popper, an expert on liver disorders at Mt. Sinai Hospital, New York City, listed Diabinese among the drugs inducing jaundice, and emphasized the great difficulties experienced by the attending physician in determining whether a case of jaundice is drug-induced or stems from another source. Dr. Samuel D. Loube, a specialist in Washington, D. C., referring to the drug under its generic name, remarked:

I do feel, however, that the side effects are distinctly of sufficient importance to be carefully brought to the attention of any physician who plans to use chlorpropamide in the treatment of his diabetic patients. The large majority of the diabetic patients in our country are treated by general practitioners who, for many reasons, may not be familiar with the results of carefully developed research studies and the evaluation by experts of such new drugs as chlorpropamide. Rightly or wrongly, they rely on the information passed on to them by the advertising media of the pharmaceutical companies.[61]

He also believed that the diabetic patient should be made

60 *Hearings*, Part 20, p. 11146.
61 *Ibid.*, p. 11185.

fully aware of possible side effects in the interest of supplying prompt information to his physician.

Senator Kefauver: Doctor, in the treating of diabetes, is it important that a patient, in order to cooperate, be aware of these matters so that he understands what side effects might occur and what might be the result? Is that an important part of the treatment?

Dr. Loube: Yes. I think nowhere in medicine is there a group of patients who ought to be as thoroughly familiar with every aspect of their disease than the diabetic patients.[62]

The Subcommittee made repeated requests to Pfizer for its summary of the clinical testing work done on Diabinese prior to FDA clearance. Finally, on the very morning that the hearings were to begin, the report was supplied. It confirmed the experts' statements on the high incidence of side effects accompanying the use of the drug, including such serious reactions as jaundice and exfoliative dermatitis. Thus, even prior to marketing and the institution of its advertising campaign, the company was fully aware of the toxicity hazards.

Despite the fact that Dr. Dominic G. Iezzoni had been in personal charge of the clinical testing program for Pfizer and had prepared the final report, he was not among the physicians accompanying John E. McKeen, president of the company, for the Diabinese hearings. The Subcommittee was, of course, particularly interested in hearing Dr. Iezzoni's views. On several occasions Mr. McKeen was asked if the physician could be present for this purpose. It turned out, however, that Dr. Iczzoni was engaged in more pressing Pfizer matters, and his absence was unavoidable. When the request was reiterated, it was explained that Dr. Iezzoni was no longer in charge of the clinical program: "The product itself and the responsibility for it has been shifted from the clinical research group over to the Pfizer Laboratories division."[63]

[62] *Ibid.*, p. 11190.
[63] *Ibid.*, pp. 11194–1195.

MER/29

The case of MER/29 will undoubtedly go down as a classic in the annals of drug history. On December 20, 1963 a Federal grand jury in the District of Columbia indicted Richardson-Merrell, Inc., on charges of withholding information on adverse toxic effects of the drug in animal testing work and making false statements to the Food and Drug Administration in connection with its new drug application. By this time the company was a defendant in over 400 damage suits brought by individuals who had sustained injuries from use of the drug, and total damages in the neighborhood of $200,000,000 were sought. Ultimately the case was ended with a *nolo contendere* plea by the company.

The drug appeared on the market in June 1960 for the control of coronary diseases. In an ad in the AMA *Journal* for June 25, 1960, Merrell "announced the availability of MER/29" in glowing terms:

"the first cholesterol-lowering agent to inhibit the formation of excess cholesterol within the body, reducing both serum and tissue cholesterol levels. . . .
"toleration and absence of toxicity established by 2 years of clinical investigation."

According to an official of the McAdams advertising agency, which handled the drug, over a million dollars was spent in promotion.[64] In its first year sales rose to 9.1 million dollars, and Merrell was able to describe it as "both the Nation's most widely prescribed anti-cholesterol drug and also our largest-selling ethical product."[65]

By January 1961 the Mayo Clinic was making its first report to Merrell of skin disorders and loss of hair associated with use of the drug. But warnings had come in earlier from another source. In 1960 Merck, in testing one of its

[64] *Hearings on S.* 1552, Part 6, p. 3095.
[65] U.S. Senate, Committee on Government Operations, Hearings before the Subcommittee on Reorganization and International Organizations, 88th Cong., 1st Sess., "Agency Coordination Study," Part 3, p. 898.

own anti-cholesterol compounds, made comparisons of its drug with MER/29. In the course of its animal testing work, Merck discovered that cataracts developed in rats and dogs treated with MER/29. A conference was held between scientists of the two firms to acquaint Merrell with the results of the Merck tests. Though Merck's compound was never placed on the market, Merrell continued its intensive promotion of MER/29.

By early October of 1961 the Mayo Clinic "notified the company by phone that both patients reported earlier with moderately severe skin and hair changes had developed cataracts" and another case had been reported through correspondence.[66] By October 11 all of the information collected by the Mayo Clinic was in the hands of the company. A few days later, at a meeting of the American Heart Association, the Mayo investigators met with Merrell officials and urged them to alert other investigators using the drug, so that more information on side effects could be secured, and to warn all prescribing physicians on the drug's dangers to the unsuspecting public.

By this time the Food and Drug Administration was also involved. On October 23, 1961 the FDA asked Merrell to supply all information in its possession on all eye changes in humans and animals, particularly the development of cataracts, in connection with use of MER/29.[67] It also asked for all other data concerning toxic and adverse reactions of the drug. By mid-November, after receipt of this information, the FDA offered the company the alternative of voluntary withdrawal of MER/29 or a warning letter to the medical profession. Negotiations dragged on for another two weeks, and it was not until December 1, 1961 that Merrell sent out its "Dear Doctor" letter warning the medical profession.

Between this date and April 1962, when MER/29 was finally removed from the market, the Senate Antitrust Sub-

[66] *Ibid.*, p. 942.
[67] "Agency Coordination Study" *op. cit.*, Part 2, p. 503.

committee conducted its hearings on medical advertising. Particular attention was addressed to the fact that as late as the November 4, 1961 issue of the AMA *Journal*, Merrell was advertising the drug as follows:

After 3 years' clinical experience:
here is what we now know about MER/29 . . .

We know that MER/29 lowers cholesterol in as many as 8 out of 10 patients, even without dietary restrictions . . .

We know that MER/29 does this by inhibiting the body's own production of cholesterol.

We know that, after use in more than 300,000 patients, few toxic or serious side effects have been reported, thus tending to reaffirm the safety margins previously established.[68]

When it was suggested to the McAdams officials that Merrell must have had knowledge of adverse side effects "for some length of time and they ought to have been communicated to you if you were not in touch with them," Dr. DeForest Ely, the advertising company's president, replied that his agency was informed by telephone late in October. He explained:

In the case of the appearance of the advertisement, I must say that as soon as our client informed us that they were working with the FDA on the issuance of a warning letter, that they might have to issue such a letter, we were asked to discontinue all direct mail and all journal advertising, and we did it. The fact that this advertisement appeared November 4 may mean simply that the possibility of cancellation at the time we were so informed by the client could not permit us to take the advertisement out of that issue of the journal.[69]

But even if the company had been delinquent in informing its advertising agency promptly, how did it happen that the ad stated "few toxic or serious side effects have been re-

[68] *Hearings on S. 1552*, Part 7, p. 3358.
[69] *Hearings on S. 1552*, Part 6, p. 3101.

ported" and yet failed to specify their nature? On this point Dr. Sackler of McAdams, Inc. replied:

You may recall that we have indicated our belief as to the role of journal advertising. We have said it was to alert the physician, and that we should seek through it to direct his attention to basic material which he needs. In this advertisement there is the following statement: "Complete bibliography and prescription information available on request."[70]

The fate of MER/29 was settled when other basic material came into the hands of FDA. The agency's chronology of events on this drug states:

In March 1962 FDA received a report from an ex-employee of the firm that the monkey study had been falsified. An investigation was begun, and, on April 9-10, 1962, FDA made an inspection at the William S. Merrell Co., Cincinnati, Ohio. Animal data on monkeys was obtained which differed from that submitted in the original New Drug Application in support of the safety of MER/29. FDA is intensively investigating this matter to determine whether false statements were willfully made in connection with the New Drug Application or whether there was a willful failure to disclose material facts.[71]

On April 16, 1962 the company formally requested suspension of its application for FDA approval of the drug. This was accepted and a month later the agency issued a formal suspension order based on a finding that the drug was unsafe under the conditions of use set forth in Merrell's New Drug Application.

THALIDOMIDE

In the course of the Subcommittee's hearings, officials of the Food and Drug Administration appeared in support of legislation to correct advertising abuses. The dramatic case of thalidomide, the sleep-inducing drug causing deformities in unborn babies, suddenly aroused public opinion to the

[70] *Ibid.*, p. 3102.
[71] "Agency Coordination Study," *op. cit.*, Part 2, p. 504.

need for corrective legislation. Although the drug was widely marketed abroad, in this country it was not cleared by the Food and Drug Administration. Nevertheless, in 1960 millions of tablets of Kevadon, the brand name for the product in this country, were distributed to doctors by Richardson-Merrell, ostensibly for clinical testing purposes. The company's written instructions to its salesmen on approaching physicians are indicative of the "hard sell" thrust:

A WORD OF CAUTION

Bear in mind that these are not *basic* clinical research studies. We have firmly established the safety, dosage and usefulness of Kevadon by both foreign and U. S. laboratory and clinical studies. This program is designed to gain widespread *confirmation* of its usefulness in a variety of hospitalized patients. If your work yields case reports, personal communications or published work, all well and good. But the main purpose is to establish local studies whose results will be spread among hospital staff members. You can assure your doctors that they need not report results if they don't want to but that we, naturally, would like to know of their results. Be sure to tell them that we may send them report forms or reminder letters but these are strictly reminders and they need not reply. Their reports or names would not be used without getting their express permission in advance.

At the beginning of your interview, don't be secretive—lay your cards on the table. Tell the doctor that present plans call for Kevadon to be marketed early in 1961. Let them know the basic clinical research on Kevadon has been done. Don't get involved by selling a basic clinical research program instead of Kevadon. *Appeal to the doctor's ego—we think he is important enough to be selected as one of the first to use Kevadon in that section of the country.*[72]

The tragic consequences of the use of thalidomide did not, in this country, reach the proportions attained abroad, but they were sufficient for swift action. On October 10, 1962 the Kefauver-Harris bill, greatly strengthening the powers

[72] "Agency Coordination Study," *op. cit.*, Part 1, p. 264. (Italics in original)

of the Food and Drug Administration with respect to pre-market testing of drugs, advertising to physicians, information on side effects, and other matters, became a part of the law of the land.

THE ROLE OF THE DETAIL MEN

A substantial factor in the industry's high advertising costs is the use of "detail men," a euphemistic term for salesmen. The function of a company's detail men is to make regular calls in their territories upon doctors for the purpose of increasing physicians' prescriptions of the company's products.

Throughout the hearings there was again much industry testimony on the "educative role" of the detail men, particularly with respect to the introduction of new products. The medical experts—themselves the recipients of numerous calls by detail men—felt differently. Dr. Dowling remarked that "When a drug is really new, information about it spreads with rapidity by word of mouth among the members of the profession and through articles in medical journals."

Furthermore, it is precisely in the case of a truly new drug that the principles upon which its dosage is based and the methods of using it are both likely to be so different from previously used drugs that the practicing physician should get a thorough knowledge of the drug from a competent authority when he first hears about it. Detail men are valuable for the purpose of getting information to physicians and pharmacists regarding the availability and prices of products distributed by their companies, but being salesmen, they cannot be expected to give unprejudiced advice.[73]

Dr. Console, speaking from his experience both in the drug industry and in private practice, said:

There is a simple maxim, I learned from detail men, which is known to most if not all in the pharmaceutical industry. "If you can't convince them, confuse them." This is a valuable tool in the industry and I have seen it in operation as a guide to de-

[73] *Hearings*, Part 24, p. 14172.

tailing as well as to other forms of advertising and promotion of drugs. It operates in what Dr. Lasagna has so aptly called the "numbers" racket with its never-ending barrage of new products, confusing names, conflicting dosage schedules and indications, claims and counterclaims; I have seen it in operation here in statements made by industry spokesmen.[74]

A rather grim example of the effectiveness of detail men is revealed in the case of chloramphenicol. This patented antibiotic, sold exclusively by Parke, Davis under the brand name of Chloromycetin, is the largest-selling trade-name prescription drug in the country. Next to tetracycline, it is the largest-selling broad-spectrum antibiotic. It is a highly useful drug in the treatment of typhoid fever, Rocky Mountain spotted fever, and other Rickettsial diseases. Unfortunately, use of the drug has also been associated with blood dyscrasias, notably aplastic anemia for which the fatality rate is at least 50 per cent. There is no known method for determining the patient's susceptibility to the drug. Blood studies may reveal the presence of aplastic anemia, but even when it is recognized the condition is often irreversible.

How does it happen that a drug with such limited uses and high potential of danger to the patient has such an impressive sales position? In part, the answer seems to lie in the effectiveness of Parke, Davis's detail men. In mid-1952, the Food and Drug Administration was so concerned with reported side effects of chloramphenicol that it suspended its sale and referred the problem to the National Research Council. Acting upon the Council's recommendation, the FDA then allowed resumption of marketing with this statement:

The Administration has weighed the value of the drug against its capabilities for causing harm and has decided that it should continue to be available for careful use by the medical profession in those serious and sometimes fatal diseases in which its use is necessary.[75]

74 *Hearings*, Part 18, p. 10368.
75 *Hearings*, Part 26, p. 15980.

Serious warnings of the drug's potentiality for harm were required on the drug's labeling, and a number of authoritative articles and editorials alerting doctors were published in the leading medical journals of the country. The effect was one of great alarm in the medical profession, and it appeared that sales of the drug might decline to the vanishing point.

The company's detail men were the focal point of inquiry among the country's doctors. During its hearings the Subcommittee secured copies of the company's "President's" and "Director's" Letters to detail men on how to handle the inquiries.[76] One such letter of August 12, 1952 informed them:

Chloromycetin has been officially cleared by the FDA and the National Research Council with *no restrictions* on the number or the range of diseases for which Chloromycetin may be administered.

Another, dated September 16, 1952, assured the detail men:

The recent decision reached by the Food and Drug Administration with the assistance of the National Research Council and a board of nationally known medical experts was undoubtedly the highest compliment ever tendered the medical staff of our Company.

On November 20, 1952 the company sent its detail men detailed written instructions on the matter. It admonished them that Chloromycetin's toxicity "should not be introduced unless the physician brings up the subject or unless you know that he has ceased prescribing the drug." Detail men were instructed to memorize the following passage and repeat it verbatim to the physician:

. . . intensive investigation by the Food and Drug Administration, carried on with the assistance of a special committee of eminent specialists appointed by the National Research Council, resulted in unqualified sanction of continued use of Chloromycetin for all conditions in which it has previously been used.

[76] *Ibid.*, pp. 15962–15977.

On the stringent warnings imposed by the FDA, detail men were ordered to commit to memory and repeat the following message:

A sensible caution against indiscriminate use, which we have incorporated into our advertising and labeling, is a welcome addition to our literature and to the label on Chloromycetin products, and in our opinion, would be appropriate in those on any potent chemotherapeutic agent. Actually, such caution is an assurance that the full benefits of well-tolerated Chloromycetin will be available and free from misuse.

Reassured by the detail men, many physicians gradually returned to their traditional reliance upon Chloromycetin for ordinary sore throats and other minor infectious disorders. By 1963 Parke, Davis's sales had reached new levels, with its leading product, Chloromycetin, reportedly stabilized at significant volume and profit levels.

The problem is all the more serious because this kind of drug promotion is not easily susceptible to corrective action. The detail man gives his sales pitch in the privacy of the doctor's office; no record is kept of the exchange that takes place. Where a personal relationship of long standing exists, a carefully worked out oral presentation, such as was used with Chloromycetin, may wash out a battery of scientific treatises and warnings in learned medical periodicals. In this area governmental prohibition can be ineffective; the need is for a competitive order in the industry which emphasizes price reductions to the public rather than excessive promotion practices.

PROMOTION OF TRADE NAMES

Great effort has been expended by the major companies to persuade physicians to prescribe by trade name rather than generic name. The reason is obvious: once a doctor has scribbled the trade name of a drug on his prescription pad, the pharmacist is required by law to supply only that com-

pany's product to the patient. The result is a complex structure of product names unparalleled in any other industry.

Dr. Solomon Garb, then professor of pharmacology at
Albany Medical College, illustrated the situation with comparisons from the food industry. In the sale of baked beans,
for example, the company's name is the brand name, i.e.,
Heinz, Campbell's and the like. He remarked:

> The pharmaceutical industry does things differently. They
> use two sets of brand names. The one set consists of the name
> of the company, such as Lederle, Pfizer, CIBA and so forth. In
> addition they add a second brand name by inventing a new
> name for the product and registering it as a private trademark.[77]

To illustrate the extent of the confusion created, Dr. Garb
described what would happen if the drug manufacturers took
over the manufacture and marketing of baked beans:

> They would all stop using the word "beans," and each would
> give the product a new, coined name. Some might use anagrams
> of beans, like "Sneabs" or "Nabes," and others might call them
> "Lo Cals" or "Hi Pro's." Picture the confusion in the grocery
> store if beans were no longer named "beans," but if each maker
> gave a completely new name to his product. Further, try to
> imagine what would happen if there were 300 to 500 additional
> new names of this type in the grocery store every year.
>
> This is approximately what is happening in medicine, and it
> is becoming exceedingly difficult for physicians to keep things
> clear.[78]

For physicians the problem is especially difficult because
their entire medical education is conducted in terms of
generic names. This practice is necessary to acquaint medical students not only with the properties of the particular
drug, but also with its relationship to allied compounds. As
Dr. Walter Modell of Cornell University Medical College
stated, "Only a name that conveys meaning lends itself to

[77] *Hearings*, Part 18, p. 10481.
[78] *Ibid.*, p. 10481.

instructive communication." He added, "We could never teach pharmacology if we attempted to cope with the confusion created by proprietary nomenclature."[79]

Dr. Modell told the Subcommittee that the current sales emphasis on trade names creates very real dangers for the patient. The sheer multiplicity of short, catchy trade names, many of them very similar, can easily result in a mistake. Even more important is the fact that the practice of rational medicine requires that the physician be familiar with the nature of the compound and its possible actions. He stated:

> If one is to take the word of the detail man, then he will prescribe whatever the detail man provides. He will not, therefore, know what the best drug available is, but he will give what he has been instructed to give, so that he may be depriving his patient of the best medication. I consider that a danger.[80]

In general, two defenses were offered by officials of the major drug companies for their heavy emphasis on trade names. The first was that generic names are too complicated and too difficult to spell and pronounce for general use by physicians. There was some difference of opinion in the hearings as to how these generic names originated. Dr. Austin Smith, president of the Pharmaceutical Manufacturers Association, testified that they were "chosen on the request of physicians and others who are interested in proper nomenclature."[81] But Dr. Lloyd Miller of the U. S. Pharmacopeia stated that generic names, like trade names, were concocted by drug companies, and that if a company persisted in using a complicated or unsuitable name, little could be done about it. To correct this situation and make the generic name a more practical device for everyday use by doctors, the Kefauver-Harris Act specifically requires the U. S. Department of Health, Education and Welfare to exercise supervisory powers.

The second defense was addressed directly to the quality

[79] *Hearings*, Part 21, p. 11602.
[80] *Ibid.*, p. 11607.
[81] *Hearings*, Part 19, p. 10623.

of generic-name products. Numerous witnesses appearing for the major drug companies stated that such drugs were of inferior quality; that they were often produced under unsatisfactory manufacturing conditions; and that the control systems in the plants were inadequate. Representatives of some of the country's leading hospitals, which purchase under generic name, opposed this view; indeed, the associate director of the New York Hospital stated that it had successfully been purchasing under generic name for 144 years.

Increasingly, state and local welfare agencies have required generic-name prescribing by physicians as a means of stretching their always inadequate budgets. To Senator Philip Hart, who presided over these hearings, the problem demanded solution. He remarked:

I am really trying to find out whether what they recommend for the welfare patient is safe for me, too. If it is safe for him, it is safe for me. If it is dangerous for him, it is dangerous for me, . . .[82]

To end any lingering doubts in this regard, the legislation passed in 1962 gives wide powers to the FDA with respect to the maintenance of good manufacturing conditions and controls by all producers of prescription drugs. It also requires regular plant inspection, insures access to necessary records and complaint files, and the like. Thus physicians may feel complete confidence in the quality of products which they prescribe under generic name. And at the same time, they know they are making available to their patients marked savings in price as compared with the brand-named product.

The Proximate Cause for Excessive Advertising

Obviously, the extraordinary advertising effort in the drug industry was made possible by the tremendous margins between manufacturing costs and selling prices; funds were available for the companies to enter into a costly promotion

[82] *Hearings*, Part 21, 11681.

warfare without disturbing an artificially high price structure. But how did excessive advertising get its start?

Strangely enough, great impetus appears to have come
from the professional organization of physicians, the American Medical Association. In the summer of 1961 the AMA
formally appeared before the Subcommittee in opposition to
S. 1552 as originally introduced. Its fire was addressed principally against the provision that new drugs introduced in
the market must be proved effective as well as safe. The
Department of Health, Education and Welfare supported
the proposal on the ground that "the time has now come in
the United States to give American men, women and children the same protection we have been giving hogs, sheep
and cattle since 1913." The Virus-Serum-Toxin Act of 1913
banned "worthless" biologicals in the treatment of domestic
animals, but no similar protection was accorded the human
population.

The AMA opposed this view. It argued that any judgment
concerning efficacy "can only be made by the individual
physician using the drug to treat an individual patient."[83]
Dr. Hugh H. Hussey, Jr., chairman of the AMA's Board of
Trustees, presented the Board's report which had been approved the previous week by the AMA House of Delegates:

The vesting of the authority suggested by this legislation in the
Food and Drug Administration would operate to limit research,
the marketing of drugs, and the exercise of discretion by the
medical profession.

The marketing of a relatively useless drug is infinitely less
serious than would be arbitrary exclusion from the market of a
drug that might have been life saving for many persons.[84]

Subsequent to the AMA official presentation of its opposition to the bill, some members of the AMA's Council on
Drugs, the drug-evaluating body of experts, appeared as individuals to support the "proof of efficacy" provision. Dr.
Louis Goodman, an authority on pharmacology and member

[83] Hearings on S. 1552, Part I, p. 44.
[84] Ibid., p. 46.

of the Council, informed the Subcommittee that this group "was not called upon to give its collective and considered opinion" of the bill. He·remarked:

This is puzzling because the Council on Drugs is the AMA's advisory body that is meant to know most about the actions and uses of drugs. I have been in correspondence with several members of the AMA Council on Drugs who strongly advocate the "proof of efficacy" requirement of the proposed law and who, like me, regret this stand of the AMA.[85]

On this issue the AMA's position was to the right of the industry's. Though considerable effort was expended to lighten various provisions of the new law, there was general acceptance within the drug industry of the efficacy provision.

In the course of the AMA's appearance, the Subcommittee inquired into major changes that had occurred in AMA's advertising policies. Until the early 1950's only drug products that had been evaluated and found acceptable by the AMA's Council on Drugs could be advertised in the *Journal* and other AMA periodicals. To enable the Council to perform its functions, the drug company wishing to advertise in the *Journal of the American Medical Association* had to supply "evidence of usefulness." In 1906 a chemical laboratory had been established for testing, and in 1949 a microbiological laboratory was added. Some plant inspection was also provided for. Manufacturers whose drugs were approved by the Council received an AMA "Seal of Acceptance" which could be used on packages and for advertising purposes.

The Council maintained high standards with respect to advertising content in AMA publications. Claims for usefulness were limited to those recognized in the Council's annual volume, now *New and Nonofficial Drugs*. If the drug manufacturer wished to make additional claims of usefulness, the ad had to be "accompanied by supporting evidence for Council consideration before it is placed in use."[86] Use-

[85] *Ibid.*, p. 216.
[86] American Medical Association, *New and Nonofficial Remedies 1950*, Official Rules of the Council, Rule 4, p. xix.

less drugs, defined as those not "in the best interests of rational medicine and the public," were unacceptable to the Council.

The AMA Council also was on record as favoring the use of generic names in preference to brand names. Medical science, it was stated, would be promoted by the use of generic names "based on scientific principles and freely available to all. This would avoid much needless tax on memory with its attendant confusion and errors."[87] Until 1950 the AMA enforced wide use of generic names by the simple expedient of permitting only the originator of the product to advertise under a brand name in AMA periodicals. All other sellers were required to use the generic name.

The effect of these requirements was generally to curtail advertising excesses in the prescription field. Doctors relied heavily on the AMA *Journal* to keep abreast of new drug products, and most manufacturers found it worth while to place their advertising where it counted. The Council's controls also tended to maintain some competitive balance between the large and small units in the industry. The Seal of Acceptance was very important to smaller manufacturers; it was prominently displayed as proof positive to physicians that the product was of high quality. The fact that only the originator of a new product could use a brand name was also a marked asset; for the small company there was a decided prestige element in the recognition that it was the contributor of the development.

Then all this changed. Early in the 1950's the AMA hired the Chicago firm of Ben Gaffin & Associates, Inc. to make a study. Its purpose was described by that firm as follows:

In the fall of 1952, Mr. Thomas Gardiner and Mr. Robert Lyon of the AMA Business Office invited us to apply survey research methods to uncovering ways in which the sale of advertising space in JAMA and other AMA publications could be increased.

[87] *Ibid.*, Rule 5.

With pardonable pride the report stated:

The utilization of the study findings netted the AMA a return of 3600% in increased pharmaceutical advertising for each dollar spent on the research. The survey of pharmaceutical advertisers played a part in bringing about a number of policy changes. . . .[88]

Among those cited was "the eventual dropping of the 58-year-old Council Seal of Acceptance Program." Indeed, within a relatively short time, the entire structure of AMA control over advertising was dismantled. The regular publication of a small volume entitled *Useful Drugs*, which had been started in 1913, was dropped in 1952. Dr. Walter Modell has referred to this volume as a "small and masterful book" whose wide use had the effect of "ensuring both safe and effective use of drugs as well as limiting their number through authoritative suggestion," and added that it helped the doctor "to clarify the confusion created by excessive numbers of unproved new drugs promiscuously and prematurely introduced into the drug market."[89] By 1957 George F. Lull, secretary and general manager of the AMA, was able to state at a convention of the drug manufacturers' association: "The consideration of advertising has been taken out of the jurisdiction of the Council. Advertising in AMA publications is in the hands of an advertising committee. No consideration of advertising elsewhere is being undertaken." He was also able to give other assurances. The Gaffin survey had gone deeply into "The Advertisers' Viewpoint" with respect to the "Rules of Acceptance" employed by the AMA. Mr. Lull informed them: "The former official rules of the Council have been superseded entirely and without wishing to bore you I would like to read what are called the *new principles, not rules*."[90]

[88] *Hearings on S. 1552*, Part 2, p. 525.
[89] *Clinical Pharmacology and Therapeutics*, Vol. 2, No. 1 (Jan.-Feb. 1961), editorial. Reprinted in *Hearings on S. 1552*, Part 2, pp. 849ff.
[90] American Drug Manufacturers Association, *Proceedings of 1957 Convention*, pp. 71–72.

The AMA's financial reports in its *Journal* revealed the change that took place. In 1949 income from dues and AMA subscriptions was twice the income from advertising—4.8 million dollars as contrasted with 2.4 million dollars. Dues and subscriptions remained virtually static in the next decade, but income from advertising rose rapidly. In 1955 the figure was 4.2 million dollars; between 1955 and 1960 it doubled again, reaching 8 million dollars. Charts were placed in the Subcommittee's record showing the substantial advertising expenditures of each of the major drug houses in the *J.A.M.A.* during these years.[91]

Furthermore, the AMA has created a built-in mechanism for deriving larger returns from stepped-up direct-mail advertising to physicians. It supplies up-to-date mailing lists of physicians for a fee based upon the number of pieces of advertising. In 1960 its income from this source was $900,000. When asked how the arrangement worked, the general counsel for the AMA replied:

Very simply, the way it works is that we maintain a directory report service which lists all of the physicians. We keep an accurate record of where they are, changes of addresses. We have eight organizations that are in the direct mail business. They have contracted with the American Medical Association and we make the lists available to them. They do the business with drug houses and other organizations, and this royalty of $2 a thousand is payable to the American Medical Association from these mailing organizations, eight of them at the present time.[92]

But the price paid for AMA's increased revenues from advertising was a heavy one. In 1963, during the hearings of his Subcommittee, Senator Humphrey referred regretfully to the role formerly played by the AMA Council on Drugs. Dr. Charles D. May, professor in the School of Medicine of New York University, replied: "Sir, they have found nothing to take its place. They lost the most valuable tool they ever

[91] *Hearings on S. 1552*, Part 1, pp. 132ff.
[92] *Ibid.*, p. 137.

had as far as being of service to the profession, and clearly appreciated by the public."[93]

The Kefauver-Harris Act

The drug hearings, which began in late 1959, eventually culminated in the passage of corrective legislation in October 1962. Basically, the new law represents a two-pronged attack—one upon the monopoly price structure prevailing in prescription drugs and the other upon existent hazards in the manufacture and marketing of these drugs.

To increase physicians' confidence in drugs sold under generic name and thus make available to the public the lower prices possible when such drugs are prescribed, the FDA's powers were greatly expanded. Today all prescription drugs must be produced in conformity with "good manufacturing practice," and adequate plant inspection is defined to include access to records, files, processes, and all facilities which are related to the final product. To make certain that all firms, large and small, are covered under these requirements, each domestic drug manufacturing establishment must be registered annually and must be inspected by FDA officials at least once every two years.

To simplify the complicated, unpronounceable generic names for drugs—as compared with the short, catchy, easily memorized trade names—the Kefauver-Harris amendments give the Secretary of Health, Education and Welfare power to designate the generic name where such action seems necessary or desirable "in the interest of usefulness and simplicity." In addition, he is required to review the generic names of all drugs to determine whether revision is necessary in the maintenance of these standards. All advertisements of drugs to physicians must contain the generic name prominently displayed in letters at least half the size of those for the manufacturer's brand name. Controversy immediately arose as to whether the new law required the

[93] "Agency Coordination Study," Part 3, p. 1066.

mention of the generic name each time the brand name is used; this issue was promptly taken to the courts by the drug companies.

With these provisions it is hoped that the prescribing physician will be encouraged to make wider use of generic names for his patients. Obviously, this road to lower drug prices is not applicable where monopoly exists under patents. Since the original provision in the bill—requiring compulsory licensing after three years with payment of generous royalty—was omitted from the final version passed by Congress, no corrective action was taken in this field. In terms of protection of the public's pocketbook, this constitutes a serious gap in the law.

The 1938 food and drug law required merely that new drugs, to be cleared for marketing, be proved safe. The 1962 amendments provide, in addition, that the drugs must be proved efficacious for the conditions for which they are recommended. This efficacy provision went into effect immediately for all new drugs submitted to the FDA after the enactment of the legislation. For "new drugs" cleared prior to that time, the drug companies were given until October 10, 1964—a period of two years—to show efficacy of such drugs already on the market.

The FDA has also been given other important powers under the new law. To secure prompt information on adverse side effects, it is empowered to require such information directly from the drug companies rather than, as in the past, relying upon published reports in medical journals and other sources. A curb on excessive advertising and promotional claims is implemented by the requirement that all advertisements must disclose information on side effects and contraindications. And to prevent a recurrence of the thalidomide episode, the FDA's supervisory powers over drugs in the investigational stage are greatly increased. Today, before a drug product is tested on humans, adequate chemical and animal tests must be performed; a sound investigational program must be submitted to a regulatory agency; qualified investigators must be used for clinical testing and they must keep careful record of their work. If the company decides to apply for approval of the drug for marketing, reports must be submitted to enable the FDA to evaluate it for safety and effectiveness.

The Congress can lay down the general lines of policy it wishes to have followed. That policy's implementation, however, must reside with the regulatory agency which provides the detailed oversight of the industry. In a field as important as the health of our citizens, there can be no compromise; here, if anywhere in our industrial system, the mores of business must be made to conform to the requirements of the public welfare. This can only be achieved, however, by eternal vigilance—not only by the industry's members and the regulatory agency but by the elected representatives of the people and the general public.

Chapter 2

*

MONOPOLY AND WASTE

The Case of Automobiles

High prices are a direct, immediate, and easily recognizable consequence of monopoly. There are other consequences, equally costly but less obvious in their impact. They arise from the kind of competitive practices which come into being when price competition is ruled out of the industry. Whenever there is more than one firm in a business, some form of rivalry is inevitable; if price competition is barred, this competitive behavior will take other forms.

But so long as it is competitive activity, what's the harm? The fact is that non-price forms of competition yield very different results from those flowing out of price competition. These results involve great economic waste and are often positively harmful to the economy.

Under price competition the total market for the product tends to expand constantly. As prices are driven lower, the product becomes increasingly accessible to additional sectors of the population. If the demand exceeds the available supply, at least for a time prices shoot upward; and the high return attracts new entries into the business. If, on the other hand, there is overproduction and oversupply, prices decline accordingly and some producers, disenchanted with the net return on their efforts, will gradually seek other more attractive business opportunities. Thus, there emerges from this restless activity a constant allocation and reallocation of human and financial resources to fit the changing needs of society.

The situation is quite different when competition is channeled into non-price forms. Instead of flexibility there is rigidity; and the machinery of the market, designed for securing the optimum use of total resources, fails to function. Prices, for example, do not rise and fall in response to the market. Their failure to decline means that demand is not quickened by bringing the product increasingly within the reach of people of lower incomes. Similarly, if sales fall off, there is no market mechanism to correct the situation. Indeed, instead of a price decline there is often a price increase; this is explained as necessary in order to allow producers to maintain their standard profit on a lower volume of sales. In this situation, producers are not attracted from the industry by better opportunities elsewhere; they are quite satisfied where they are. Thus the entire industrial structure becomes fixed and immobile under a system of administered prices, while non-price forms of competition run rife.

Often this non-price rivalry builds unnecessary costs into the fabrication of the product, representing sheer economic waste for the general public. The producing firms become embroiled in activities which involve vast expenditures of funds; yet these added costs neither enhance the quality of the product nor add to its convenience or usefulness to the public. The rationale usually employed by the industry in defense of this state of affairs is that it is acting in response to the demands of the buying public. True, these added costs mean higher selling prices, but if the public is insistent, what can the industry do about it? Too often this is the industry's own rationale for preferring non-price forms of competition.

A double penalty is thus imposed upon the consumer. Not only are prices for the product higher than they need be; emphasis is often placed upon a course of development that actually detracts from the usefulness of the product. Instead of trying to achieve real improvements and lower prices for its product, the industry is concentrating attention upon superficial gimmicks which will spell success in the market-place while prices remain immobile. The inventive and creative talents available within the industry are siphoned off into socially unproductive ends, and the genuine progress that could have been made never takes place. Indeed the steps taken may actually be backward rather than forward: in the interest of securing product differentiation, real sacrifices may be made in quality, durability, safety, and the like.

The automobile industry provides an arresting illustration, because the situation just described is represented on a gargantuan scale by that industry. Within a few decades the automobile has been converted from a novelty for the wealthy to a necessity for all. Almost at the moment it completed its shift from luxury status to widespread acceptance, the automobile deserted its role as an instrument of economical transportation and became a costly showpiece. This peculiar development in the automobile industry has occurred nowhere outside the United States. Basically it is a tribute to the intensity of non-price forms of competition in an industry where active price competition is effectively barred.

There can be little objection to the freakish whims of fashion on perishable items of low cost. They provide variety and pleasure, and the fun of acquisition outweighs the relatively small expenditure involved.

The purchase of an automobile is different. For the average family it is, next to the purchase of a house, the largest single item in the budget. Even if the car is purchased under a credit plan, the monthly payments constitute a heavy and insistent drain on the budget, usually over a three-year period. Furthermore, the automobile performs an essential function in transportation. In the complex traffic conditions of our age, the public is entitled to the best that modern technology can provide, as well as the safest and most efficient in operation. Like the household refrigerator, the automobile is a durable good whose design should be attuned to its specific function; and the buying public should have a reasonable expectancy that, in both service and appearance, the new car should give satisfaction for several years.

Instead, the automobile industry has devoted its creative energies to converting its product from a durable good into a perishable item as ephemeral as the latest fashions. The annual production of new models, with its accompaniment of saturation advertising, involves heavy costs for the manufacturers which inevitably are passed on to the public in the form of high prices for automobiles. The dictates of the styling engineers take precedence over everything else. Even safety of operation—not to speak of fuel economies and problems involved in parking—are subordinated to the whims of the fashion experts. This strange fixation on forcing speedy obsolescence, through new annual models, of a durable good is a relatively new development. It is the direct result of non-price competition carried to a logical extreme.

The Extent of Concentration

Of this country's major industries, automobile manufacture represents the apex in economic concentration. In recent years the four largest companies producing passenger cars have accounted for about 99 per cent of the output. Even this figure does not reveal the full extent of the concentration that exists. In 1963, one company produced over half of the cars manufactured in the United States. General Motors' share in 1963 was about 53 per cent, as contrasted with 26 per cent for Ford, 14 per cent for Chrysler, and 6 per cent for American Motors.

In terms of new car registrations, this general relationship is only slightly different when imports are considered. In 1963 General Motors had about 51 per cent of U.S. sales. Ford had 25 per cent, Chrysler, 12 per cent and American Motors, about 6 per cent. The remaining 6 per cent was divided among Studebaker, Checker, and, particularly, foreign imports.

This structural imbalance is relatively new. In 1921 there were 88 firms in the automobile industry. This was the era that E.B. White, the noted essayist, termed "paradise" for the consuming public. "Thirty or forty years ago, when a man wanted a car, he had a fabulous assortment to choose from—everything from a jackrabbit to a bearcat. Big cars, medium-size cars, cheap cars, expensive cars, moderate-priced cars, high cars, low cars, open cars, closed cars, gas cars, steam cars, electric cars; it was paradise."[1] In those days the new industry was in the throes of creation, and a vigorous competitive and experimental spirit characterized its activities.

As compared with the situation today, prices varied enormously. In late 1923 a Ford Model T touring car could be purchased for $380; the Chevrolet Superior and Overland 91 models were going for around $500. The Maxwell, Dort, and Studebaker—each produced by an independent company—were priced at around $1000. Touring cars such as the Hudson, Hupmobile, and Willys-Knight were a little more, but were still under $1500. Another group, including the Marmon and the Cadillac, were in the $3000 range. Then, for the more affluent of our society, there were such showcases as the Duesenberg and the Pierce-Arrow in the $5000 class.

The sedan, which was just coming into vogue, was also available in a wide price range. The Ford Model T was the lowest priced, selling for $685. Chevrolet and Overland models were available for $795. A number of cars—including Oakland, Cleveland, Buick, Gardner, and Jewett—were in the $1500 range. Then came the Hudson and Chalmers, selling for around $2000; and from there, there was a steady climb to such models as the Lafayette for $6500 and the Duesenberg for $7500.

In those days rivalry among auto manufacturers occurred on all fronts. Not only was there unremitting effort, through

---

[1] *The New Yorker*, March 16, 1958, p. 37, partially reprinted in *Hearings*, Administered Prices, Automobiles, Part 6, p. 3058.

improved engineering and design, to provide greater comfort, safety, reliability and performance; there was also intense price competition, resulting in good part from the aggressive competitive behavior of Henry Ford. In 1909 the Ford touring car was selling for $950; by 1912 the price had been reduced to $600; and by 1916 it was available for $360. World War I sent the price up again to around $600, but by 1920 a sagging economy resulted in a sharp curtailment of automobiles sales and Ford announced drastic price cuts on his products. The touring car was reduced from $575 to $440, the sedan from $975 to $795.

The first response of his competitors was hostile. Several —including General Motors, Dodge, Hudson, Maxwell-Chalmers, and Paige—took the position that sales are not stimulated by price reductions. Buyers, it was argued, would suspend purchases, waiting for even further reductions. This argument, incidentally, was persistently voiced in the Subcommittee's steel and drug hearings to explain the absence of price competition. Henry Ford was unconvinced: "It was said that we were disturbing conditions," Ford is reported to have remarked later; "that is exactly what we were trying to do."[2]

At one time it appeared that the extraordinary Selden patent could be used to curb this business revolutionary. As early as 1879, George B. Selden, as enterprising patent attorney in Rochester, New York, filed a patent application on the entire automobile. At this time the automobile was in a state of embryonic development; numerous European and American inventors, professional and amateur, were making improvements in the construction and arrangement of components. Specific patents were being secured on the new combinations, but none of these inventors attempted to secure a patent on the entire vehicle in the belief that the concept was so well known as to be in the public domain.

A patent would have served little purpose in 1879, since

[2] Nevins and Hill, *Ford: Expansion and Challenge, 1915–33*, (New York: Charles Scribner's Sons, 1957), p. 154.

the automobile had not yet reached the stage of profitable commercial production. By a series of delays and intricate maneuvers in handling his patent application, Selden managed to prolong the proceedings for 16 years in the Patent Office. Then in 1895—to the vast astonishment of the burgeoning automobile industry—Selden received a patent. An alliance was quickly formed between the patentee and a group of Eastern financiers who saw in the patent an opportunity to impose private monopoly control over a new, swiftly growing industry. One by one the automobile manufacturers succumbed to pressure and secured a license under the Selden patent; such licenses contained production limitations as well as price-fixing requirements.

In 1903, Ford made application for a license but was refused. His continuance in the industry resulted in the institution of an infringement action under the Selden patent. The legal battle, which lasted for eight years, ended in victory for Ford, and the industry was freed to develop in a competitive environment. Perhaps in consequence of this litigative history, the automobile industry was one of the first to recognize the problems created by a mass of patents in separate hands on an interlocked technology. Very early, therefore, the industry established a patent pool under which patents were freely licensed to all comers.

During most of the period from World War I to the depression of the early 1930's, Ford was the leading producer. The cause was not difficult to find. Not only were the Ford cars lowest in price; they had an established reputation for reliability. As one historian remarked, "Nobody ever called the Model T handsome, much less beautiful; nobody ever rhapsodized over its silhouette; nobody ever praised its comfort. It could plow through bogs, surmount hills, skitter along slopes, and take stumps and rocks in its stride. Summer cloudbursts and winter blizzards merely gave it stronger heart."[3]

By the beginning of the 1930's, Ford's position as leader

[3] *Ibid.*, p. 394.

was in jeopardy. In 1929, Ford and General Motors each held about a third of the market; in 1930, Ford's share rose to over 40 per cent. This was its last year as the country's top producer. In 1931 General Motors took the lead with 43 per cent—never to lose it again. Throughout this period it became increasingly clear that the public wanted something more than sheer utility. Given the choice between an economic and dependable but rather ungainly Ford and a Chevrolet which, for a hundred dollars more, offered not only a better appearance but greater speed and better transmission, cooling, lubrication, ignition, and springs, the public was willing to pay the added price.

General Motors was well equipped to take command of the automobile industry. As early as 1917, when the company was in financial difficulties, the Du Pont Company had made substantial investments in General Motors and even, for a time, assumed responsibility for the financial policies of the automobile company. In the relationship of these two companies reciprocity in buying and selling was developed into a fine art, for each of these giant corporations manufactures products that are useful to the other. The effect, of course, is to provide on the one hand, assured markets for certain products; and, on the other, assured sources of supply. Large quantities of goods are removed from the marketplace; the flow is channeled exclusively between the parties, and outsiders are denied access to the market. It was in this context —its effect upon competition—that the Antitrust Division sought and recently secured severance of the partnership between Du Pont and General Motors in the courts.[4] Undoubtedly, one of the consequences of this corporate alliance was to provide General Motors with the financial resources to assert its dominance in the automobile industry.

Indeed, its association with Du Pont was a significant element in the development of General Motors as one of the world's greatest conglomerate concerns. Regularly, in the *Fortune* listing of the 500 Largest Industrial Corporations,

[4] U. S. vs. DuPont, 353 U. S. 586 (1957).

this company has ranked first, with annual sales now in excess of 15 billion dollars. The Subcommittee's report on the automobile industry in 1958 shows that approximately 35 per cent of all sales—then 11 billion dollars—involved activities *other than* the manufacture and sale of passenger cars and trucks. This contrasts markedly with the situation for Ford and Chrysler. Of Ford's total sales of 5.6 billion dollars, only 18 per cent—1.2 billion dollars—involved areas other than the manufacture of passenger cars and trucks. In the case of Chrysler, the smallest of the "Big Three," with annual sales of about 2 billion dollars, almost all of that figure came from automobile manufacture.

Most of General Motors' widespread activities appear to be confined to industries in which the degree of concentration is relatively high and in which the company itself ranks among the top producers. It is one of the four largest companies producing diesel engines, trucks and truck tractors, motor buses, railroad locomotives and switchers, bicycles, and aircraft engines and propellers. It is a major producer of household refrigerators, service and household machines, cast-iron heating boilers, household electric ranges, and the like. And it is, of course, a leading supplier of equipment and parts for these products.

A question of particular interest to the Subcommittee during the hearings was the manner in which this vast economic power has been used. For example, were profits enjoyed in a sheltered market used to subsidize losses in more competitive areas? In these latter industries, were prices deliberately driven down to such levels that smaller firms were forced out of business? What devices were employed to discipline competitors whose activities were confined to just one industry? In a word, how does a giant conglomerate, with substantial monopoly power in some industries, throw its weight around in the competitive areas in which it operates?

The answer of General Motors' officials provided little clarification. Information showing a breakdown of profits by operating divisions was held to be "confidential." Subsequent to the hearings a statement was filed by the company to clarify testimony by its officials, but was phrased in such generalities as to intensify, if anything, the confusion that already existed. The net result was to suggest that, insofar as General Motors was concerned, its actual exercise of the vast economic power in its hands was a sensitive subject that preferably should remain undiscussed.

Over and beyond its conglomerate operations are other important sources of General Motors' dominance in the automotive field. It has a strong dealer organization embracing the largest number of dealerships of any automobile company in the world. Its advertising and sales efforts are unparalleled. It has been a beneficiary of substantial Government contracts, both for production and for research and development work. Because of the manner in which used car prices are arrived at, the prices of GM used cars—and, thus, their "trade-in" values—are higher than the comparable models of its competitors. This, of course, greatly aids dealers in swelling the sales of new GM cars. Any catalog of the operations of GM should also include General Motors Acceptance Corporation, the wholly owned automobile financing company. The auto finance company is the most costly way of financing the purchase of a car; its "6 per cent add-on finance charge" over a three-year period adds up to an interest rate of over 11 per cent annually. For the ten-year period 1950-60, GMAC's net profit, after taxes, regularly exceeded 15 per cent.

The Strange Pattern of Competition

The imbalance between General Motors and its smaller competitors determines the competitive pattern in the automobile industry. A single event will highlight the present scene. In the fall of 1956, rumors were abroad in the industry that prices on the 1957 models would be increased 5 to 7 per cent to help maintain "a competitive pricing position for higher cost producers such as Chrysler, American Motors, and Studebaker-Packard." However, the first announcement was made by Ford, and the average increase was only 2.9 per cent. At the time a Ford representative explained that the increases were "no more than our actual costs for materials and labor have gone up." Two weeks later General Motors announced its prices on its new Chevrolet models only. The average price increases amounted to 6.1 per cent. Ford waited one week, and then revised its prices upward to be in line with those of General Motors. With the situation clarified, Chrysler then made its announcement of prices which conformed to those of its larger rivals.

This episode illustrates the almost complete replacement of price competition with price leadership accompanied by non-price competition. In autos as in steel, lesser companies may make the first announcement of a price increase, but it does not become effective until the leader acts.

During the Subcommittee's hearings in 1955 and 1958, the situation was further clarified by the testimony of automobile company officials on how their prices were determined. Ordinarily, under competitive conditions, prices represent the summation of costs plus a reasonable profit for the more efficient producers; high-cost producers who cannot sell at these prices are weeded out of the business. General Motors, according to its officials who testified before the Subcommittee, approaches the problem differently. It starts with a projected "target" profit rate—the return it expects to make on its investment. Usually this is stated as 15 per cent net return on capital employed, or alternatively, as 20 per cent on net worth.

Basically, this is the method employed by a public utility which, because of the nature of its product or service, is free of the pressures of competition. However, a distinction should be noted. The public utility is a monopoly subject to Government regulation; its cost structure and pricing practices are scrutinized and often revised by an administrative agency acting on behalf of the public. In determining the

reasonableness of price, the regulatory body sets a limit—
6 per cent or 8 per cent—as a fair return upon the capital
employed. Though it uses the same method as public utilities
for determining its prices, General Motors, in contrast, is
free of regulation. It sets up its own cost system, determines
its own method of allocating joint costs, and fixes its own
prices in terms of the particular profit rate it wishes to enjoy.

The Subcommittee's report on the automobile industry in
1958 shows that General Motors has been remarkably successful in adhering to its "target" profit rate. Save for the
Great Depression in the early 1930's and the "recession" of
1938, it has met or exceeded its goal. Even during the
years of depression, when many firms showed substantial
losses, General Motors made profits. For the ten-year period
1948–57, preceding the Subcommittee's report, the company's average annual return, after taxes, on its stockholders' investment was an impressive 25 per cent. In the worst
of these years, 1957, the rate of return was 17 per cent, a
figure that any public utility would regard with some awe.

The best year was 1950, when the company made 37½
per cent. It is an interesting fact that the company's pricing
policy has been fully capable of compensating for the rise in
income tax rates over the years. The rates of return in 1929
and 1950, after taxes, were very similar—36 per cent as
against 37½ per cent. The 1929 rate was achieved with a
before-tax earnings rate of 38½ per cent on stockholders'
investment. By 1950, the tax rate had risen greatly; therefore the company had to make a before-tax profit of 77 per
cent in order to earn 37½ per cent after taxes.

None of the other automobile manufacturers is in quite
the same position. Their predicament was summed up by
Dr. Theodore O. Yntema, vice-president of Ford, when he
was asked during the Subcommittee hearings whether his
company also employed a projected "target" rate of return.
The reply was: "We are not in that fortunate position—we
would like to do better than we are doing." When asked how
then Ford arrived at its prices, Dr. Yntema explained more
fully:

. . . in our own particular company, we do not have a simple cost-plus formula. We do not have any simple way in which you go just from cost to price. We have to look at our competitive situation. Ordinarily, what we find is this: We have very little leeway. If we would reduce the price substantially to meet competition, we could not make a respectable profit.[5]

The testimony of the president of Chrysler was very similar. He too stated his company projected no "definite profit figure," and remarked: "All we know is our profits in recent years have been far too low and we are trying to improve them." When asked why the prices in comparative models were similar for the three major companies, the reply was:

We have got to price our cars as near as we can to theirs to compete with them. We do not get them quite as low because we have not got the volume. If we had their volume, maybe we could make it lower, but you have got to make a reasonable profit to stay in business at the end, and we just price ours as near as we can and that is what it amounts to.[6]

George Romney, president of American Motors, put the matter even more simply. He explained his company's pricing policy in this way:

I cannot ignore the prices of my competitors in setting the prices on my cars because I cannot sell my cars if my cars are not priced on the basis where they will sell in relationship to the price of the other fellow's product. So one of the things I have to take into consideration in pricing my cars is the price of the competitor.[7]

Mr. Romney was less reluctant than Ford and Chrysler officials to discuss the dominant pricing role of General Motors. He remarked that the GM "target" profit rate was designed to average out over a period of years; for that reason "in good times they have not moved their prices up as far as they could" and "in bad times they have not gone down." This has resulted in an absence of price flexibility in

[5] *Hearings*, Administered Prices, Automobiles, Part 6, p. 2683.
[6] *Ibid.*, p. 2779.
[7] *Ibid.*, p. 2946.

the automobile industry. He left no doubt, however, that GM's pricing policy fixed the stage on which Mr. Romney could maneuver his own company.

Under these circumstances it is not surprising that the Subcommittee found a close similarity in prices of comparable automobile models among the automobile manufacturers. Because of the sizable outlay represented in the purchase of a car, there is no need for absolute price identity; a few dollars one way or another will not dictate the particular make that is selected by the buyer. In general, however, there is very close price conformity among the companies, arising out of the fact that none of the lesser manufacturers can afford to price much beyond the range set by the dominant producer.

Thus, in a subtle fashion, General Motors plays the role of price leader, even when Ford or Chrysler leads in the price announcements. As the 1957 episode shows, the aim of the smaller manufacturers is to anticipate the prices of General Motors; and on the occasion when the guess is wholly out of line, the mistake is hurriedly rectified. Had the move been in reverse in 1957, with price reductions rather than increases, Ford would undoubtedly have matched the cuts made by General Motors. Thus there can be no doubt that the key role in pricing is played by GM; its decisions establish the price level for the industry.

Car Fancification—Competitive Waste

The disappearance of price competition has engendered the socially wasteful competition embodied in annual style changes. To an extent unparalleled by any other durable goods industry, this type of rivalry represents a concerted, unrelenting effort to make quickly obsolescent a product which, by its very nature, is designed to give service for many years. To convert a durable type of consumer product into an ephemeral perishable of fashion is a difficult art. Every conceivable form of pressure and inducement is invoked to make the consumer dissatisfied with his old car while it is still a useful instrument of transportation. An endless stream of "improvements" is presented which have little or no real significance insofar as the public is concerned. Each new offering, however, is hailed as "revolutionary," and every advertising device is skillfully employed to shame the consumer into discarding his current automobile in the interest of presenting a more prosperous appearance to the world with the latest automotive fashion.

A number of experts appearing before the Subcommittee stressed the unsuitability of the automobile as a style guide. Dr. Ruby Turner Morris, in remarking that the annual model changes are "wasteful of our natural resources," stated that "Automotive engineers themselves must regret when perfectly good dies, capable of putting out millions of more excellent cars, have to be thrown in the dust heap as a sacrifice to the great god of fashion and change for change's sake."[8] Indeed, one of the difficulties involved in annual change is that no company can anticipate all of the problems that arise when a pilot model is translated into a mass-produced product; some "bugs" are inevitable. Where the model is kept standard for some years, design errors or mechanical defects can be corrected. Under the present system, however, there is little incentive to make these corrections, particularly if they involve substantial alterations in jigs or dies, because in a few months the equipment will be discarded for a different model.

In consequence, it is not surprising that many experts feel there has been actual deterioration in the quality of cars now being produced. In part, this has been due to the fact that emphasis on styling is so dominant that function is sacrificed. Speaking on this point, the automotive consultant of Consumers Union, a testing service for consumers, remarked that it often appears that "modern styling was created only

[8] *Ibid.*, p. 2448. Dr. Morris, a professor at Connecticut College, is an expert in consumer economics and author of the article "Product Fancification, Optional and Otherwise," p. 2455 ff.

to hinder both car and driver." He added that "when a styling feature vies with a practical feature, or a safety feature, styling usually wins."[9]

As an example he cited the fact that, back in 1937, Chrysler had the idea of flattening off the dashboard by recessing all knobs. This important safety feature did not, however, survive the vicissitudes of new styling changes. Most of the new cars of today are characterized by highly decorative dashboards containing protruding objects which are a hazard to front-seat occupants.

Industrial designers frequently draw a distinction between style and innovation. The stylist is concerned with superficial changes to give the appearance of newness where the reality is absent. Innovation occurs when advances take place which affect both the product itself and its visual appearance. In the latter instance there is genuine progress when the two essential factors—function and style—are combined. The problem faced by the stylist is that he has a limited palette; the number of acceptable variations can easily be exhausted, and little by little he is pushed into creating ridiculous changes. In the automobile industry this has been reflected in the rise and fall of fins, the multitudinous lighting components, gingerbread chrome and glitter, bucket seats, ornate but functionless bumpers with protruding lights, and the like.

The cost of annual model changes can only be described as staggering. Recently a trio of college professors presented to the American Economic Association a paper on the costs of automobile model changes in recent years.[10] For the five-year period 1956–60, they estimated that these changes contributed about 25 per cent to the average price of four-door sedans currently available in the market. Over-all expenditures for the entire industry for model changes amounted to about 3.9 billion dollars annually during this period.

[9] *Ibid.*, p. 3067.
[10] Franklin M. Fisher, Massachusetts Institute of Technology; Zvi Griliches, University of Chicago; and Carl Kaysen, Harvard University. (Papers and Proceedings of the 74th annual meeting of the American Economic Association, Vol. LII, *American Economic Review*, May 1962, p. 259.)

But this is not the whole story. Accompanying the annual model changes has been the horsepower race which started in the early 1950's. The ever larger power plants have necessitated bigger and heavier cars; this situation, in turn, has created greater expense which is not exhausted with purchase of the car but is expended throughout its life. Important among these is increased gasoline consumption. These economists estimated that the owner of the average 1956–60 car pays for gasoline about $40 more per 10,000 miles than would have been necessary if models had remained constant as of the period just prior to the horsepower race. This represents another 20 per cent increase in total gasoline costs, or an additional annual expenditure of about 968 million dollars. And this increased cost is bound to continue during the useful lives of the existing stock of cars. For all cars built through 1961 the economic team estimated that the cost to the public of additional gasoline consumption would run to about 7.1 billion dollars.

Altogether, their estimates of costs of model changes run to about 5 billion dollars annually over the 1956-60 period, as compared with the prehorsepower-race years of 1949 or 1950. And they emphasize that these figures are, if anything, underestimates. No attempt was made to assess the higher costs to the public of repair bills and replacement parts, the added costs arising out of the increased use of highly skilled mechanics and the complex tools made necessary by the huge automotive mechanisms, and the frightful expense involved in the repair of bodywork damage. Nor, of course, could any monetary values be placed upon the heavy social costs arising out of the parking problems created by these larger vehicles in areas already heavily congested.

For a brief time a halt appeared to be called by automobile manufacturers to the costly horsepower race. In 1957, as a result of the investigations of traffic accidents by the House Subcommittee on Health and Safety, an informal agreement was entered into by manufacturers to arrest this form of non-price competition. Company officials, meeting under the auspices of the Automobile Manufacturers Association, pledged themselves "to encourage owners and drivers to evaluate passenger cars in terms of useful power and ability to afford safe, reliable and comfortable transportation, rather than in terms of capacity for speed." The resolution also banned auto factory participation in auto racing and speed and acceleration tests, and the use of such tests and race results in company advertising. Apparently this latter step was taken because of increased expenditures for these activities, as well as the danger of unfortunate publicity for manufacturers arising from racing accidents.

Being in the nature of a gentlemen's agreement, this truce depended upon voluntary adherence to its terms. Though it could not wholly stem the pressure among the manufacturers to emphasize speed and power in their advertisements, it served a useful purpose. In 1962, this agreement came to an end. According to a *Wall Street Journal* report, "the spirit, if not the letter, of the agreement has been well shattered." The 1957 pact simply gave way before the industry's "urge to woo customers by bragging about the number of horses under the hood."[11] As further evidence of the return to this form of rivalry, the *Wall Street Journal* cited the latest showings at the Chicago Auto Show comparing the increased horsepower of the newest models with their earlier counterparts. In addition, a renewed interest has been shown by manufacturers in auto racing, ostensibly for advertising emphasis on speed and power. In 1962 the *Wall Street Journal* characterized the automobile companies' participation as "concealed": "But reporters at the recent 500-mile stock car race at Daytona, Fla., noticed that engineers and officials of GM's Pontiac division were much in evidence in the pit area. Pontiacs placed one-two-three in the race."

One year later Ford eliminated all pretense by directly entering special racing cars under its own name in the Indianapolis Sweepstakes. In addition to the larger financial outlays involved in "souping up" the engines and the mainte-

[11] *Wall Street Journal*, March 5, 1962.

nance factors involved, the social costs must also be taken into account. A member of the House Subcommittee, in expressing concern for the companies' abandonment of their 1957 agreement, stated:

The need for such an agreement was reflected in the rising death toll on America's highways. At that time, each manufacturer based his claims on massive horsepower and high speed figures. Competition being what it is, the public was caught in a race of spiraling high performance figures and death statistics to match.[12]

The House Committee's report in 1962 states that, in the last ten years, nearly 400,000 persons have died in the United States as a result of motor vehicle accidents. In 1959, there were 4,172,000 injuries from motor vehicle accidents. *In the age group from five to twenty-four, the motor vehicle is the principal cause of death in the United States.*

Curiously enough, annual style changes appear to have little influence upon the total number of new cars that are sold each year. Because of the present high prices, a customer who would prefer a new car but is financially unable to make the purchase is forced into the used-car market. Here he may get a good buy or he may end up with a "lemon" requiring heavy expenses for maintenance or repair.

In the course of the 1958 automobile hearings, General Motors officials expressed great pride in the "styling leadership" of their company. At one time, major style changes involving some advances in technology were made every four or five years; intervening years were marked by superficial "face lifts" designed to give the appearance of change. Under the leadership of General Motors, however, this period has been shortened until now the companies boast of completely new models each year. Alone among the major manufacturers, GM has the financial resources to play this costly game successfully—a game which both Ford and Chrysler have

[12] *Congressional Record*, 87th Cong. 2d Sess., Vol. 108, No. 32, March 6, 1962, p. 3199.

felt compelled to follow. According to Mr. Romney of American Motors, this situation developed after the postwar period when the two companies could easily have been eliminated from the industry; in an effort to solve their dilemma "they simply adopted the GM product philosophy, and the result is all three of them began to build products based on the same product idea."[13] This was not conspiracy, he thought; GM's competitors were simply doing "what the champ had done" with proved success.

Neither the officials of Ford nor those of Chrysler revealed much enthusiasm for the annual style change. Mr. Yntema of Ford explained simply that his company had no choice; it would like to lower tooling and other costs but when "the competition" comes out with a new model, Ford is compelled to do likewise or lose business. Chrysler officials took the same view; if their company presented the same car year after year "when General Motors or Ford or both of them are changing to new cars each year, you'd pretty soon be out of business."[14] Thus both feel themselves caught in a real dilemma. Major model changes are necessary to maintain sales, yet the staggering costs such changes entail are a threat to the companies' continuing survival.

The Biggest Little Midgets

At the time of the Subcommittee's hearings in 1958, the new compacts had yet to make their appearance. However, foreign imports of small cars were making threatening inroads in the United States market. From 1 per cent of new passenger car registrations in 1955, the figure for this group had risen to over 5 per cent by 1958 and was to reach 6½ per cent in 1959. Yet American cars, bigger and fancier, were being produced each year. Who dictated these styles? Who decreed the social waste involved in the enormous expenditures for annual model changes?

General Motors' response was prompt. "Fancification,"

13 *Ibid.*, p. 2858.
14 *Ibid.*, p. 2828.

said the president of GM (and he used that term), "is the result of the demand on the part of the public." When asked whether the consumer took the initiative or was receptive to auto companies' advertising, he replied, "I would say that the customer now has the pressure on us to make changes."[15] He went on to explain that consumer preference was determined by surveys constantly being conducted, and added significantly, "There is no indication that there will be a change in the trend in the near term."

Officials of the other auto companies were less dogmatic with respect to the origin of style changes. An official of Ford pointed out that, unlike most consumer-goods industries, there is a "4-year gestation period" on automobile production; the 1962 models, for example, were worked up in 1958. This time factor, of course, presents serious problems; there is always the danger that one may produce cars consumers wanted four years earlier. Indeed, according to one authority, this is exactly what happened in the case of the Edsel. Richard S. Latham, industrial designer, told the Subcommittee that "The Edsel, a wholly new product said to have cost 250 million dollars to develop, is the result of four years' research into 'what the consumer really wanted in a middle-bracket car.' The conclusion that one cannot fail to reach, for its apparent and proven lack of success, is that it was, indeed, research in what people wanted—four years ago."[16]

Testimony by Ford officials indicated that the role of the consumer is not that of dictator of style changes, but rather of final arbiter in the marketplace. To a large extent, styling is a guessing game; the risks are extraordinarily great and "a few wrong decisions can wreck a company."[17] The Chrysler position was very similar. "You decide what the consumer wants at the time and you do your best to adjust yourself to what you think he is going to want, and if you guess wrong, you are in bad shape."[18]

George Romney of American Motors pointed out that the

[15] *Ibid.*, p. 2512.
[16] *Ibid.*, p. 3150.
[17] *Ibid.*, p. 2730.
[18] *Ibid.*, p. 2798.

introduction of a significant change in design is very difficult for the smaller producers; they lack the large volume necessary to secure immediate acceptance by the public. A company of the size of General Motors can, however, create public adoption of the new style immediately. With saturation advertising and a strong dealer organization, the public can quickly be prevailed upon to believe that the change represents a substantial improvement over the older models. As an example Romney cited the wraparound windshield introduced by General Motors. This development did not significantly improve vision but immediately became high style. As he put it, "A small company could not have made the wraparound windshield a successful thing because when you get right down to the guts of it, it has no basic advantages over the straight windshield, and yet through advertising and promotion you can make an item of that type become absolutely the hallmark of a modern car, if you have got a large enough percentage of the total market to do it."[19]

To further illustrate his point, Romney likened the automobile business to the millinery trade. If one milliner had over half the country's hat business, his decision to put cherries on ladies' hats would determine high fashion for that year. All other milliners would have to think twice before omitting cherries from their models if they expected to get some business. The introduction of cherries by a small milliner, however, might well be disregarded as an unattractive, if not ridiculous, adornment. Thus, he suggested, the introduction of the wraparound windshield by a small manufacturer "probably would have been a flop, but the fact that it was put on cars by a company doing as much business as the company that put it on helped to make the thing a success, because in the field of fashion, Senator, familiarity brings acceptance."[20]

The introduction of the compact car represented a triumph of public demand for smaller and more economical

[19] *Ibid.*, p. 2879.
[20] *Ibid.*, p. 2983.

instruments of transportation. The burgeoning of foreign imports and the success of American Motors were a direct refutation of the GM position, in the Subcommittee's 1958 hearings, that "there is no indication that there will be change in the trend for the near term." Instead, in a flurry of activity, the large automobile manufacturers suddenly reversed their accustomed course and adopted the philosophy of one of their smaller, upstart competitors.

Yet the new compacts had hardly made their appearance before the pressure began anew for bigger and fancier versions. At the present time the major manufacturers are vociferously vying with each other in P.T. Barnum's term for the "biggest little midgets in the world." Indeed the talk is now in terms of the "fresh new compact in the large economy size." A supercharged version of Chevrolet's compact Corvair has been given the imposing name of Corvair Monza Spyder, the last two names suggestively referring to an Italian race course and a West German racing sports car. The new models enjoy the delightful contradiction of being "too roomy to be a compact" but "too darn thrifty to be anything else."

Reflecting the extent to which the 1957 agreement to ban speed and horsepower promotion has been abandoned, these "sleek, sparkling newcomers" in the automotive field are also "spirited." In the case of the Dodge Dart, you no longer have to settle for "weak-sister power"; "you get the kind of standard horses you pay extra for in most other compacts." And you have the best of two possible worlds, for Dart not only "saves with the rest of 'em," it "outstrides the best of 'em." And the Pontiac Tempest 4 "goes around acting like a V-8," as you will realize when you get those "horses atrotting." All accounts indicate that the horsepower race has been moved to a war footing by the major manufacturers. The stepping up of power has extended from the more modest compacts to the fanciest models.

Ominous rumblings in response to this state of affairs have been heard from several quarters. The public's genuine interest in smaller and more economical cars is indicated by the fact that so-called compacts now have over a third of U.S. sales; counting foreign imports—composed almost entirely of small models—the figure is around 40 per cent. Sales of imported cars appear to be on the rise again; they are edging up to the levels prevailing at the time that the American companies made the defensive move of introducing their own smaller models. The increased popularity of imports may reflect the growing realization by United States consumers that the "biggest little midget" is something of a contradiction in terms.

The renewed emphasis on speed and horsepower has also awakened some concern in the Congress. Members of the House Health and Safety Subcommittee at various times have voiced their alarm at the current trend among the country's auto makers. Unless the industry takes voluntary action to curb the trend, the Congress may be forced to act.

The situation in the automobile industry epitomizes the kinds of problems that develop when price competition has atrophied and rivalry among firms is limited to non-price forms. The public, allegedly the impetus for the annual style changes, is in reality the victim. It is called upon to foot the bill for a kind of competition that is neither healthy for the industry nor useful to the consumer. Indeed, in the aggregate, the social wastes involved may be more important than the pecuniary costs, great as they are. Unfortunately, the social losses—absence of the real technological progress that could have been achieved, loss of human life arising out of the industry's emphasis on speed and power, the traffic problems that have multiplied in the wake of today's automotive monsters—are not susceptible of ordinary measurement. Nor, indeed, is the loss to society of the benefits that would have arisen were this highly important industry constantly revitalized by the free play of industrial rivalry in all its forms, including price competition.

Chapter 3

*

MONOPOLY AND JOBS

The Case of Steel

In our society the practices of monopoly are often secreted behind a front of "competition." In the sale of automobiles, for example, the public is confronted with a vast array of retail dealers, all of whom competitively assert that they can offer "the best deal" to the prospective buyer. The marketing pattern for gasoline is characterized by an overbuilt, wasteful, and costly structure of retail stations often located adjacent to each other along the highway. The appearance is one of intense competition as each retail outlet sells at the identical price and blazons the superiority of its particular national brand over those of nearby competitors. Even the stations selling under private brand names, with prices slightly lower in order to get customers, are careful to maintain the customary price differential and thus avoid shaking the sensitive price structure in the retailing of gasoline.

Yet behind these competitive façades exist highly concentrated industries controlling the production of these essential goods. Here there is little of the competitive bombast attuned to price which characterizes the retail forum. Prices are administered; what competitive behavior exists is channeled into non-price forms.

Similarly, the basic materials used in the production of many commodities are the subject of monopoly control, without any real awareness of this fact by the general public. The consumer buys canned tomatoes; he does not buy tinplate. He buys automobile tires, not carbon black. He purchases high-octane gasoline, not tetraethyl lead. He buys pots and pans, not sheets of aluminum. In all of these cases monopoly pricing affects our lives, but it is furtive and indirect. The toll is taken from our pockets, but it is done unobtrusively in the competitive clamor of the retail marketplace.

For this reason I have found myself unsympathetic to the "market-basket" concept of the consumer's interest. There is an understandable tendency for consumer agencies to concentrate their efforts on products directly purchased by the general public—to provide useful tips on how to spend one's dollars most wisely. This is a useful function, but it is not the only function for the protection of the public. I tried to indicate this in introducing a bill in the Senate for the establishment of an independent Federal agency to represent the interests of consumers. This was in June 1963, and represented the third attempt on my part in three successive Congresses. At the time I stated:

I do not visualize the Office of Consumers as being solely concerned with the housewife with a market basket under her arm. The problem is far more complicated than is represented by the market-basket concept. It is just as easy to victimize the consumer behind the front lines—at a point remote from where direct contact is established between buyer and seller.

The Crucial Role of Steel

We consumers shop for hammers, lawnmowers, equipment of all sorts made of steel. Steel supports are essential in the construction of our homes, in the factories and office buildings we occupy during the day to earn our livings. Most of the forms of transportation we utilize are heavily dependent upon the steel industry in one way or another. Even the routes of railroads are dictated by the steel rails over which the movable steel structures must make their way. The spanning of waterways with bridges, the construction of tunnels, the massive development of automotive thruways are mute testimony of the importance of steel in our lives.

The average consumer never thinks of buying a pound of steel, yet the steel industry's role in our economy is fundamental. Our machine economy, with its heavy dependence upon steel, makes us peculiarly vulnerable to the pricing decisions in the steel industry. If the price of steel goes up, the inflationary impact is felt throughout the entire economic structure. And the increase is not limited to a mere increase in the cost of steel. All along the productive line, from the basic material to the final fabricated product, there is an effort to maintain traditional margins or "markups." As a result, increases are pyramided upon increases as one fabricator after another seeks to preserve his customary percentage of profit on the orders moving through his plant. Thus it is not surprising that a $6 a ton increase in the price of steel, according to one expert, results in a $75 increase in the price of a tractor; nor that a $25 increase in sheet steel prices ultimately means an increase to the purchaser of an automobile of over $50.

But the impact does not end there. Steel executives are prone to describe the demand for steel as a "derived demand" —that is, it arises out of and is an aspect of the resiliency of the economy. In an economic slump, when orders fall off, jobs decline, and profits melt away, the market for steel suffers. When the economy is booming, with production and job opportunities rising, the demand for steel quickens.

No one who has lived through a depression—or even a recession or a "downward dip" or a "healthy readjustment period"—can doubt the authenticity of these statements. But there is another side of the picture. Just as steel, in its pervasive importance in our economy, is a sensitive barometer of industrial conditions, it is also a significant element in determining the economy's state of health. Our industrial system is a highly complex mechanism; it both *reacts upon* and *reacts to* an industry of such major significance as steel.

In industries of lesser importance, escape valves can sometimes be found by industrial users to avoid—and strike at—existent structures of monopoly pricing. Considerable ingenuity is often displayed by industrial consumers in searching out substitute materials that are as good as or even better than the original product. If the opportunity permits, goods may be imported from overseas at prices which, even including costs of transportation, are more reasonable. Or, if the industrial consumer is large enough and has the financial resources, he may engage in vertical expansion; that is, he will extend his corporate domain to include production for his own use of some essential materials needed in the fabrication of the company's products.

In an industry as important as steel, these techniques are less successful. Some substitution has occurred; industrial users have shifted, wherever possible, from high-priced steel to aluminum, plastics, and other materials. There has been an increasing driblet of imports; between 1955 and 1961, annual United States imports of steel mill products rose from 973,000 net tons to 3,164,000 tons.[1] In 1963 imports reached 5,400,000 tons. However, this latter volume is insignificant in terms of total supply. In 1961, the U.S. steel industry accounted for nearly 100,000,000 tons of ingot production and over 66,000,000 tons of shipments of finished steel products. In 1963 ingot production was 109,000,000 tons; and steel product shipments were 75,500,000 tons.[2]

For the most part the economy has been forced to live with the administered pricing structure in the steel industry and to abide by its dictates. The industry's turgid pricing posture, its unwillingness to expand production and develop new markets for its products, its failure to engage in price competition, have left deep marks on employment within the industry. In 1955, the U.S. iron and steel industry employed 625,000 workers; by 1961, over 100,000 had been cut from

[1] *Hearings* before the Committee on the Judiciary, U.S. Senate, 87th Cong., 2nd Sess., Sept. 1962, Steel Companies (Subpoenas), p. 52.

[2] American Iron & Steel Institute data.

the payrolls. In 1963 there were fewer total workers than in 1961 but they turned out 14 per cent more shipments than in 1961.

It is impossible to estimate the spurt that would be given to the sales of the vast array of products containing steel if the industry allowed full play to the forces of competition. No one can doubt that there is a great untapped demand for goods in this country; that all of us would buy more if we could. Even the family enjoying the pleasures of full employment has its miscellany of unfilled wants; for those suffering the deprivations of technologic displacement, underemployment, or total inability to find a place in the job world, the fact of want is inescapable. Obviously, it would be unfair to place the major onus of a limping economy upon any one industry, no matter how important its role in the scheme of production. But certainly if shares are to be allocated among the major industrial participants in this drama, the steel industry would to many observers be a leading candidate.

Unused Capacity and Maintenance of Profits

In September 1962, the president of Republic Steel informed the Senate Judiciary Committee that the steel industry was then operating at 50 per cent of its capacity.[3] The particular occasion was a dramatic moment. Earlier that spring the industry had announced an increase in steel prices, but the direct and personal intervention of President Kennedy resulted in a recision of the increase. At the time there was considerable comment in industrial circles that the price increase was justified but that the manner in which the matter was handled by the steel industry was not. The nature of the public controversy that followed made it evident that another effort—not too far in the future—would be made to increase steel prices.

It was in this atmosphere that the Subcommittee on Antitrust and Monopoly determined to secure information on

[3] *Hearings,* Steel Companies (Subpoenas), *op. cit.,* p. 30.

steel costs to ascertain whether or not the impending price rises were justified. Particular effort was made to assure that the identities of the particular companies and their costs would not be disclosed; that figures would be combined in such a fashion, or that ranges would be used in place of specific numbers, so as to obviate the possibility of corporate disclosure. A Subcommittee proposal was even made that the data be submitted to the General Accounting Office for analysis to insure the confidential nature of the companies' submissions. Subcommittee subpoenas were served upon the major steel producers requiring the submission of necessary information. Four companies—Bethlehem, Republic, National, and Armco—refused to comply. The members of the Subcommittee then met in executive session in August 1962 and, by a majority vote, reported a resolution to the full Senate Judiciary Committee calling for contempt citations to be reported to the Senate against the non-complying corporations. This resolution was defeated within the Judiciary Committee in September, and the matter ended then and there. That is, it ended so far as the Subcommittee was concerned. Some months later—in the spring of 1963—the steel industry again announced an increase in prices, slightly tailored in manner but equally pervasive in its impact upon the economy. This time the price hike "stuck."

How can a price rise be made to stick in an industry operating at only half of its capacity? This is a crucial question, and its answer lies in the organization and long-established pattern of behavior in the steel industry. During his appearance before the Senate Judiciary Committee, Thomas F. Patton, president of Republic and speaking for all four of the non-complying companies, supplied information on United States steel capacity in 1960. This was in answer to an inquiry by Senator McClellan. It is of interest that U. S. Steel alone had 28.2 per cent of the country's steel capacity; that second in order was Bethlehem with 15.5 per cent; that Republic accounted for 8.6 per cent. Thus, the three largest companies controlled over half of the total. The inclusion of the next five producers—Jones & Laughlin, National, Armco, Youngstown, and Inland—brought the figure up to nearly 75 per cent of total steel capacity in this country.[4]

Statistics on actual ingot production in 1960 and shipments of finished steel products in that year support the finding of high concentration in the industry. But even this does not tell the whole story because of the specialization of the companies both in products and in geographical areas. For example, the Subcommittee's report on steel shows that in 1957 the four largest producers of railroad products —axles, joint bars, rails, tie plates, and wheels—accounted for all shipments. Most probably this situation remains unchanged today. The same concentration by the largest four existed in the case of certain types of structural steel, such as piling, and various kinds of steel sheet and strip. In tin mill products, the four largest producers accounted for around 80 per cent of electrolytic tin plate and black plate, and almost 90 per cent of hot dipped tin and terneplate.[5] The same principle applies to geographic areas. The four largest producers of hot-rolled merchant bars held 65 per cent of the country's total capacity for this product; in the Northeastern states the four largest accounted for 75 per cent.

Under these circumstances it is not entirely surprising that the steel industry can so price its products that the "break-even" point occurs slightly below an operating rate of 33 per cent. That is, for the steel industry as a whole and specifically for the largest producer, U.S. Steel, when the production rate approaches 33 per cent of capacity, operations are profitable.

This calculation by the Subcommittee was confirmed during the steel administered price hearings in 1957 by Fred V. Gardner, a prominent management consultant and author of treatises on the subject.[6] Using a different method of

4 *Ibid.*, p. 63.
5 Administered Prices, Steel, 1958, p. 70.
6 *Hearings,* Administered Prices, Steel, Part 3, p. 713 ff.

computation, he arrived at a break-even point of around 35 per cent. In his view, a pricing structure that achieved this result was dangerous to the health of the economy and acted as a brake upon economic development. He stated that the average break-even point for all U. S. industry was around 50 per cent, and that this figure constituted the minimum for the operation of a sound economy. In his twenty-five years of computing break-even points for 1500 companies, he said, U.S. Steel's break-even point was the lowest he had ever encountered. In terms of prices prevailing in 1957—prior to the 1958 and 1963 increases—it was Mr. Gardner's opinion that U. S. Steel could lower its prices 10 per cent and still maintain a break-even point near 50 per cent of capacity.

The Subcommittee's report on administered prices in the steel industry for 1958 made a comparison of the steel companies' average rates of return after taxes for ten-year intervals. U. S. Steel, during the period 1920-29, enjoyed an average profit rate of 8.7 per cent on investment; from 1930–39, including the depression years, the figure was 1.4 per cent. For the decade 1940–49, excluding the war years when prices were controlled, the rate was 9.4 per cent. The rise continued in the 1950's; omitting the brief Korean War period, the average for the period from 1950 through 1956 was 11.5 per cent.

The Subcommittee's steel hearings in 1957 followed directly upon the heels of a uniform increase in steel prices in the summer of that year. Since the companies were then operating well below capacity, the price hike provoked a number of questions by members of the Subcommittee. To some of us, a price increase at that time hardly appeared to be the right formula for stimulating increased steel business and restoring utilization of facilities then lying idle.

In most industries, great variation in costs frequently exist from one company to another. Steel is no exception. Such variations may reflect differences in the kind of operations engaged in; to some extent they also reflect the degrees of efficiency of operations. Bethlehem and National are generally regarded as among the more efficient steel companies, and both have consistently enjoyed higher profit rates than U.S. Steel. For this reason it was particularly mystifying that Bethlehem and National found it necessary to join in the uniform price rise. At that time it would have seemed more logical for those companies to have cut prices to get additional business.

Perhaps anticipating the line of questioning from the Subcommittee, Arthur B. Homer, president of Bethlehem, met the problem head on in his opening statement. At the time of his appearance in October 1957, when Bethlehem was operating at 90 per cent of capacity, he stated:

As a general rule, Bethlehem does not expect to operate at capacity for any extended period of time. Capacity operation gives us so many problems in the way of maintenance and other fields that we have a feeling that we are probably doing better at, say, 85 to 90 per cent of capacity than at 100 per cent, and we do our long-range planning with that in mind.[7]

However, questioning brought out that even when Bethlehem was operating well below 85–90 per cent capacity, it still did not initiate lower prices to stimulate additional business. The following colloquy occurred:

Senator Kefauver: I notice here in 1954 that in the first quarter you were operating at 77.7 per cent of capacity, the second quarter 73.3, third quarter 67.1. Did you lower your prices then to get more production?

Mr. Homer: No, no. We felt, in 1954, that we had a depressed situation. It might have been due to a lot of things that had nothing to do with the price of steel. Again lack of money . . .

Senator Kefauver: You said yesterday that 85 to 90 per cent capacity operation was desirable, and here in 1954 you were down to 67 per cent. I wonder why you did not lower your price then to get more production?

Mr. Homer: Well, again, Senator, we feel that under those conditions that the lowering of the price would not stimulate

[7] *Hearings*, Administered Prices, Steel, Part 2, p. 549.

business. There are other conditions that affect the dropping off that a change in price would not have any effect upon at all. That was our judgment.[8]

Mr. Homer was asked whether there would not have been greater competition if Bethlehem had refrained from raising its prices to the full extent of the 1957 increase. Mr. Homer replied:

Well, we did not need the business, Senator. A reduction in price, in our opinion, would not have increased the business. We were operating at practically full capacity and, therefore, any reduction in price would not have stimulated any more business.[9]

Mr. Homer's statement to the Subcommittee contrasted markedly with the reasons he gave for his company's desire in 1957 to acquire Youngstown Sheet & Tube, the fifth largest steel producer in the country. Here the argument moved in the opposite direction; the purpose of the merger, according to Mr. Homer, was the need for greater competition in the steel industry. In defense of the proposed merger, he argued:

The merger will result in another company capable of waging effective competition in many of the markets of U.S. Steel, to the benefit of suppliers, customers, and the public alike.

The merger will result in salutary strengthening of the forces of competition in the steel industry, and do so without impairing, or even tending to impair, the vigor of competition in any market area and without tending to create a monopoly.[10]

This view, however, was not shared by the U. S. Department of Justice, which instituted successful action to halt the merger under Section 7 of the Clayton Act.[11]

The appearance of George M. Humphrey, chairman of

[8] *Ibid.*, p. 623.
[9] *Ibid.*, pp. 621–22.
[10] Affidavit of Arthur B. Homer, September 15, 1957, in *U.S. v. Bethlehem Steel Corp. and The Youngstown Sheet & Tube Co.*, U.S. District Court, Southern District of New York, Civil Action No. 115–328.
[11] 157 Fed. Supp. 877.

the board of National, was of particular interest to the Sub-committee. In a press conference late in June 1957, President Eisenhower had expressed the view that control of inflation could not be left solely to the Federal Government. He said:

The only point I make is this: Government, no matter what its policies, cannot, of itself, make certain of the soundness of the dollar in this country, that is, the stability of the purchasing power of the dollar in this country. There must be statesmanlike action, both by business and labor.

Frankly, I believe that boards of directors of business, of business organizations, should take under the most serious consideration any thought of a price rise and should approve it only when they can see that it is absolutely necessary in order to continue to get the kind of money they need for the expansion demanded in this country.[12]

Just one day later newspapers over the country featured a press release from the U.S. Steel Corporation announcing increases of $6 a ton in steel prices, effective July 1. Within a week every major producer had followed the steel corporation's lead.

In his capacity as Secretary of the Treasury under President Eisenhower, Mr. Humphrey had frequently deplored the inflationary impact of price increases. The Subcommittee was interested in learning Mr. Humphrey's views after his return to private life:

Senator Kefauver: You would not contend, Mr. Humphrey, that this increase in July of $540 million to the direct consumers was not inflationary; would you?

Mr. Humphrey: Any increase, Senator—and I think I testified to this while I was still a bureaucrat—any increase is inflationary to some degree. Any increase in the price level, in price levels, does have some effect upon the depreciation of the dollar. It does have some effect upon the cost of living. I think that until increases which come all at once and become effective at once,

[12] *New York Times*, June 27, 1957.

until they can be leveled off through increased productivity and the development of increased productivity, I think they are temporarily inflationary.

Now, as they can be leveled off through increased productivity, they gradually will be absorbed. It cannot be done all at once.[13]

At the time of Mr. Humphrey's appearance before the Subcommittee in 1957, National's utilization of capacity had declined from 98 per cent to 80 per cent. Asked if an increase in prices was warranted under such circumstances, he replied that it was the "proper policy at this time," and added "because very frankly from the effect upon our earnings and our operations so far . . . we certainly are not in any position to take any less price, and we can't get any more."[14] This view resulted in the following exchange:

Senator Kefauver: Mr. Humphrey, in the first quarter of 1957 you were running at 98 per cent of capacity. You are now down to 80 per cent of capacity. How far down in reduction of capacity do you have to go before you think your formula here takes application?

Mr. Humphrey: To the point where we believe that a change in the price would make a difference in the demand and would stimulate demand and increase total demand, and that is not at the present time.

Senator Kefauver: I would think that getting down from 98 per cent to 80 per cent ought to be coming somewhere close to putting into application your formula here of getting more business by reducing your price increase from $6 to $5.

Mr. Humphrey: Not at the present time.

Senator Kefauver: Do you not think that it would stimulate your sales as distinct from the industry sales, that is, it would increase your sales, give you more production, raise your operating revenue, be a wonderful example and a tonic to the country at this time?

Mr. Humphrey: Senator, your experience and mine is a little different and I just do not agree.

[13] *Hearings,* Administered Prices, Steel, Part 3, p. 821.
[14] *Ibid.,* p. 814.

Senator Kefauver: You do not think it would?

Mr. Humphrey: I do not, and I said so yesterday.

Senator Kefauver: Can you give us any idea on how far you would let your production go down before you would put in your—

Mr. Humphrey: No. It depends upon a great many conditions, as I have just told you, and I cannot estimate at what point that would be true.[15]

The problem faced by the steel industry is a serious one. Currently it has the capacity to produce about 170,000,000 tons of steel annually; yet the United States market demand at present prices appears to hover in the neighborhood of 100,000,000 or 110,000,000 tons. At best, it is difficult to envision a domestic consumption—again at present prices —that exceeds 125,000,000 tons. Until 1959 the industry sought to solve this problem of excess capacity by moving into the export field. The difficulty has been that foreign steel producers have been vigorously competing on a price basis for the same business; the American companies, by failing to bestir themselves, have lost out. Indeed, not only have they lost out abroad; they have watched with growing alarm the inroads of foreign firms in their own backyards.

The industry's dilemma was dramatically illustrated during the 1963 hearings of the U.S. Tariff Commission on so-called "dumping" of wire rods from Belgium.[16] The president of Springport Steel Products Co., Springport, Michigan testified that for several years he had purchased wire rods used by his plant from a number of domestic steel mills. He shifted to foreign suppliers because of the rigid identity of price that prevailed among domestic mills. He described his experience in this manner:

I became quite concerned about the fact that the price was so identical, and I deliberately set out to try and find some little bit

15 *Ibid.*, p. 872.

16 In the Matter of Hearing on Hot-Rolled Carbon Steel Wire Rods from Belgium, Investigation No. 27, U.S. Tariff Commission, Official Report of Proceedings, Vol. 2, pp. 242–243 ff.

of price competition among the American mills, and I deliberately called them in one by one, their salesmen, and we checked every possibility. But if I ordered a train load of wire from Sparrows Point, from Buffalo, from Colorado, from Kokomo, Indiana, when it got to my plant there wasn't a dime difference in the whole train load.

He then offered to buy an entire years' supply—roughly 3000 tons of wire rod—if he could get a slight price reduction. He stated:

I called the salesman from one of the mills in and told him that I would give him a contract for the entire tonnage if he would give me a price concession of 10¢ a hundred pound. He said he did not think there was a chance, but that he would try. He reported back later that they had taken it to the top management, and that his district sales manager had even offered to refund me the money out of his bonus if they would let him do it. They said it was not to be allowed.

An attempt was then made to purchase at the mill plant, with the buyer taking over the task of delivery.

At the time I had trucks delivering boxes to Ford and Plymouth down in Indiana, and I had trucks coming back empty from Indiana, but I was not able to pick up my wire at Kokomo at the Kokomo base. They would not allow me to pick it up in my own trucks because that would give them a better price than their competitors, a lower price, and they were afraid that would offend the other mills.

Out of this experience developed his entry into the foreign market for supplies in 1959. He explained:

I am a stubborn sort of a guy, and I got an idea to try and beat the price by a penny and I was not able to do it. In fact, I heard one of the wire salesmen say, "Why don't you draw your own wire?" I said "Why not?" He said, "You need about $100,000 worth of equipment," but I found a wire-drawing operation in

Chicago that was going bankrupt and I bought the wire-drawing setup at a much lower price. So then I began to draw my own wire. So at that time I began to buy some foreign rod. After I had been buying foreign rod for several months or maybe a little over a year, then one of the mills did call me in and asked me to come down to their offices and they did offer to cut the price, but not sufficient to meet the price I was paying.

When asked if this offer to cut the price was conditioned upon ceasing to purchase wire rods from abroad, he replied, "Well, it was conditioned on my buying a substantial quantity from them which would have amounted to the same thing."

How Prices Are Made

No doubt the device of price leadership far antedates the passage of the Sherman Act in 1890. Yet it sometimes appears to be an instrument perfectly and deliberately designed to frustrate the purpose of the antitrust statute, for under price leadership the process of pricemaking is completely removed from the competitive forces in the marketplace while, at the same time, the usual evidence of conspiracy—so essential in our pattern of antitrust enforcement—is often totally absent.

Senator Burton K. Wheeler, then Chairman of the Interstate Commerce Committee, probed this question in the mid-1930's. After listening to testimony from steel executives for some days, he remarked:

All the witnesses thus far give the impression that their prices were set only to meet competition. In other words, they indicate that they only follow the bellwether. Somebody, somewhere, must set the original price. During the era of the "Gary dinners" we knew how the prices were set. They were set because, when they got together in these dinners, they set the price. In earlier days they got together and sat down and agreed in writing what the prices should be, but at the present time it seems to be extremely difficult to find out who the bellwether is and who fixes the price originally that they follow to meet that competition.[17]

At this particular moment William A. Irvin, then president of U.S. Steel, was on the stand:

Mr. Irvin: I would say we generally make the prices.

The Chairman: You generally make the prices?

Mr. Irvin: Yes, sir. We generally make the prices, unless some of the other members of the industry think that that price may be too high, and they make the price.

The Chairman: You lead off, then, with a price charged, either up or down, at Gary; is that correct?

Mr. Irvin: Yes.

The matter was gone into again during the hearings of the Temporary National Economic Committee. At that time Eugene C. Grace, then president of Bethlehem, was interrogated by A. H. Feller, an official of the Antitrust Division in the Department of Justice.

Mr. Feller: Mr. Grace, do you recall any occasions on which your company took the initiative in announcing a lower price on any steel commodity?

Mr. Grace: I can't recall whether we have or whether we haven't. I know, generally, we haven't.

Mr. Feller: Then I take it . . .

Mr. Grace (interposing): I know—I am telling you what the general practice is from our company standpoint. Whether we have ever initiated any, I just couldn't say, but in the main we would normally await the schedules as published by the steel corporation.

Mr. Leon Henderson [TNEC staff]: That went back as far as you can remember the policy of the Bethlehem?

Mr. Grace: Yes.[18]

It is of interest that Mr. Grace never employed the trade name in referring to U.S. Steel; in an apparent reversal of

[17] Hearings before Senate Interstate Commerce Committee, 74th Cong., 2d Sess., on S. 4055, p. 595.

[18] Hearings before the Temporary National Economic Committee, 76th Cong., 2d Sess. Part 19, pp. 10601 ff.

the practices of the major drug companies, he preferred the generic term, "the steel corporation." He went on to explain in a little greater detail.

Mr. Grace: When we put out a schedule, what we call our official prices, they usually represent and are the same as our competitor has put on the market, and, in most instances, as a general practice, not looking for a little difference here and there, as a general practice, that pace is set, if that is a good word, by the steel corporation.

Mr. Feller: Now, it wouldn't matter, however, in an actual case, if some company would come out at some time in the future, some company other than the steel corporation, with a different published price. You would still follow that, and you have done that in the past?

Mr. Grace: I would still follow that.

A decade later the issue of price leadership came up before Senator Joseph C. O'Mahoney, Chairman of the Joint Committee on the Economic Report. This time Mr. Homer, president of Bethlehem, was on the stand. The questioning related to a price increase that had been instituted by U.S. Steel and was immediately followed by Bethlehem.

Senator O'Mahoney: Did you make the same increase with respect to these semifinished products that the U.S. Steel did?

Mr. Homer: Yes, sir.

Senator O'Mahoney: Did you have any conference with U.S. Steel about it?

Mr. Homer: No.

Senator O'Mahoney: How did you happen to make the same increase?

Mr. Homer: I think my statement outlines that, Senator. We learned of the increase in the market price through our sales people who had heard from customers that they were in contact with that the market price had changed.

Senator O'Mahoney: And you did not take the initiative?

Mr. Homer: No, sir.

Senator O'Mahoney: Would you have taken the initiative if U.S. Steel had not?

Mr. Homer: I cannot answer that question; it depends upon what the situation is. We have taken the initiative in some cases, and at other times we have not. It depends on what the product is.[19]

A year later Senator O'Mahoney was back at it again with Mr. Homer:

The Chairman: . . . I have observed that in the steel industry you all move as a unit. When U.S. Steel announced the price, then the others came right along, and it is substantially the same price. That was what was shown in the hearings a year ago, it is what is shown now.

Mr. Homer: And it will probably be shown in the future, Senator, because in order to stay in business you have to meet the market level; if you are going to get in there and get it, you cannot have your prices way up high and expect to get business.

The Chairman: Well, I confess that I am a little bit puzzled in trying to understand the position of Bethlehem a year ago and the position of Bethlehem today, a very substantial producer, feeling that for purposes of competition when U.S. Steel raises its prices, it must also raise its price.

I should think that the competitive effect would be quite the other way and that if you retained your price, you might get a better market.[20]

Because of this earlier testimony, the Subcommittee made a determined effort to ascertain how U.S. Steel arrived at its decision to raise prices in the summer of 1957. At the hearings Roger M. Blough, then chairman of the board, appeared on behalf of U.S. Steel.

Senator Kefauver: . . . You talked about the factors that you considered when you decided upon this $6-a-ton increase. Who do you mean by "we," Mr. Blough? Who is on that committee or who makes the decision? Do you make it or who makes it?

Mr. Blough: . . . In our management team we have many mem-

[19] Hearings before the Joint Committee on the Economic Report, March 2, 1948, 80th Cong., 2d Sess., p. 55.

[20] Hearings before the Joint Committee on the Economic Report, January 24, 1950, 81st Cong., 2d Sess. p. 513.

bers. There are a number of those gentlemen who were involved in trying to arrive at a point of agreement with respect to this, and I would mention Mr. Hood, Mr. Tyson, Mr. Sentner, who are here.[21]

Mr. Blough explained that the ultimate decision was, of course, in the hands of the Board of Directors. As he put it,

This matter was discussed with the Board of Directors. We made the recommendation. If the board would have felt that we were out of line in the light of all of the factors, I am sure that they would have said so, and we probably would have revised our recommendation. I would say the answer to your question is, the ultimate decision lies in the board of directors of the U.S. Steel Corporation.

When asked if alternative proposals had been submitted to the board, Mr. Blough replied that a single recommendation has been made, and he indicated that this same procedure had been followed in connection with earlier price increases.

Senator Kefauver: They are not equipped to go into all the technical cost and difficulties and problems to arrive at a price, are they, Mr. Blough? That has to be done by a smaller group.

Mr. Blough: I think our directors are pretty well equipped, but I agree with you that in the management of any corporation, the active management should be in a position to make a recommendation with respect to any material change.

The inquiry then turned to the manner in which the small group of executives had arrived at their judgment:

Mr. Blough: I would say we make it as a team.

Senator Kefauver: I know. But suppose you disagree. Who is the referee?

Mr. Blough: I would have to cross that bridge when we came to it.

[21] *Hearings,* Administered Prices, Steel, Part 2, *op. cit.,* p. 304. Clifford F. Hood was president of U.S. Steel, Robert C. Tyson, chairman of the finance committee; Richard F. Sentner, executive vice president in charge of sales.

Senator Kefauver: You mean you never disagree?

Mr. Blough: We talk things out until we agree.

Senator Kefauver: Did anybody recommend a higher increase or a lower increase in this little group?

Mr. Blough: I do not recall any such recommendation.[22]

Did this mean, it was asked, that all four of the individuals had each independently arrived at precisely the same amount? Mr. Blough replied that he could not remember who had first mentioned the amount; nor could he "recall any other figure" that had been suggested. However, he added that the group did have the benefit of knowing what others in the industry hoped for in the way of price increases.

We had, through newspaper accounts and trade journals, estimates of what other figures in the steel industry—I mean connected with other companies—had said the price should go up or it needed to go up, and that sort of thing, and those estimates ranged all the way from, as I recall it, $8.50 to $12, or something in that area, maybe, I think, as high as $14. I have no doubt that figures such as that with reference to other elements of the industry were discussed among us.[23]

The Game of "Follow the Leader"

The tribal mores in industries tend to fall in distinctive patterns. Many people have noticed that pets seem to take on certain characteristics of their masters; they often exhibit similar preferences and dislikes. There is also some evidence that long service in an industry creates a distinctive kind of executive. As the officials of the leading corporations in an industry parade through a Congressional hearing room, they often seem to have been constructed from the same mold. Sometimes this similarity is not confined to the rather uniform way they view the industry's problems and defend its set of trade practices. On occasion it extends to general

[22] *Ibid.*, p. 305.
[23] *Ibid.*, p. 306.

physical appearance, pattern of dress, and even sense of humor, which becomes manifest at one time or another during the hearings.

The rationale for an industry's price structure follows rather set patterns. In drugs, the magic word is "research." In automobiles, it is "the public's insistent demand" for style changes. In steel, it is "high labor costs." In each of these industries, something sacrosanct has become attached to these particular concepts, and there is little disposition to subject them to critical examination.

Time and again during the drug hearings, expert witnesses with long experience in the field of drug manufacturing pointed out that many expenses wholly unrelated to the development of new drugs are charged against the category of "research"; these include the costs of processing a patent application through the Patent Office, attorneys' fees in waging an interference fight in the Patent Office, the costs of appeals, and the like. They include the expenses for developing mixtures and special dosage forms which have little medical value but will increase the sale of the company's products. More properly, these expenditures belong elsewhere than in the category of research.

In the automobile hearings, a real effort was made to shake the industry's asserted conviction that style changes are the result of consumer demands. From whence came the great public demand for fins? Where was the public outcry for headlights on bumpers that led to the style of G M cars? Who has insisted upon a speed capacity which, if exercised, will land the driver in jail or in Kingdom Come? Outside the teenage set, how many motorists are really concerned about a pick-up that will allow them to best all rivals when the stoplight flashes green? Yet the industry which has created these advertising lures, as a device for avoiding price competition, has remained adamant in its position that they are a response to insistent public demand.

In steel the defense for high prices centers around the level of steel wages as compared with those in other industries. The unit of measurement preferred by the industry is cost "per employee-hour." Now, if the steel industry were selling man-hours of work, as happens in a law office or in a firm of consulting engineers, that would be one thing. But, as everyone knows, the industry is engaged in the marketing of steel and steel products. The incidence of technological progress is constantly to lower man-hour requirements in production; according to a variety of estimates, the average annual rate of increase in man-hour productivity in the steel industry is between 3 and 4 per cent. As a result, employment costs per ton of steel shipped may decline or hold even, while employment costs "per employee-hour" rise. This simple fact was pointed out again and again during the Sub-committee's hearings in 1957. Yet "cost per employee-hour" was used as justification for higher prices by the industry in 1962 and again in 1963.

The rules of the game of "Follow the Leader" are quite understandable when the price movement is downward. Steel mill products, though characterized by great variety, can be highly standardized by specification. Further identity is achieved through wide use of the same "extra book" which quotes standard charges for specific metallurgical properties, for size, shape, surface treatment, and a host of other characteristics. Steel that meets the specifications lacks quality differences. Industrial consumers are very knowledgeable purchasers; they know what they want and they know whether they are getting it. In this kind of environment slight shavings in price are significant in determining which steel company gets the business. Mr. Blough summed up the views of the steel industry in these terms:

. . . I have a very high respect for our competitors and they are very able people and they are well able to take care of themselves. But I would like to clear up, shall I say, misconception or illusion with respect to other steel companies. There isn't certainly any steel company in the first 10 or in the first 20 that couldn't require us to change our prices overnight simply by taking action which is different than the action that we take.

Now I want to be sure you understand what I am saying. If Inland or Bethlehem or J. & L. or any one of those companies chose to sell steel, as they have many times in the past, at a different price in different marketing and competing areas in this country it would definitely have an effect upon our decision. Now, if you have the impression that there is some kind of a ukase that determines all things in a competitive industry such as steel, it is simply a wrong impression.[24]

But what if the situation is in reverse—and the price movement is upward? Would not some of the companies see an opportunity to expand their sales by raising their prices to less than the amount set by U.S. Steel? Would not this opportunity appear particularly attractive to those companies whose profit rate was superior to that of "the steel corporation"?

This question was put to the president of Bethlehem.

Mr. Homer: Well, we sell at the competitive price, Senator, and if that results in our making a better performance than our competitor, that pleases us very much and pleases our stockholders, and makes a much better situation.

Those are some of the things I talked about yesterday, where we have many competitive situations and are striving to improve in all respects, and if, after you sum it all up, we find that we end up with a little better result than our competitor, based on getting business on a competitive basis in the competitive market, that is fine; that is what we are trying to do.

We would like to be better than the other fellow. I do not see that that is any reason whatsoever that there should be any reduction in prices because of that. . . . We go out and get business at the competitive level, and we make a better performance than somebody else, fine; fine.[25]

It was suggested that perhaps the consumer might be given a "little break" with price reductions.

Mr. Homer: Then you can carry it on to the point where you

[24] *Ibid.*, pp. 308–309.
[25] *Ibid.*, pp. 631-632.

would not be making any money, if you do embark on that process.

Senator Kefauver: Nobody is talking about that.

Mr. Homer: If you embark on that process, step by step, you will end up without making any money at all. That certainly would not be in anybody's interest.

It was pointed out to Mr. Homer that a basic tenet of competition is that the more efficient producer passes on benefits to the public in the form of lower prices; and that these lower prices force other producers to improve their outmoded techniques or go out of business.

Senator Kefauver: But the trouble is, Mr. Homer, you are operating under the umbrella of those who are not as efficient as you, as indicated by the profit figures. If you would lower your prices, which might bring your profits down a little bit, not much, then the inefficient would have to get more efficient or they would fall by the wayside, and that would be true competition.

Mr. Homer: . . . I cannot see that you would get anywhere at all by a process such as you are suggesting, because one company is more efficient than the other. You are, in effect, saying that to be efficient is a bad thing, because you want to turn around and give a lower price, and then your competitors meet that, and then the next time you give them another one, and pretty soon you end up with a zero proposition.[26]

No one, it was argued in return, was suggesting that efficiently operated companies should be denied good profits and dividends for their stockholders. Nor was it being suggested that prices should be driven into the ground. But, under competitive conditions, the public also participates in the benefits of industrial progress; and this is accomplished by reducing prices. Mr. Homer's answer came very close to an assertion that monopoly pricing is necessary to maintain a competitive system.

. . . if you keep going at the process you are suggesting, of cutting down and cutting down, pretty soon no one gets anything

[26] *Ibid.*, pp. 632–633.

out of it, and we are not able to maintain our plants, even though we may be efficient; we have no money left to do the job that we have got to do, as I outlined in my statement yesterday. . . .

Your suggestion is a route that is disastrous, as I see it, for any industry to go, and you will end up that the last one to be in the business will be the most efficient one, and the rest of them will be out, and you will have a monopoly with one company supplying our country with whatever steel they can supply them, and it will not be enough, and the rest of them will be out of business.[27]

The same question was put to Mr. Humphrey of National.

Senator Kefauver: So you have an economical operation, an efficient company, operating at low cost. Why would it not be in line with what you were working for as Secretary of the Treasury —that is, in bringing about deflation and lowering of prices— for you to pass on to the steel consumers the benefit of your better operation, your greater efficiency?

Mr. Humphrey: We do not know that we can at the present time, and we have no intention of making a move until we know what we can do.[28]

Mr. Humphrey went on to elucidate a kind of thinking decidedly reminiscent of Mr. Homer's.

Mr. Humphrey: We cannot go up because our competition has set a limit on "up." We might even consider that if we did not have a limit on it, but there is no use considering that because we cannot go up, and we certainly are not going to go down.

Senator Kefauver: You cannot go up because your competition has set a ceiling, but you could go down and your competition would likely come down to your lower base, would it not?

Mr. Humphrey: It is not going to help this country or anyone else if we go down to a point where this industry does not make any money, and it will hurt the Government very seriously if that should occur.[29]

[27] *Ibid.*, pp. 633–634.
[28] *Ibid.*, Part 3, p. 822.
[29] *Ibid.*, pp. 822–823.

In fact, as Mr. Humphrey disclosed his views, it became increasingly apparent that he saw no relation between high profits and the need for lowering prices. When Senator O'Mahoney asked him whether National would follow U.S. Steel up even if his own company's costs were substantially lower, he replied:

So long as U.S. Steel's pricing were such that we believed there was a fair general price to expand the general market, I would say yes, sir. I think there is no reason in the world why, if National Steel can make more money than U.S. Steel, we shouldn't do it, so long as we are looking at a long-range picture and are building and developing and expanding markets for our product.[30]

Senator O'Mahoney's interest in the "target" pricing system used by General Motors led him to inquire whether National too had a "general, long-term pricing policy." Mr. Humphrey's formula was simplicity itself. "It is to keep ourselves competitive with prices that we find that we have to meet." But the Senator's curiosity was not fully satisfied, and he asked to have this remark explained. Mr. Humphrey's reply was strikingly characteristic of the climate of opinion prevailing in the steel industry. National's pricing policy, he said, was to

quote prices that are as near the prices of our competitors as we can learn and determine and work out so that we will get at least as much as they do, and we ought to be ashamed of ourselves if we do not, and so that we will not price ourselves over them and thereby not get any business.[31]

Throughout his testimony Mr. Humphrey sought to equate price conformity with his company's success in the steel industry. History does not bear him out. In the company's early days, when it was a young upstart, it was quite independent in its pricing policies. During the NRA days of the 1930's, National was the only company that resolutely cut

[30] *Ibid.*, p. 816.
[31] *Ibid.*, p. 812.

IN A FEW HANDS

prices and refused to conform to the pricing practices of its established competitors. The radical shift in policy that has occurred in the intervening years was made clearly evident in Mr. Humphrey's eulogy of U.S. Steel as price leader:

> . . . I think that U.S. Steel is the largest producer, a very well managed, a very conservatively managed concern over a long period of years. Since the days of Judge Gary they have been very public minded, very conscience minded. They have been very thoughtful and very wise in trying to determine the long-term best interests of the business, and they know that the long-term best interests of the business is to produce a product that will gain in volume and gain in use, and that to do that they must make the best product for the purpose for the least cost, to get the public over a long period of time to buy their product instead of somebody else's, and to continue the expansion of the business as a whole.
>
> I think in view of that wise publicly minded long-term thing, I think it has paid off in the industry because of the rapid growth of the industry and the continued growth of the industry and the continued fact that steel is better than most other products for most things within its field; that that expansion is due to that; and I think, as a result of that sort of management and that sort of thinking, probably most of the time the steel corporation has been the low man, and most of the time the steel corporation's prices have been lower than other people, than a number of other people, not all, but than a number of other people in the steel business would have been glad to have and thought might have been desirable.
>
> I think they have been an influence in operating their own business for the best interests of a long-pull operation. From my point of view, I would like to compliment them on their wisdom over the time that I have been in the business.[32]

Philosophy of Competition

Just as the practices of the steel industry represent a departure from competitive norms, so does the philosophy of

[32] *Ibid.*, p. 870.

those in command of the country's largest steel corporations. Mr. Blough made this evident when he was questioned about uniform bids on Government purchases, where prices of the steel companies matched each other to the thousandth of a cent per pound. His position was clearcut: "My concept is that a price that matches another price is a competitive price. If you don't choose to accept that concept, then of course, you don't accept it. In the steel industry we know it is so."[33]

The point is, of course, that price identity may reflect a highly competitive market or it may indicate a united front by sellers. The real question is how that identity is arrived at. Under genuinely competitive conditions, producers must meet the lower prices of their rivals or lose the business. Under other circumstances, price identity is achieved through lockstep action of sellers, all following the price leader. Mr. Blough's failure to take account of this distinction is indicated in his remark: "For anyone to assume that prices are not competitive because some producers raise the price the same as other producers, I think is, as I said before, simply an erroneous assumption."[34]

It was also evident in his prepared statement to the Subcommittee when he likened R. H. Macy's pricing practices to those of U.S. Steel. The important difference is that, when Macy's increases the price on one of its products, it has no certainty that Gimbel's and other retail stores in New York will follow. But when U.S. Steel raises its price, it does so in the comfortable assurance, based on years of experience, that other steel companies will follow in almost military formation. In an effort to clear the haze, it was pointed out during the Subcommittee's hearings:

When Macy's increases the price of any given product, it has no certain knowledge whatever that Gimbels is going to increase its price by a like amount.

In other words, its area of discretion in price making is

[33] *Ibid.*, Part 2, p. 312.
[34] *Ibid.*, p. 314.

strongly limited not only by the presence of Gimbel's but by Gimbel's conspicuous independent behavior. But when U.S. Steel raises its price, it does so with the almost certain knowledge, based on years of experience, that its so-called competitors will make the same increase.

Inasmuch as Mr. Blough brought up the matter of Macy's pricing let us follow it through and see where we come out. Would Mr. Blough say that Macy's and Gimbel's are not in competition because their prices are different? Would he say that New Yorkers would have the benefit of greater competition, of greater freedom of choice, if the prices of Macy's and Gimbel's were invariably identical? Would he consider that competition between Macy's and Gimbel's would be greater if every price increase by Macy's was immediately matched by Gimbel's? If Macy's and Gimbel's turned to what we have heard here about the steel industry, then a new Macy's slogan might wave over Herald Square, "Our prices are always exactly as high as Gimbel's."[35]

The president of Bethlehem presented the standardized approach to the problem. Differences in costs among producers, he felt, "have little, if any, effect on the prices at which products are sold."

Mr. Homer: Differences in costs, by and large, the same as differences in operating and other efficiencies, are reflected principally, if not entirely, in differences in net earnings.

I believe that the economists teach that the market price of a product reaches a level slightly above the cost of the marginal producer. In such case, I do not think that all the producers who are more efficient than the marginal one make the same amount of profit.[36]

In his discussion of Bethlehem's favorable profit record, this statement was expanded.

If Bethlehem showed a little bit better performance than anybody else, that may be because the results show we have been a little more successful than anybody else.

[35] *Ibid.,* pp. 324–325.
[36] *Ibid.,* p. 612.

And, if that is so, fine. That is what we are supposed to do if we can possibly do it, but still operating on a strictly competitive basis as far as the sale of steel is concerned. . . .[37]

It was suggested to Mr. Homer that the benefits of competition lie in the efficient producer's reduction of prices, thus forcing the less efficient to introduce economics in operation or go out of business. At this point Mr. Homer developed his economic philosophy more fully, explaining that it was not original with him but acquired in an economics course in 1915.

Mr. Homer: I think the question resolves itself down to the fact that it is the marginal operation of any company or plant that really establishes the price level, and they are the high-cost operation. And if they cannot survive at a certain price level, they go out of business.

Now, that price level is pretty much established by the marginal producer. If you want to talk theory about this as to why prices get to where they do, I think you have got to go back to the theory of marginal operation, because I think that really controls the level of prices.[38]

As Mr. Homer explained it, the alternative to his system was monopoly or even public ownership.

If you do not operate on that basis, you eventually get to a point where you have monopoly, because if you keep the most efficient producer cutting prices every time that he has a little margin in there or makes a little money, he drives out of business the rest of the producers, and you end up with a monopoly.

Now, that is the theory of it, and it is not a new theory at all. It is not a new theory at all.

But the surest way to drive us into Government operation or public ownership of the steel industry is to operate on the basis that you suggest, as I see it, because you are going to gradually get down to the point where no one is able to stay in the business, and then who is going to take care of it?[39]

[37] *Ibid.*, p. 635.
[38] *Ibid.*, pp. 635–36.
[39] *Ibid.*, p. 636.

Mr. Homer's economic doctrines fail to fit the facts of his own industry. One of the major assumptions in classical theory is that each producer is operating at full capacity, and the high-cost marginal producer—whose output is needed to meet the public demand for the product—will establish the price at almost zero level profit on his operations. Then if demand drops off, a still lower-cost producer will become the marginal operator, and prices will fall to reflect the lower costs. On the other hand, if demand increases, prices will rise to bring into operation the high-cost producers who previously could not have functioned in the industry. Thus prices are presumed to fluctuate constantly in response to market conditions, and an industrial order exists in which no company defers to another in the initiation of price changes. But in the steel industry prices are set by the price leader, and the fluctuating element is production which responds to demand at the established price.

The theory also presumes easy entrance to and exit from the industry. This is not the case in the steel industry. According to an analysis made by the U. S. Department of Justice in connection with the Bethlehem-Youngstown merger, the structure of the industry has remained virtually unchanged in the last twenty years.[40] Between 1935 and 1957, thirty-one companies with ingot capacity were added, but altogether they represented less than 7 per cent of the total ingot capacity in 1957. And few of these were genuine newcomers. Most of them had been in the steel industry prior to 1935, either as members of the steel industry lacking ingot capacity or as consumers of steel products engaging in some fabrication. During the intervening years they merely added ingot capacity, primarily for their own use. Genuinely new entrants—such as Kaiser Steel Corporation—were usually

[40] Affidavit of S. Robert Mitchell in Support of Plaintiff's Motion for Summary Judgment, *U.S. v. Bethlehem Steel Corp., and the Youngstown Sheet & Tube Co.,* United States District Court for the Southern District of New York, Civil No. 115–328. The information was compiled from the *Iron and Steel Works Directory* published by the American Iron and Steel Institute.

the beneficiaries of sizable financial aid from the U.S. Government. The new additions did not alter the basic structure and organization of the industry. All of the major steel companies that exist today have remained in their position of dominance for several decades.

Mr. Humphrey's philosophy was akin to Mr. Homer's, but was couched in less doctrinal language. In a hearing before the Senate Finance Committee, the head of National Steel had explained his thinking with respect to the price rise that had just occurred. If a competitor increases his price to $6, he stated, "I am just a little ashamed of myself if I cannot sell equally with you and not get $6. But if I cannot, rather than shut down, I will take $5 and take some business, and that is the way it works."[41]

During the Subcommittee's hearings, Mr. Humphrey was asked if this meant that, unless he raised his prices to meet those of the price leader, "you are a little ashamed of yourself if you cannot sell equally with him and get $6 for your steel." Mr. Humphrey replied: "If he is the low man, if he is the man that sets a price that I think is the low price and is a reasonable and proper price and adequate price, then if I cannot get that, I feel that there is something the matter with my sales."[42] It was pointed out that, where all producers sell at the same price, there is no "low man"; that the "low man" is also the "high man." The following exchange occurred:

Senator Kefauver: Suppose the low man raised his price to $25. Would you feel ashamed of yourself if you did not get your price up to $25?

Mr. Humphrey: I would think that if the low man went to $25, there would be some very good reason for his doing so. And if the reasons that affected him in doing so affected all the rest of the industry in doing so, it probably would affect me in doing so. It would mean that something had happened that required a

[41] Committee on Finance, U.S. Senate, 85th Cong., 1st sess., *Hearings, Investigation of the Financial Condition of the United States,* July 11, 1957, p. 613. Also reprinted in *Hearings, Administered Prices, op. cit.,* p. 867.

[42] *Hearings, Administered Prices, Steel, op. cit.,* p. 868.

substantial increase in price, and if it were justified, then I would feel very badly if I could not get it. If it was unjustified, it would not last a minute.

Senator Kefauver: Would you be ashamed of yourself if you did not get $25, too?

Mr. Humphrey: I would be ashamed of myself if I could not get the price that was justified, that conditions justified, yes, sir; that other people could get.[43]

Thus Mr. Humphrey ended up in company with Mr. Homer, though the route was pragmatic and less adorned with theoretical abstractions. It could only be summed up in these blunt terms: "As I interpret that, Mr. Humphrey, you would be ashamed of yourself if you did not get what the traffic would bear."

[43] *Ibid.*, p. 868.

Chapter 4

MONOPOLY AND SMALL BUSINESS

The Case of Bakeries

Monopoly also leaves its heavy imprint upon small business. In many industries, the activities of small independent units have been almost extinguished; in others, they are "contained" to "fringe" areas of an industry's activities, such as highly specialized fabrication, custom-designed products, and the like.

In the ethical drug industry, for example, the large companies have almost totally pre-empted the sale of prescription drugs through retail pharmacies; increasingly the business of the smaller companies has been limited to sales to institutional buyers purchasing in the competitive generic-name market. In automobiles, the genuinely small manufacturer is limited to the production of parts and components, and even this market is shrinking with the disappearance of the independent auto makers. In the steel industry the little fellow is usually a nonintegrated fabricator whose material must be purchased from one of the major mills with whom he also competes in the marketplace.

The surest protection to competition, and thus to the consumer's interest, is the existence of a large number of producers none of whom has an appreciable share of the market. Even when an industry desires to achieve "price stabilization," as price-fixing is sometimes euphemistically called, if that industry is made up of many independent units its attempts at price-fixing will be short-lived or impossible. The women's garment trade is a case in point. For years that industry marketed its products on the basis of specific price lines, with "house dresses" at the foot of the price ladder. To the consumer's gain and the manufacturers' continuing distress, the house dress branch persisted in upgrading its product but selling at house dress prices. On occasion the manufacturers met and reached a common agreement on the price lines to be followed and the quality to be put into each of these lines. After one such meeting a number of the manufacturers immediately returned to their offices and notified their customers that they would maintain their former low prices and further upgrade the quality of their merchandise. Thus, with each producer acting according to his own independent best interests the industry remained as fiercely competitive as ever.

It is this free spirit of individualistic behavior which gives to the public the benefits of competitive enterprise, namely, lower prices and better quality. It is this same spirit which earns the enmity of monopoly for its unsettling and disturbing impact upon established ways of doing things, not to speak of the disrupting consequences on monopolistic pricing and profits.

The Wholesale Bread Industry

The effect of monopolistic power on the small businessman is well illustrated by the wholesale bread industry. The baking of bread and related products is an important area of economic activity; in 1958 this industry shipped nearly 4 billion dollars worth of merchandise at wholesale prices. The bread industry by nature has been one of the provinces of the small businessman. The official 1958 Census of Manufactures showed that there were 5300 separate wholesale baking companies.

Despite the large number of independent companies, however, only four firms accounted for 22 per cent of the market, and the eight largest held 37 per cent. These market shares were much larger than in 1947 when there were nearly 6000 separate firms. The big companies have been getting bigger very rapidly, while the small ones have been going out of business by the hundreds. A number of small bakers who appeared before the Subcommittee in 1959 described from their own experiences the practices which explain what the statistics show.

Central to the problem is the fact that the large companies have their operations spread out over many local markets. They can keep the price of bread high in some areas and make substantial profits—profits that can be used in other areas to finance competitive practices which are ruinous to the independent bakers there.

In virtually all of the major cities of the country independent bakers have experienced the aggressive tactics of their well-heeled larger competitors. At the present time the penetration is extending to communities of more moderate size, and more and more small bakers are succumbing to the new economic order in the industry. Even where large-company entry into a particular market has not yet occurred, the independent bakers feel insecure. They are familiar with the competitive practices used by the major companies in nearby markets, and often personally know small bakers who have been destroyed by engaging in competitive warfare with the newcomers. It is not difficult to understand why submission to the price policies of their large competitors may be viewed as the better part of a dangerous—perhaps suicidal valor.

One of the case histories presented to the Subcommittee bears eloquent testimony to the methods used to destroy the small businessman. The witness was a businessman who had taken over a bakery in Meadville, Pennsylvania, from his father-in-law in 1944. At that time the business had sales of $150,000 a year. By 1950 the witness had built sales up to nearly one million dollars a year. In August 1958 his company closed its doors. This was not only a disaster to the owner; it left employees without jobs and deprived the home town of what in that area was a substantial payroll. The sequence of events is instructive.

As soon as this baker began to expand his share of the local market, he attracted the attention of two competitors, Ward and Continental, among the largest firms in the industry. Both served the market from plants in Youngstown, Ohio, some 60 miles away.

The first move was from Ward Baking Company, which in 1948 made inquiries about buying out the smaller firm. The owner set a price of $240,000 and, according to his testimony, was assured by Ward that this was fair enough. Thereupon he forwarded to Ward information on his routes, costs, customers—everything, in short, that might be of interest to a competitor. Called to New York to complete the sale, the witness was informed that the price would only be $160,000, which he refused to accept:

They informed me then, of course, that if they wanted that bakery badly enough there were other ways to get it, and they cited, for instance, price cutting in a market; and they illustrated a bakery, . . . I am pretty sure it was in South Bend where they brought the price of bread down as low as 5¢ a loaf in that market until this particular baker was out of business.[1]

The evidence indicates that the witness was subjected to just such a price squeeze after his refusal to sell out. The wholesale price of bread baked in Youngstown was raised several times; by September 1958 it sold in Youngstown and most localities served by the Youngstown bakeries for 15.6 cents a pound. But in the market area served by the witness, the price of his major competitors' bread, shipped from the Youngstown bakeries, did *not* go up. The wholesale price was 13 cents a pound in 1950, and, in the words of the witness, "That 13 cents price prevailed right up to August 19, 1958, when I closed my doors." The testimony of the major com-

[1] *Hearings*, Administered Prices, Bread, Part 12, p. 6435.

pany witnesses before the Subcommittee established the fact that it costs at least half a cent a pound to ship bread 50 miles. Thus, solely on the basis of costs, the price of the major brands would be expected to be higher in northwestern Pennsylvania than in Youngstown where it was baked. Since this was not the case, we can guess that the failure to raise prices in the marketing territory of the independent, while they were being raised in other areas supplied out of Youngstown, was part of a deliberate competitive strategy by his large rivals. Significantly, within two weeks after this independent went out of business, these companies raised their prices substantially in the very territory where for nearly a decade there had been no price increases.

In addition to price discrimination, this independent baker was subjected to harassment by two labor unions, the Teamsters (which had organized his drivers) and the Bakery and Confectionary Workers (representing his plant personnel). Both of these unions had been expelled from the AFL-CIO because of corrupt leadership. Several years ago Senator McClellan, in a series of hearings, exposed the close ties which existed between top officials of the leading bakery companies and the very union leaders whose activities led to the expulsion actions.

In 1950 two Teamster officials were sent up from Pittsburgh to handle current negotiations for the Meadville local. They demanded terms which were higher than those prevailing at the Youngstown bakeries, stating that Ward and Continental would not negotiate until the Meadville independent baker had first agreed to the new terms. When the latter insisted that he could not compete if his pay scale were raised above those of his competitors, the answer of the Teamster representatives, according to the small baker, was simple and direct: "If you can't compete, get out of business. We don't want to do business with small fellows anyway." But the baker's drivers remained loyal to him and dropped out of the Meadville Teamster local.

Then a strange thing happened. The business agent of

the Teamster local was appointed to serve simultaneously as business agent for the Bakery and Confectionery Workers' local! The pattern of union harassment continued, this time through the bakers' organization. Finally, when the plant workers, like the deliverymen, made evident their loyalty to and support for their employer, the national office of the Bakery and Confectionery Workers simply deprived the Meadville local of the power to do its own bargaining. Responsibility for negotiating the Meadville contract was taken away from the Meadville local and given to the Youngstown local.

In 1955 the Meadville baker was approached by Continental Baking Company in regard to selling the business. He provided the president of Continental with all available information on route sales and the like, but was then informed that Continental was no longer interested in the transaction. At the time the Meadville baker operated a profitable depot or agency at Jamestown, N.Y., with a number of house-to-house retail routes. Two of his supervisors who wished to go into business for themselves agreed to purchase the agency. Soon thereafter, within three months after the baker's conversations with Continental, the two former supervisors sold the Jamestown routes to a subsidiary of Continental.

Throughout this period in Meadville, as in many other communities across the nation, there was heavy mortality among the independent grocery stores in the face of chain-store supermarket expansion. Over four or five years, more than half of the town's small grocers went out of business. The witness testified that, with this development, he was forced to turn to the business of baking private-label bread for grocery chains. But even here he ran into difficulties. Time after time he would enter into a private-label agreement, only to have the deal bested in one way or another by the national wholesale bakers operating in his area.

One example of the methods used relates to the matter of "stale returns." In selling his own brand of bread, a baker regularly agrees to take any unsold merchandise back from the retailer; thus the retail store pays only for the bread it actually sells. In supplying private-label bread to a chain grocery, on the other hand, the wholesale baker normally operates on a "no returns" basis. Indeed, the major companies explained to the Subcommittee that this policy is one of the principal reasons why they can sell private-label loaves to grocery chains at lower prices than those charged for their regular brands. On occasion, however, the Meadville independent baker found that when he was negotiating a private-label agreement, his major competitors would undercut him by offering to meet his price and at the same time to allow full credit for the return of unsold bread. This is the sort of competition which no independent baker, operating in a single market area, can hope to meet. After being subjected to this kind of competition from the major companies for a period of nearly three years, the witness stated in his own words, "I simply closed the doors; I had nothing to offer."

This story of the Meadville baker whose business was destroyed is told not merely because it describes what happened to one individual. Instead, it is typical of the experiences related to the Subcommittee by small businessmen all over the country. It dramatically suggests the reasons why small producers, unable to stand up under the pressures directed against them by the giants of the industry, are disappearing from the American scene.

Efficiency and Competition in the Baking Industry

Baking is an industry which singularly lends itself to localized operation and control. Bread is a product that must be sold soon after it is produced. At the same time, shipping it any distance is relatively expensive. Thus, bread is produced by plants within each of the narrow geographical markets within which it is consumed.

Both small and large bakers agreed that there are no

technological advantages possessed by the national multi-plant baking companies over locally owned single-plant businesses. The president of the industry's largest company, Continental, asserted: "I would say that, by and large, the average independent can outoperate Continental . . . I would say that his costs are lower than our costs, and I think that is· borne out by the fact that independents make a higher percentage of profit."[2] The presidents of both General Baking and Ward testified that their plants are no more efficient, and in some cases much less efficient, than well-managed locally owned baking plants. The witness representing Campbell-Taggart Associated Bakeries, today the second largest and consistently the most profitable of the major companies, stressed the fact that his company's success rests upon a foundation of autonomous local management in each of its plants, with a minimum of central office advice or control.

Even small plants—with capacities of, say, 30,000 pounds per shift or less—can be operated efficiently. In 1958 nearly two-thirds of Campbell-Taggart's plants were relatively small operations, and fifteen of the seventeen plants operated by Southern Bakeries, another of the more profitable companies, were in the small-size category. And both of these companies operated predominantly in areas of low bread prices. This supports the considerable evidence in the record that in this industry operating efficiency does not increase directly with the size of the plant—that, indeed, the reverse may be true.

Throughout the hearings the small independents reiterated their belief that they could easily hold their own under conditions of "free and reasonable competition." Their basic complaint was that these conditions no longer existed in most areas insofar as bread baking was concerned. The Subcommittee's inquiry disclosed a vast network of discriminatory practices in the industry which, in the aggregate, have had a serious impact upon the ability of these smaller units to survive.

[2] *Hearings, op. cit.,* p. 6196.

Forms of Discriminatory Practices

PLANT PRICE DISCRIMINATION

One of the most common devices used by the large baking companies is plant discrimination. This involves charging widely differing prices for the same bread produced in different plants of a company. The existence of this type of discrimination was amply demonstrated in figures on plant prices as of September 1, 1958—data provided to the Subcommittee by the major baking companies themselves. The Campbell-Taggart plant in Des Moines, Iowa, for example, —was selling the same bread at the same time for 16 cents. The same company's plant in Cedar Rapids—less than 100 miles away—was selling the same bread at the same time for 16 cents. Continental's bread baked at Omaha, Nebraska, sold for 13 cents a pound; not too far away, at the Sioux City, Iowa plant, the price was 16 cents. These cases were not exceptional; examples can be multiplied many times over in every part of the country and for each of the major baking companies.

Why does the practice exist? The first explanation that comes to mind is difference in production costs. But the cost data secured by the Subcommittee and the testimony presented in the hearings made it clear that differences in production costs were not sufficient to explain the price differentials. Indeed, in some cases the evidence indicated that costs of production had little relationship to the prices charged. Frequently, plants of a large concern operating in the same general area and with similar labor and other costs had widely differing prices.

It was not so much costs as the state of competition that was cited as the cause of the price differentials. The position of the large companies was that they were "meeting competition" in each local area. According to the president of Continental, "We have different competitive situations in every city, and, going back to the remark I made earlier, we either have to match existing prices or go out of business." The president of General Baking Company pointed out, "But competition is again the thing that we have to take into consideration in determining a price to sell on the market. We can't price standard white bread over the market." Strangely enough, the major companies insisted that low prices in almost any given market could be traced to small independent bakers who derived all of their sales income within that market. As the president of Ward stated, "In every one of these [low-price] towns there are independent bakers who have established this price for one reason or another, whether it is keeping it low to keep out competition or whether it is a fair price based on their cost figures."

The small, independent bakers saw things differently. To them, a price structure had been imposed on the bread industry under which all of the financial resources of their larger competitors were being marshaled to drive them out of business. This viewpoint was expressed by the spokesman for a leading association of independent bakers. He stated that independents have two great fears with respect to their major competitors. The first is "Spotted destructive pricing. The use of underpricing in one market, while maintaining normal prices in others. The corporation with a large number of plants can easily stand a loss for a long time in a certain percentage of its units while making a profit in others." The second, "a danger which could accelerate and which we also fear, is a practice called waltzing or private price battles between two or more large companies with the independent in the middle." Here the spokesman for the independents was referring to the fact that while the major companies never engage each other in any large-scale competitive battles, they may sometimes engage in isolated tests of strength in one or two local markets. Regardless of the purpose, however, the effect is still the destruction of the independent businessman in such markets.

In a sense both sides were right. Where competition was minimal or nonexistent, the large companies had no check upon their impulse to charge what the traffic would bear.

However, in local areas where small baking establishments still survived, they were prepared to meet the competition—and then some. The point is that this is a game which only the large company, with a wide distribution of regional plants, can play effectively. Losses that may be incurred in Des Moines can be made up by gains in Cedar Rapids. But if you happen to have only one plant, and that is in Des Moines, you will be in for some hard sledding.

ROUTE PRICE DISCRIMINATION

Closely allied to plant price discrimination is "route price discrimination." This concerns the sale of a product at points on routes radiating out from its place of manufacture at prices lower than that which prevails where it is made. Obviously there is no "cost defense" here. It costs half a cent to move a loaf of bread 50 miles, and yet a number of charts placed in the record showed that prices for bread are frequently lower in outlying communities than in the cities where it is made.

Continental, for example, has a plant in Columbus, Ohio which sold bread wholesale at 16.4 cents a pound. A big truck trailer carries the bread to what is known as a "loading station" at New Lexington, 55 miles away. At the loading station the bread is transferred into smaller delivery or route trucks. One of these trucks goes to Parkersburg, West Virginia, a distance of over 120 miles from where the bread is baked. But in Parkersburg the bread sold for 15.2 cents.

One of the most striking examples of route price discrimination concerns General Baking Company's operations in the Philadelphia area. In the city, itself, General is the leading producer; the bread baked in Philadelphia sold wholesale in that city at 18.8 cents. Trucks carry it to Reading, Allentown, and Easton, all about 55 miles north of Philadelphia. In each, the bread was a cent cheaper. The delivery truck moving out of Easton transports the bread farther out to Stroudsburg, where it was sold two cents cheaper. The Allentown truck in turn moves out to such smaller communities as Ashville, Snyder, and Tamaqua, where the wholesale price was also two cents less.

The same pattern of price variations appears south of Philadelphia. At the time of the Subcommittee's investigation, the cheapest places to buy bread baked in Philadelphia were such distant localities as Stroudsburg or the Eastern Shore of Maryland. The most expensive place to buy it was in the city of Philadelphia, within a few blocks of the bakery!

When asked for an explanation of this state of affairs, officials of the large companies explained again that they were merely meeting "competitive conditions." But what were the "competitive conditions"? The variation in Continental's prices in Columbus, Ohio, and Parkersburg, West Virginia, is suggestive. Prices were high in Columbus, where Continental's competition in the wholesale bread market consisted primarily of General, Ward, and American, all among the largest baking companies in the nation. Prices were low in the Parkersburg area. When asked to comment, the president of Continental explained: "In the Parkersburg-Marietta area there are four bakers. . . . All we are doing is meeting their price." Significantly, all four of these bakers were small independents.

Thus, there is real price competition in a market where a giant firm is faced by a few tiny rivals, but it is conspicuously absent when the giants face each other alone. Where the small independent bakers have been weeded out of the business, prices remain high. But in communities where the independent baker has built up an established reputation for his product, prices are driven down sharply by the large companies in an effort to capture the market. It is therefore not surprising that most of the independent bakers appearing before the Subcommittee felt that their own future survival was highly problematical.

FREE BREAD, STALES CLOBBERING, SPECIAL DISCOUNTS

Other forms of discrimination are prevalent in the bread industry. When a large company plans the invasion of a new market, it has to take into account the fact of sales resistance. Local loyalties have been developed for the independent baker in the community; often his product has won an established reputation for quality. To overcome whatever consumer resistance may exist, the grocers are induced to give prominent display to the new product with free bread or fixtures. The latter often consist of new bread racks or a new paint job for the store front. The large multi-plant firm can, of course, make these financial investments, recovering its outlay later or in another community. Indeed, temporary losses on business are usually regarded as a necessary cost for invading a new market.

One example of this behavior cited in the hearings concerned the efforts of the American Bakeries Corporation to break into the Topeka, Kansas market in 1955. According to witnesses, the company gave away thousands of loaves of free bread over a period of time—bread placed in customers' cars, free merchandise offered to grocers, supplies of baked goods to institutions, and so forth. Local bakers had complained to the Federal Trade Commission, but the agency's field investigators apparently decided that American's activities were simply "promotional." As one witness commented, "It is not promotion and it is not a one-shot promotion, and even if it was, giving a grocer a month's free bread is a little vicious. That is worse than cutting the price. That is giving it away."

Another device, perhaps peculiar to the bread business, is "stales clobbering." In the baking industry stale bread which is unsold is customarily returned to the baker, and the grocer is reimbursed for his stale returns. Obviously, it is to the baker's interest to sell as much as possible but to hold stale returns to a minimum. On the other hand, it is generally accepted in the trade that consumers are influenced by the "pile psychology"; that is, they tend to select a loaf from the largest pile on the grocery shelf. Thus a conflict is created. Though the baker wishes to keep stale returns to a minimum, he feels he must maintain a respectable pile on the grocer's bread rack to entice the customers. The large pile also has another advantage; it crowds the wares of the smaller independents off the shelves.

A typical example was described by an independent baker from Hastings, Nebraska. Campbell-Taggart—under the name Rainbo Baking Company—had acquired a plant in Grand Island, Nebraska, from which it began to enter the Hastings market in 1955. One of the practices utilized was "slugging" the market with more merchandise than could possibly be sold, both to attract consumers and to force rival merchandise off the limited shelf spaces available. As a result, the witness stated,

Our percentage of stale or returned merchandise was running approximately 4.9 per cent which is a normal percentage of returns. In 1955 when the Rainbo Bread Co. began operating the Grand Island plant, our stale returns jumped to 5.7 per cent; in 1956 to 9.3 per cent; in 1957 to 9.5 per cent.

The reason for the increase in returned merchandise is due to the fact that the Rainbo Bread Co. put merchandise in the stores in large quantities, more than could ever possibly be sold.

We were forced to increase the amount of merchandise that we put in the stores, otherwise we would lose sales and rack space to this concern.[3]

This witness had one plant. If he lost money there, he lost money in his whole business. Compare this to Campbell-Taggart's position. The spokesman for that company told the Subcommittee, "In 1958 none of our bakeries lost money." But then he had an afterthought:

Wait a minute, I'm sorry. I might have to make an exception in the case of Grand Island. . . . I would have to check the record, because if they made any money they just barely did. They have been in the red. I sometimes forget about Grand Island.[4]

This game tends to be one-sided. The larger companies are financially able to squeeze the independents by flooding the

[3] *Ibid.*, p. 6476.
[4] *Ibid.*, p. 6301.

grocery stores with their brands and absorbing the losses on stales. The small baker is in a dilemma. He can match the practices of his bigger competitors or lose volume. In either event, he is bound to suffer. If he tries to match piles with the bigger companies, his stale returns will increase drastically and his profits will be reduced to a minimum. If he remains aloof from this form of competitive activity, his sales volume falls.

Here is another form of competitive activity in which there is no real gain to the public. The studied creation of mountains of stale bread serve no useful end to society; nor is there any social benefit to be derived by catering to the fiction that the height of the pile is an indication to the consumer of the freshness of the bread.

The record of the Subcommittee also shows that special discounts to preferred customers is a common practice in the bread industry. Instead of cutting prices across the board, the large baker often attempts to maximize profits through selective price reductions. In this fashion he hopes to keep captive the retail grocers with large volume, but to withhold the price cut from those retailers lacking real bargaining power. The chief beneficiaries in this practice are, of course, the national chains.

A dramatic illustration of the problem occurred during the Subcommittee's hearings. An independent with a single supermarket in Pomona, California, submitted a sworn statement relating his failure, over a ten-year period, to secure discounts approximating those granted to super-markets operated by the national chains. When the Subcommittee began hearings on bread, he was suddenly showered with attention; representatives of both Langendorf and Interstate informed him he was eligible for a 5 per cent discount. Prior to this time, however, he had been repeatedly informed that a minimum of five retail outlets was necessary to secure a discount. In contrast, throughout this period the chains were given a 7½ per cent discount, and some reportedly were getting 10 per cent. Indeed, the Subcommittee's hearings show that the large bakers plied the big retail chains with offers of ever better discounts; and the latter, concerned about possible attack under the Robinson-Patman Act, actually became reluctant to accept the ever increasing discounts.

"Money under the table" is a phrase used in every industry for the granting of pecuniary favors for which no record is kept. According to one of the larger independents operating in Michigan, this phrase is inadequate for the bread business. To indicate its diversity, he preferred to speak of money "over the table" and "under the table" and then, as an afterthought, included "and through the table." Often these cash payments are made ostensibly for prominent display space or a "preferred rack position." This practice, which is both widespread and growing, is really a form of commercial bribery. Since these payments are secret, seldom appearing on an invoice, it is virtually impossible to counteract them effectively.

The existence of phoney "promotional allowances" was openly acknowledged by R. A. Jackson, president of Ward Baking Company. Paul Rand Dixon, Chief Counsel to the Subcommittee, placed into the record a "contract" for eight promotions of Ward products by National Food Stores; the allowances were $610 per promotion, for a total of $4880. The strange thing was that this "contract" contained nothing at all about specific performances to be fulfilled by the customer.

Counsel for the Subcommittee asked Mr. Jackson, "Could you tell us exactly what sort of promotional services you paid nearly $5000 for and what was the duration of this contract?" Mr. Jackson's answer was direct and honest: "In effect, it is nothing more than a discount, to meet competition." Later, agreeing that no promotional services were expected, he reiterated, "But the name 'promotional' is a misnomer, so to speak, because in the final analysis it is nothing more than a discount."[5] Indeed, the only disagree-

[5] *Ibid.*, p. 6277.

ment on this point came when payments of this type were referred to as "money under the table." The Ward vice-president assured the Subcommittee that there was nothing "under the table" about it either for Ward or its customers—"It is on our books and on their books."

The use of these secret payments sets loose a vicious cycle that imperils the survival of the independent baker. Grocers who are approached with cash offers are immediately tempted to play off one baking company against another. The force of competitive rivalry places the small baker, with his limited resources, at a distinct disadvantage; with the best will in the world, he can scarcely hope to match the secret inducements of his larger competitors.

Other discriminatory practices involve tampering with the loaf. In some markets the larger bakers sell a "fighting brand" of bread. Sometimes referred to as a "secondary loaf," this bread is made from a leaner formula and sold under a different brand name. Often it is expanded with air to give it the appearance of a standard loaf. Its price is, of course, lower and the consumer thinks he is getting a special bargain.

The situation occurs in reverse when the large baker meets the prevailing price in the market, but offers a larger loaf. This is frequently employed as a temporary device when a large baker plans the invasion of a new territory. After a short time, when he becomes established as an important factor in the market, he abandons the practice and few consumers are aware of the change.

An unusual case of preferential price treatment disclosed in the Subcommittee hearings was that granted by Ward Baking Company to the Grand Union grocery chain. In 1959 Ward entered into a contract to supply Grand Union's private-label bread and bakery products ("Freshbake" bread and "Nancy Lynn" baked goods). No firm prices were specified; instead, Ward agreed that the prices charged Grand Union would be 20 per cent under prevailing chain-store retail prices in the market in which they were sold, *regardless* of what the prevailing retail prices were. In other words, where the chain-store private-label price was 18 cents a loaf, Ward supplied Grand Union stores at 14.4 cents a loaf wholesale. If the prevailing retail price was 14 cents a loaf, Ward's price to Grand Union was 11.2 cents.

Such an arrangement had two very strange effects. In the first place, the Grand Union stores supplied by Ward were almost completely insulated from changes in the local chain-store market price. Regardless of what happened to chain-store prices in the market, Grand Union continued to receive its 20 per cent margin on baked goods. In the second place, the arrangement prevented Ward from expanding the sales for its own TipTop bread in any market where it also supplied Grand Union stores, for any price reduction on its own products would lead to competitive reductions by chain stores in the area, and these would be matched by Grand Union. This would necessitate decreases in Ward's wholesale prices on Grand Union's private-label goods in order to maintain Grand Union's contractual margin. Under this arrangement a major baking company is, in effect, subsidizing one of its own principal competitors. And it subsidizes in such a fashion as to forestall any action on its part to increase its own share of the market at the expense of its competitor's.

None of these discriminatory practices is either new or unique to the bread industry. Their danger stems from the fact that they widen the gap between big and small units and virtually guarantee the extinction of the smaller firms. As many of the independents pointed out, they had no fear of their ability to survive on the basis of their efficiency under conditions of free and honest competition. The real threat created by monopoly power in the bread industry is the temporary establishment of such competitive conditions that all but those with sizable financial resources go under. Once this is accomplished, the rest is easy; an administered price structure becomes established in the industry. As R.

Norman Jordan of the Jordan Bakers in Topeka summed up the whole situation:

The independent in that market is in a pretty unfavorable situation because he has only one bakery from which to draw his profit, and if the national wholesalers concentrate on him, he will either operate at no profit or a loss for so long as his finances permit. Then eventually close his doors or sell out at the best price he can get.[6]

Why, it was asked, had the small bakers not invoked the sanctions of the Robinson-Patman Act which is aimed precisely at such discriminatory practices? Or the "unfair methods of competition" provision contained in the Federal Trade Commission Act? On this point Mr. Jordan provided some interesting information:

We have a file of correspondence, directed to these FTC offices that must weigh 6 pounds. We reported to FTC investigators many of the questionable practices in which American Bakeries Corp. and Continental Bakeries were engaged. Finally one investigator came to Topeka and saw a few of the grocers whom we had listed for him. . . . Most of the grocers we listed and felt he should see were not contacted. We suppose that this man did not have time or was not sufficiently interested. At any rate he reported later that he could not find out much. We went into such unfair competitive activities with the FTC again, and they eventually sent another man to see some of the grocers listed. He too seemed unable to find out anything.

A major problem, of course, is the difficulty encountered by a Government investigator in securing proof of violation. As Mr. Jordan remarked,

We realize that the grocers who accept free bread for two weeks or more or accept money or rebates probably do not choose to discuss these things with an FTC man, because they are afraid that they are guilty of some offense or they don't want

[6] *Ibid.*, p. 6453 ff.

to let down the baker who makes the offer or they don't want the revenue department to get interested.

Nor can the complainant himself be of much help. Normally, it is easy enough to ascertain the nature of the offense on an informal basis from a good customer; it is quite another thing to ask him to supply a signed affidavit on the subject. Mr. Jordan put the problem quite simply when he remarked that an independent baker could hardly say to a good customer: "You remember what you said yesterday. Now I want you to sign that, because the FTC says they have to have an affidavit to that effect."[7]

On one occasion the FTC, after its investigation, informed this complainant that the violation appeared to be a "one-shot competitive event." But Mr. Jordan told the Subcommittee, "If that is so, then the one shot has lasted four and a half years, because American Bakeries is still offering money, free bread, discounts, and the same things they started in January of 1955."[8]

In general, the institution of a Government investigation in a particular market appears to have a salutary effect for a brief period. As another witness stated: "We received temporary relief from this kind of competition during the time the Federal Trade Commission was investigating our market, but just as soon as the Federal agency was not observing our market, the same practices commenced again."[9] Obviously, this kind of relief can, at best, occur only at infrequent intervals. It is axiomatic both in the Federal Trade Commission and in the Antitrust Division that staff cannot be spared for repeated investigations of the same complaint; the agency's scanty resources must be deployed in other industrial areas which too long have been free of Government scrutiny.

[7] *Ibid.*, p. 6463.
[8] *Ibid.*, p. 6454.
[9] *Ibid.*, p. 6466.

AN ADMINISTERED PRICE STRUCTURE

The administered price character of the bread industry in most markets today is revealed by the Subcommittee's price survey. This disclosed a remarkable absence of competitive pricing in most major cities. Prices changed infrequently, and when they did, the change was almost invariably in one direction—upward. Price reductions were noticeably absent except in those small and medium-sized cities where there were still some "troublesome" independents who resisted being driven out of their home markets.

Another important indicator is the way in which price changes occur. Ordinarily, the dominant firms in a market raise their prices simultaneously; or if a single firm takes the lead, the others follow within a day or two. The mechanism by which prices change may vary from time to time and place to place. The most direct method, of course, is outright collusion. There is evidence of collusion in several Department of Justice cases against bread companies in various local markets. Thus, in a case arising in western Tennessee, Campbell-Taggart's local manager testified, "I have drank coffee with my competitors at the Pig 'n Whistle," and went on to describe how he, Continental's plant manager, and various local bakers reached agreement on price changes.

In other cases the price leader may simply notify his competitors of his intentions to raise prices. Many instances of this practice are contained in the files of the Subcommittee. A typical example is a letter, dated June 4, 1957, from the Los Angeles plant manager of Interstate Bakeries to the San José manager for Langendorf United Bakeries, both companies being among the eight largest in the nation. The letter from the Interstate manager informed his competitor that Interstate's prices would be raised on June 10 by specified amounts for different products. On June 10, both Interstate and Langendorf raised their prices by identical amounts.

In still other cases, neither collusion nor notification appears necessary. The price leader simply increases his prices. His competitors learn of this almost immediately from their route drivers and then raise their own prices to the leader's level. This procedure is common in most of the major bread markets of the country. When the president of Continental was asked whether he had ever failed to follow a competitor's price increase in a major market he replied, "St. Louis is the last that I recall. It was three or four years ago." The president of General Baking Company could not recall any instance in which his firm had failed to follow an increase initiated by one of the other major companies, although he did mention three instances (none later than 1948) in which competitors had failed to follow General's lead. Ward's president found it equally difficult to recall any instances in which any of the major companies failed to follow one another up the price ladder. The Campbell-Taggart spokesman could not remember any such cases either, although he felt sure that there had been some. After checking his company's records, however, he subsequently wrote to the Subcommittee:

I am unable to cite any specific instances during the last few years where one of our subsidiary companies failed to meet a competitor's price increase with the result that such increase had to be rescinded . . . Of course, one reason . . . is because there have been very few instances of that type.[10]

It seems clear that the major bakers have adopted the rationale employed by other industries that practice administered pricing. When prices are raised, it is "to meet competition." The files of the Subcommittee are full of examples, in the form of letters from plant managers to regional and company headquarters officials requesting approval for price increases, which show the extent of the administered pricing rationale:

[10] *Ibid.*, p. 6652.

As of Thursday, August 7, our competitors in the Seattle area increased the price of their bread, and . . . we are raising the price of our bread effective August 11 *in order to meet the competitive situation.*

This is to advise that Interstate Baking Company, in the Greater Chicago area, made the following changes in the whole-sale price of their bread products this morning. . . . I recommend on our following bread products *we meet this competitive in-crease.*

Learned in market this morning that Ward has notified its customers of new wholesale prices effective Tuesday, September 2, 1958, as follows. . . . Request authority *to follow this compe-tition* in Metropolitan New York City market including north Jersey on Wednesday, September 3.

There are indications that Ward will increase the price of white bread, rye, wheat, and package rolls on Thursday, September 25, 1958. May I have approval *to meet this price increase?*

We have been notified by one of our local competitors that they plan to [increase] some of their wholesale bread prices effec-tive on Wednesday, February 12, 1958. If this happens *we will meet their price.*[11]

Like the steel producers the large bakers regard them-selves as "competitive" only when their prices are just as high as those of their brethren in the industry.

[11] *Ibid.,* pp. 6599–6651.

Chapter 5

*

MONOPOLY AND THE COMMUNITY

What are the social costs to a community whose economic life is dominated by a single industry? What are the effects on its development when its major corporations are dominated by an officialdom located far away? What are the human consequences upon a town whose miscellany of small, independent enterprises have largely atrophied, and have been superseded by branch plants, district offices, and chain stores of every description? What kind of community is created by these changes?

All of these questions were brought sharply home to me in June 1963 when I introduced a bill to establish an Office of Consumers. In pointing up the special need for an independent consumer agency, I found myself contrasting life today with the kind of life with which I was familiar as a boy in Madisonville, Tennessee:

In our present highly industrialized society we are all actively consumers buying most of the necessities and amenities of life in the marketplace. This fact constitutes the outstanding difference between our way of life and that of our grandfathers. A hundred years ago most of our population lived on farms, and many of the family's needs were supplied from this source. The canning of surplus food production was a commonplace practice on the farm; "store-bought" foods were limited to such items as coffee, tea, salt and similar staples not grown in the area. The fashioning of clothing was then a home activity; some of us here today can recall our first "store-bought" suit as a significant event which marked the shift from childhood to maturity. Even in the smaller towns and cities, the family constituted a largely self-contained unit able to satisfy much of its material needs. A truly pecuniary economy had not yet come into being; it was just around the corner but at this time it only touched the fringes of people's lives.

Indeed, thinking of Madisonville specifically, I remarked:

I can remember, for example, when "store-bought" bread was an exciting novelty in our household; in my youth, bread was made in the home in sufficient quantities to last a week or longer. Today home-made bread is an almost unattainable luxury. We are now all consumers operating in a pecuniary economy; when we need something, we go to the store and buy it.

No doubt all of us feel a certain nostalgia for the way of life that existed in our childhood, and at the same time fiercely reject any notion that we are resistant to change and the forces of progress. The point is, I think, that in the social and economic currents that carry us, heavy costs are frequently involved. These costs must be paid by someone, either in the present or in the future. Unfortunately, they are not susceptible to precise measurement, and often neither the nature of these costs to society nor their magnitude can be fully understood while the change is taking place. For example, which of the early tinkerers who made the Industrial Revolution a reality could have guessed that in the wake of their creative work would come the blight of employment of young children in factories for 12 or 16 hours a day? Who of the early traders in human cargo from Africa dreamed that in supplying slaves for Southern plantations they were setting the stage for a moral and social crisis in this country which today, even after a bloody civil war, is still unresolved?

Probably one of the most dramatic illustrations of the

social costs to a community of tight industrial concentration accompanied by absentee ownership occurred in the anthracite and bituminous coal mining regions. For decades the ugly spectacle of the company town, with its accouterments of company-owned housing facilities, company-owned stores, inadequate educational and recreational facilities was an affront to the human conscience. Eventually the sheer abuse of private power, as reflected in the hazardous conditions in the mines, the high accident and disease rate, and the exploitation of workers in the excessive charges for company-owned houses and goods purchased in the company-owned stores, resulted in belated action. The vigorous growth of labor unions in this industry during the early days of Franklin Roosevelt's administration resulted in the correction of some of the worst abuses. But even to this day a trip through these mining regions provides evidence of the terrible scars left by an economic way of life offering few of the benefits and opportunities our society regards as inherent rights for every American.

This historical example of human exploitation we tend to dismiss today as being nineteenth century in character and therefore, basically an obsolescent phenomenon. Certainly it is true that the modern company town—as exemplified by some of the one-company oil communities and other cities whose economic life is dominated by one or two large corporations—presents a more pleasing external picture. Private corporate philanthropy in the form of company-owned recreational facilities, bus transportation to and from the portals of employment, attractive and inexpensive luncheon facilities at the plant, has come to be regarded as good business practice. It helps in the recruitment and retention of highly skilled personnel who could easily move to other sources of employment. It also reduces problems at the job levels where replacement is relatively easy but involves administrative costs inherent in a high turnover.

But does this external picture tell the whole story? Are there basic, fundamental differences between communities whose industrial activities are characterized largely by small independent enterprises owned by the local residents and communities dominated by one or two large corporations that are controlled from outside the local environs? What happens to the organized life in the community? What is the impact upon its educational institutions, its political pattern, its agencies of civic welfare, its sense of civic responsibility?

During my service in the Congress, both in the House and in the Senate, I have frequently been struck by the plethora of statistical data accessible to the economic and social investigator. I have been told that no other society has compiled and published such a wealth of information on its operations; that historians of the future will be burdened with such mountains of documents on our time that their major problem will be to winnow out something that has meaning from the weltering confusion of the twentieth century. And this situation, it is said, will be particularly true of the United States, where statistic-producing factories abound both within and outside of Government. Generally speaking, the European countries have been more reticent, particularly with respect to the operations of private industry. The types of economic statistical data—such as products manufactured, volume of production, market shipments, list prices, corporate profits and the like—which are routinely reported in private trade journals and obscure Government reports in this country are generally neither compiled nor released for publication abroad.

The amazing fact is that, with all the whirl of the printing presses in this country, there are vast and important gaps in information. Time and again it has been my experience as chairman of an investigating committee in the House or Senate to find that crucial economic facts of vital consequence to the whole economy were shrouded in mystery. Sometimes these facts were deliberately withheld by the interested parties; just as often, I think, the important questions had not been raised by the statistics-gathering bodies. There has been something of a tendency to gather statistics which *might* be valuable in the examination of a "controversial" topic. In some Government agencies, I suspect, the motives are mixed—the purpose is to show, by sheer physical bulk, the magnitude of the agency's accomplishments for the year and at the same time to publish such information as will not invite criticism of the agency and possibly jeopardize its budget. Whatever the purpose, the end result is something less than satisfactory.

For reasons not quite clear to me, the area of the social effects of monopoly and high industrial concentration upon community life is particularly barren of study and analysis. Here we are, confronted with vast transformations occurring in the established patterns of private controls over the instruments of production and distribution in our economy. And yet we have no idea of (and, judging from the amount of study in the field, no real interest in) the effects these alterations in the economic field will have upon our present mode of life and the lives of our children.

The few limited studies that have been made in this field are enlightening; they are also alarming in several respects. Though piecemeal and inadequate in character, they do supply an outline of the nature of the problem that faces us.

The Rochester Study

In the late 1950's the Chamber of Commerce of Rochester, New York instituted a study of the effects of corporate merger and consolidation upon that city.[1] Because of the city's history of attracting highly specialized industries and because it is recognized as a center for the newest technologies, it was probably one of the first communities to feel the impact of the trend toward industrial concentration. According to the Committee report, between 1950 and 1957 a dozen major independently owned local firms lost their identity in mergers with larger corporations located else-

[1] Report of a Committee of the Rochester Chamber of Commerce on the Out-of-Town Acquisition of Rochester Companies (1959, unpublished).

where. In addition, a large number of other independent enterprises were approached with merger offers by outside concerns which, for one or another reason, were at that time declined. Since then undoubtedly a number of such proposals in the Rochester area have been accepted, as the merger movement has accelerated throughout the country.

The study showed that the initial reaction by employees to the merger announcement was one of alarm that the plant would be closed. In general, however, their fears were unfounded; in none of the cases studied was there a shutdown. Indeed, some of the plants commenced the manufacture of additional new products. Nevertheless, despite efforts in some cases to dispel in advance the employees' reaction of job insecurity, the morale of the entire work force was affected. Particularly in those plants where real momentum had been developed under the creative leadership of existent supervisory personnel and local owners, the losses were great. An attitude of resignation prevailed; an atmosphere of stagnation set in as men felt they were mere "cogs in the machine" and their personal identity was being lost. This kind of situation, of course, exists in any management change-over; it tends to be greatly intensified when the new corporate control is alien to the community and key posts are taken over by the new occupation group.

According to the Rochester report, the corporate consolidations "presented a real challenge to such agencies as the Community Chest." The outside owners were neither as sensitive to the rising community needs nor imbued with the same sense of loyalty and responsibility when faced with these needs as the local owners had been. In this kind of situation the branch operation tends to be faceless; the new local management has little feeling of identity with the community. In any event, the decision to dig more deeply into the corporate pockets beyond the assigned "quota" lies elsewhere, in the central corporate office hundreds or thousands of miles away; and there is little expectation that appeal in that quarter would meet with much response.

In Rochester, lay and professional officials very early anticipated this problem, and at the outset attempted to ameliorate it. A prompt welcome was extended to new local and general managers as they arrived, and every effort was made to acquaint them with the city's traditions in this field and the nature of the local problems. Subsequent analysis of the statistical data showed varying response by the recently merged plants; in general, however, it was clear that these absentee-owned companies lagged behind the locally owned firms in response to rising community needs.

The situation was made graphic by the economic recession in 1954. Since the quota allocations for charitable purposes were, in the merged plants, apparently based upon the general prosperity of the whole corporation, there was a marked drop in contributions at the very time that the need was intensified. In Rochester these losses to the community agencies were more than compensated for by the increased generosity of individual workers in these plants. Whether these workers, as permanent members of the community, were more alive to the crises faced by other families in their locality, or whether they were grateful for their good fortune in retaining jobs despite the hard times, is unknown. But because the generosity of the employees offset the reduced corporate gifts, the budgets of the community agencies were sustained during the economic emergency.

Other consequences of mergers were also felt in the city of Rochester. Local banks reported that several of the merged plants no longer did a major portion of their banking in Rochester. This reduced the deposits in the local banks, which in turn restricted their ability to make loans to homeowners, contractors, and the remaining independently owned plants. The funneling of business, resulting from the acquisition by large companies of independent Rochester firms, into the country's major banks strengthened these institutions at the expense of the local Rochester banks. This kind of change is probably an inevitable consequence of industrial mergers; undoubtedly it is one of the leading causes for the flurry of merger activity in recent years in the banking field.

A similar trend was noticed in the insurance industry. Here again a corporation's policy with respect to the types of insurance carried for all types of industrial hazards is a matter for determination by top management. It is a general practice for a large corporation to place large blocks of insurance, covering several of its plants, with a few of the major insurance companies; negotiations are carried on in the top echelons of both companies. As a result, local insurance agencies in Rochester suffered a decline in business when firms were merged.

This decline in business extended far beyond the banking and insurance fields. A number of local firms paid the price of lessened sales as a result of the mergers. The purchase of supplies in a large corporation is generally a prerogative of a special department set up for this purpose. It is common knowledge that "reciprocity" in business relations is an established practice in most industries. Large firms, particularly, like to keep careful check on the size, dollar volume, and identity of the companies from whom they purchase to insure that such firms reciprocate with equivalent dollar purchases from them. This constitutes an additional incentive for centralized purchasing of goods and services—in addition to the more obvious advantage of lower prices achieved through large volume. In consequence, there is a continuing economic fallout from mergers upon the local community. As corporate decisions become centered in top management remote from the particular locality, local firms formerly dependent upon the custom of their business neighbors lose out when mergers take place in their community.

Even the professions do not escape. The law is a good example. An independent locally owned firm tends to use the services of a lawyer in the community; often a personal relationship of long standing exists in addition to the business association. All of the legal problems faced by the company are frequently handled by the same lawyer or some member of his firm. Once a merger takes place, the situation is radically altered. Large corporations, with home offices usually located in a large city, tend to maintain a separate legal department for their routine legal problems. If they happen to run afoul of the antitrust laws, they call in a major law firm, located in New York or Washington, that specializes in this type of work. The same is true of an important tax problem, a litigative struggle in the field of patents, an effort to secure or prevent the passage through Congress of a particular legislative proposal.

The Smaller War Plants Study

A more comprehensive analysis of the sociological effects of concentration was made by the late Professor C. Wright Mills, who, at the time of his death in 1962, was a professor of sociology at Columbia University. In 1946 he prepared a report entitled "Small Business and Civic Welfare" for the Smaller War Plants Corporation, published by the Senate Small Business Committee.[2]

Under the chairmanship of Maury Maverick, the Corporation was then making the prediction (at the time derided in many circles, only to be fully borne out by later data) that as a result of centralization in the hands of a few giant corporations of most of the war contracts, research contracts, and surplus plants and facility disposals, over-all concentration in the postwar era would be substantially higher than it had been prior to World War II.[3] The question naturally arose as to what effect this greater centering of economic

[2] 79th Cong., 2d Sess. Senate Doc. #135, "Small Business and Civic Welfare," Report of the Smaller War Plants Corporation to the Special Committee to Study Problems of American Small Business, U.S. Senate (1946).

[3] 79th Cong., 2d Sess. Senate Doc. #206, "Economic Concentration and World War II," Report of the Smaller War Plants Corporation to the Special Committee to Study Problems of American Small Business, U.S. Senate (1946).

power in a few hands would have upon the general welfare of our cities and their inhabitants.

For the purpose of this study, three pairs of cities were compared. In each pair was one "big-business city" and one "small-business city." The members of each pair were so selected that they had a number of basic factors in common —geographical location, physical size, make-up of population, and the like. The important difference was the business structure of the community. In one, a few large firms employed all or most of the workers; absentee ownership was prevalent; business activity was largely concentrated in one or a few industries. In the other member of the pair, workers were employed by a large number of independently owned small firms, and there was considerable diversity in the types of products manufactured.

Of particular interest was the historical development of these two types of communities. In 1890 all six cities were established trading centers, largely servicing the immediately adjacent agricultural areas. At that time the small-business cities were flourishing communities, larger in size than their big-business counterparts. The growth of the latter arose out of the establishment of large branch plants in these communities and the recruitment of workers to fill the job openings.

By 1940 one pair of these cities under study had each attained a population of 150,000. For the small-business city, this represented a normal growth of roughly double the 1890 figure of 60,000 inhabitants. In the big-business city, however, there had been a fifteen-fold increase from the original population of 10,000 in 1890.

The second set of cities had a population of 60,000 by 1940. This represented a threefold increase for the small-business city, which had 20,000 people in 1890. The big-business city had increased its population 11 times, from 5000 in 1890.

The third pair of cities had a less clearly differentiated pattern. By 1940 each had a population of 30,000, representing increases in both cases of about double the original size in 1890. For this pair the dichotomy of big-business against small-business city was somewhat less sharply defined. These two were included in the study to serve as a check upon the findings for the other pairs of cities.

It is not surprising that a sudden population boom leaves its imprint upon the physical characteristics of a community. In the big-business cities, where growth had been rapid, there was an accompanying real-estate boom. As a result of real-estate speculation, the residential areas were widely dispersed and capriciously located, with ugly slum sections in the center of the city. Only a fraction of the numerous real-estate subdivisions were developed. In consequence of this scattered pattern, operating costs of the city were high for such minimum civic services as street lighting, road maintenance, garbage and trash disposal, and the like. Increasingly, the better residential areas were developing in suburbs farther and farther from the city.

All of this was in sharp contrast to the small-business cities where the population growth was slower; new housing facilities evolved naturally as expanding needs required. In consequence, the physical contours of these cities were more pleasing in appearance; city costs were lower; and the new structures, better and less hastily built, were not subject to the rapid deterioration common to many of the housing developments in their big-business city counterparts.

A marked difference was found in the two types of cities with respect to stability of employment. A serious economic depression, such as occurred in the 1930's, had a strong impact upon both types of community. Generally speaking, however, a city with a miscellany of diverse manufacturing establishments appears to be better able to weather an economic storm. Where most of the employment in a community is dependent upon one or two large plants, a shutdown is catastrophic; indeed, the first portents of a management decision to reduce production has an immediate effect upon retail stores and service trades in the area.

Not unexpectedly, bankruptcies of small concerns were higher in big-business cities.

The report also disclosed a marked difference in the occupational distribution of gainful workers. The small-business city had, of course, a relatively larger number of independent proprietors and officials of corporations, though wage earners constituted the bulk of the work force. Almost a quarter of the gainfully employed, however, fell in the first category. In contrast, in the big-business city only 3 per cent were in the self-employed category, and 97 per cent were wage earners.

This difference was further reflected in the distribution of income in the two communities. In the larger big-business city examined, roughly 5 out of every 10,000 gainfully employed people earned $10,000 or more annually. For its small-business counterpart, the number was doubled. For the next set of cities, with population of 60,000 at the time of the study, the contrast was even greater. Here the rate was 2 per 10,000 earning $10,000 or over in the big-business community, as against 18 per 10,000 in the small-business city.

Thus it would appear that one of the community costs of high industrial concentration is an imbalance in income —a small sprinkling of the wealthy at the top with the vast majority of the population in the lower-income classes. Virtually eliminated is the independent middle class which normally serves as the backbone for progress in the community.

Traditionally, the small businessman is a leader in the management of local civic enterprises. He is usually well educated, either through the conventional academic channels or through self-study, and his experience in the conduct of a small business trains him for initiative and responsibility.

It is also in his self-interest that civic improvements be made. If he is a retail merchant, better highways and streets increase his sales; city enforcement of health regulations in restaurants, hotels, and the like attracts shoppers from outside the community. By participating actively in civic affairs, the small businessman widens his circle of contacts. This can be of strategic importance; traditionally, businessmen in small-business cities constitute each other's best customers. There is also personal satisfaction in being a leader in the community where he spends most of his life. And success in such endeavors as better schools, city parks, and playgrounds is not only a personally satisfying accomplishment; it promises greater enrichment of the lives of his children and those of his neighbors.

Most of these incentives are absent for officials of absentee-owned corporations. If their competence is outstanding, their stay is temporary; they are grooming themselves for the next rung in the corporate ladder which ultimately may land them in a key spot in the central office of the giant enterprise. Even if they remain longer, they often have little real interest in betterment of the community. Family ties lie elsewhere; often the social life of these executives is confined to their business colleagues.

Frequently this isolation is institutionalized through suburban communities composed largely of the families of big-business executives. The focal social center becomes the country club, which bars most of the local townsfolk as intruders. Thus a new social elite comes into being, in which interest in local community affairs is an indication of absence of sophistication and worldliness. At one time the gap between town and corporate officialdom of this sort could be closed through the mixing of children in the schools. Increasingly, however, families with higher incomes have turned to private schools for the education of their children, and the public school system—once hopefully regarded as the great social leveler—has no opportunity to serve its appointed function.

The prestige element in being a civic leader in a small community appears to atrophy in the large city. The report states:

Field investigation has revealed that such social standing as the local middle class in the big-business cities may secure is obtained through association with the leading officials of the great absentee-owned firms, through following their style of living, through moving to their suburbs, attending their social functions, duplicating in miniature, so to speak, their behavior. Since the chief interests of the corporation group do not characteristically include civic affairs, the local middle class correspondingly tends to drift away from civic enterprises.[4]

Interviews with well-informed residents of a big-business city—school board members, local businessmen, librarians —revealed that plant managers and chief executives of the large corporation occupy the apex of the city's social structure. Acknowledgment of this fact was indicated by the efforts of the former civic leaders to get invited to their social affairs, to send their children to the same private schools, even to marry into the new social circle. One of the most obvious symptoms of the change was the movement of the old leading families into the exclusive suburbs built largely by the corporation officials.

According to the report, the element of social prestige weighs heavily in the degree of participation in civic affairs. This is particularly true of women who, in addition to being motivated by a desire to be of service to the community, are also concerned with enhancing their family's social prestige and being helpful in their husbands' businesses. In the small-business community, civic activity is "the thing to do"; and there is often real rivalry for leadership in civic enterprises. The result is a higher level of social welfare in the community.

The situation is quite different in the large-business city. Wives of the corporation's executives often have little interest in civic affairs; their concern is with trips to metropolitan cities, trips abroad, new developments in the world of fashion, social functions, and the like. Thus a woman

[4] *Op. cit.*, p. 27.

may make substantial contributions to the community and still be unknown in the society that "counts."

The second factor of helping in her husband's business is also absent in the big-business city. Officials of the large corporations are concerned primarily with regional or national markets; their contracts are basically with businessmen outside the city. Even when the official enters into negotiation with local businessmen, it is not on a plane of equality; the difference in corporate size between the two creates its own chasm. The mere name of the corporation is enough to establish contacts within the city; no friendly relationship is required.

This does not mean that the large corporation does not wield the power which its very size commands. The report states:

> Although the officials of the large absentee-owned firms have little interest in civic affairs, they, nonetheless, actually run the big-business cities studied in this report. The answer to this apparent paradox is that corporation men, in fact, take action in civic affairs only when these civic affairs impinge upon corporation interests. In such cases, the influence of corporation men is often exerted surreptitiously, behind the concealing façade of local puppets and official figureheads. It is in this sense that officials of the great absentee-owned firms in big-business cities possess the real power in civic affairs, although the apparent power may reside elsewhere.[5]

One of the most powerful weapons in the possession of the large corporation is the threat to leave town. According to the report, this threat is employed as a veto power only on civic projects seriously opposed by the corporation. Such projects involve matters of such direct corporate import as a proposed increase in taxes, the demands of organized labor, and the like. A more common procedure followed by the large corporation to indicate opposition to a local proposal is the withdrawal of support. In one big-business city under

[5] *Ibid.*, p. 29.

study, the chief officer of the local chamber of commerce supported a policy contrary to that of the corporation officials. The latter simply withdrew from the organization and did not return until a new officer was appointed.

Another device frequently employed is the exercise of control over the city affairs through one or more small local businessmen. This, of course, is not a novel method; any seasoned Congressman or Senator can cite offhand a score of instances where legislation of benefit to large corporations is pressed by small-business groups who are financed by and act as a front for shadowy figures behind the scenes. The report cites the case of a local businessman in one big-business city who speedily attained acceptance in the social circle of the big corporation officials. He received membership in the best clubs and was given a social position out of proportion to his business attainments. Efforts were then exerted by these officials to secure his election to high posts in the leading civic organizations. Since big corporations usually control an undivided bloc of votes, this was accomplished without difficulty. The report states:

The result was to place the local man in a highly strategic position. Whether or not he was maintained there, however, depended entirely upon his behavior—specifically, on whether or not he followed orders promptly and expeditiously. In this case the local businessman was at one point induced to visit Washington to protest against a Federal decision involving his town. This decision, local residents agreed, would have benefited the small businessman's own economic interests, but would have interfered with the operations of the plant of the big absentee-owned corporation.[6]

The differing structural base of communities has a direct effect upon business vitality. It is not merely the fact that in communities whose industrial life is dominated by one or a few absentee-owned firms there is continuous uncertainty that plants will remain open. This uncertainty, of

[6] *Ibid.*, p. 30.

course, is hardly conducive to expansion or modernization of facilities. The human tendency under these circumstances to "wait and see" explains the present lackluster appearance of many of our towns which once were flourishing.

The report shows that retail sales per capita in the small-business cities actually exceeded those of the big-business cities. In large part this was attributed to the fundamental conditions existing in the two types of cities. Retail stores in the small-business cities not only serve the members of their community; they attract buyers from adjacent areas. In contrast, many of the residents of big-business cities go elsewhere to shop. To some extent the practice gets established by corporate executives of the large absentee-owned firm whose purchasing habits historically were formed elsewhere. If business trips to a large city are necessary, they also become the occasion for periodic shopping sprees. And as the local shopping facilities deepen their stagnation, the urge to shop elsewhere is intensified throughout the whole community.

Though admittedly difficult, the measurement of the relative level of welfare in cities is not impossible. A city is certainly "better" if fewer of its children die during their first year after birth, if it has more parks for children to play in, and more recreational facilities for all age groups. A city is "better" if it has more housing, better health, more utilities, more cultural facilities, and higher per capita income.

One of the nation's leading sociologists, Dr. E. L. Thorndike, developed a measure of civic welfare originally including 300 different measurable items, but narrowed to 37 important items—called by Thorndike a "G-score"—which was used in the report. In this index weights were given for infant mortality and general death rates (reversed); per capita expenditures for schools and teachers' salaries, libraries, museums and recreational facilities; per capita acreage of parks; per capita installation of gas and electricity, telephones, and the like; frequency of home ownership; average wage rates and number of children gainfully employed; and other social factors. In each case it was found that the level of civic welfare was substantially higher in the small-business cities. The score in one small-business community was 17 per cent above that of its big-business counterpart. In the second small-business center, the score was 19 per cent above that of the big-business city. In the intermediate pair, the difference was much smaller.

Housing conditions were found to be clearly superior in the small-business cities, when judged by a standard commonly used for this purpose: namely, the number of dwellings with an average of more than 1.5 persons per room. In one big-business city, more than 3.5 per cent of all dwellings were overcrowded, when judged by this standard, as against only 1.4 per cent of all dwelling units in the small-business city. In the second big-business city, 5.1 per cent of all dwelling units were overcrowded, as against only 1.8 per cent in its small-business counterpart. In the third group, the big-business city was more overcrowded than the small-business city.

The chance that a baby would die within a year after birth was found to be appreciably greater in the big-business than in the small-business cities. The death rate of infants within a year after birth was 40.4 per 1000 live births in the big-business city as against only 33.9 per 1000 in the small-business city. In the second group, the death rate was 45.7 in the big-business city as against only 24.9 in the small-business city. For the intermediate pair, the big-business city had a somewhat higher death rate.

Although public expenditures on health per capita were the same in the first pair, they were substantially greater in the other two small-business cities than in the corresponding big-business cities. An exception to the pattern was the fact that public expenditures on sanitation per capita were in every case greater in the big-business city.

Public expenditures on recreation, per capita, were substantially greater in small-business cities than in big-business cities—$1.31 as against 87 cents, and $1.63 as against 59 cents. Public expenditures on libraries were also greater in small-business cities than in the corresponding big-business cities.

Judged by magazine circulation, the interest of residents in literature and educational subjects appeared to be greater in small-business cities than in the corresponding big-business cities. The proportion of residents who were church members was in every case greater in the small-business city.

The record on education was also better in the small-business cities. Expenditures on public schools per student were greater in the small-business cities of two of the pairs, while the expenditures in the third pair were the same. Children were maintained in school for a longer period of time in two of the small-business cities. Residents in small-business cities were in every case more adequately provided with the common utilities—telephones and electricity—than were the residents of the big-business cities.

In short, in terms of the over-all index as well as these individual items (which are included in the Thorndike index), the level of civic welfare proved to be substantially higher in the small-business cities. The small-business cities had a lower percentage of slum dwellings, lower infant death rate, lower incidence of school dropouts. Correspondingly, per capita expenditures for community cultural and recreational services were higher, as were the incidence of home ownership, installations of electricity and telephones, and the like.

The Arvin and Dinuba Study

A similar report was prepared at about the same time on the effects on civic welfare of differences in the scale of farm operations.[7] This study was prepared by a group of sociolo-

[7] U.S. Senate, Report of the Special Committee to Study Problems of American Small Business, "Small Business and the Community—a Study in Central Valley of California on Effects of Scale of Farm Operations," (1946), 79th Cong., 2d Sess., Senate Committee Print No. 13.

gists from the University of Southern California under the direction of Dr. Walter R. Goldschmidt of the sociology department of the University of California.

The report on the California communities consisted of a contrast between two communities in the same general area. At the time this study was conducted, 1943-44, these two communities were similar in all important respects except one: the first community, Arvin, was surrounded by large-scale corporate farming; the other, Dinuba, by small-scale, independent farming. It was the purpose of the report to compare the levels of community welfare in these two centers. Which had a higher and more even distribution of income? Which had the better schools, better civic organization? Which showed greater participation among its citizens in social activities? Which had less juvenile delinquency? Which was taking more aggressive and effective steps to combat it? Which offered greater opportunities for young people to build independent, prosperous lives of their own? In short, which was the better place in which to live and rear one's children?

On all counts, the advantage lay in the small-farm community, and the reason was the difference in size of the farm organization. The report states: "Large scale farming does, in fact, bear the major responsibility for the social differences. . . ."

At the time of the study Arvin farms were about nine times larger, averaging 497 acres as contrasted with 57 acres in Dinuba. Numerous modest operations existed in Arvin, but seven farms operated 42 per cent of the cropland and orchards, and 22 farms operated two-thirds of all such land in the community. In Dinuba, on the other hand, 94 per cent of the farms were less than 160 acres. The five largest farms operated less than 4 per cent of the total acreage tilled in the community.

As in the case of the small-business cities discussed above, the Dinuba area—the example of small business in agricultural production—was the result of more gradual growth and development. For example, its first school was established in 1879, whereas the first school in the Arvin area began in 1902. Similarly, Dinuba's population maturity was reached in 1920; Arvin's growth came later when the community expanded sharply during the period of migration of destitute persons from the Dust Bowl.

The two communities showed marked differences in their form of government. In 1906, early in its existence, Dinuba became incorporated. Biennial elections of a council of five were concerned with local problems involving projects for the improvement of the community. At the time of the study a heated election had just occurred and the civic issues debated were still lively subjects of conversation among the local electorate.

In the course of its history, Dinuba had paved miles of sidewalks and streets, established a water system, sewage and garbage disposal facilities, set up police and fire departments, built parks and recreational facilities, developed a program of tree-planting and other measures designed to beautify the city. Its school system was a matter for pride in the community; teacher turnover was negligible.

At the time of the report Arvin had not yet constituted itself a civic body but was governed by the county. A number of explanations were given for this situation. One was that Arvin's inhabitants were quite satisfied with things as they were, that there was no real need for local government. Other explanations were less flattering. One of the ministers remarked that the large property owners did not want incorporation because they were fearful that their laborers "would run the town." Since it was not difficult for them to make their voices heard with county officials, it was suggested that there were no advantages to be gained by giving the local people a voice in their own affairs. Another possibility was that taxes would be increased. Since the large corporations and absentee landholders saw no direct benefit to themselves in civic improvements, they were opposed to higher taxes for such expenditures.

As a result, many civic advantages enjoyed by Dinuba citizens were not available in Arvin. At the time of the study water and garbage service in Arvin was provided by private companies, with no direct popular control over their activities. Street paving and lighting and the building of sidewalks were, of course, supplied by the county, and the latter appeared to be less alert to social needs than the city council of Dinuba. If Arvin citizens wished a new school, a park, or more adequate street lighting, it was necessary to form a committee to wait upon the county officials. Customarily, such county officials conferred with the operators of the large farms. Thus in the making of decisions important to the whole community, only a small segment of the community was consulted. Even when the decisions were favorable, there was some local resentment over the manner in which they had been reached.

The absence of a high school in Arvin was a matter of particular concern. At the time the study was made, it was pointed out that for the previous twenty years there had been enough children of high school age to warrant construction of a public high school. To secure a high school education, Arvin children had to travel daily a distance of 20 miles or more to another city; the need to catch the homeward-bound bus deprived them of all opportunities for extracurricular activities at the school. A rigid social barrier had developed in the community where the high school was located between the local city children and the "foreigners." This was further reflected in the attitude of the high school authorities themselves. The children from Arvin and other outlying areas possessed basically second-class citizenship in the school; automatically they were assigned to trades classes on the assumption that they were going to be farmers or laborers and had no interest in college preparatory work.

In many small communities the local high school is the gathering center for cultural and civic activities. It supplies playground facilities, gymnasium, and auditorium. It is used for lectures and musicals, school dances, and the like. It has library facilities, art classes, and often adult education programs. At the time the study was made, the Arvin students were denied all of these advantages in their home community, presumably because it would have meant an increase in the tax rates.

The economic conditions in the two communities also showed marked contrasts. The small-farm community showed twice the number of independent business establishments. Its volume of retail sales was substantially higher; and the expenditures for household supplies and building improvements were three times greater than in the large-farm community.

It was also discovered that the small-farm area supported a larger number of people per dollar volume of production. Despite this fact, people in this community enjoyed, on the average, a higher standard of living. In the large-farm community less than one-fifth of the gainfully employed were independent businessmen, white-collar workers, or self-employed farmers. In the small-farm community, this group constituted one-half of all employed. A marked difference also showed up in the numbers of agricultural wage laborers, a group in our society characterized by great economic insecurity, subsistence living standards, and little opportunity for either social or economic advancement. In the large-farm community, Arvin, nearly two-thirds of all the gainfully employed fell in this category. In contrast, less than one-third of the workers in the small-farm area were agricultural wage laborers.

The physical evidences of a higher level of civic welfare in the Dinuba community were also clearly apparent. Its trim outward appearance was made possible by the array of community services provided for its citizens; its schools, parks, and public recreation centers, widely distributed, indicated the community's concern for the betterment of all its citizens. An ironic commentary contained in the report on the large-farm community was that its single playground was on loan to the public by a private corporation.

In summary, the per capita income in the small-farm community was higher; income was much more evenly distributed; there was a much larger middle class and a much smaller lower-income group. Reflecting these differences in income, living conditions were better in the small-farm community. The small-farm community had a higher proportion of homes with running water and telephones; they spent much more for household supplies and building equipment.

But the differences between communities cannot be measured only in terms of material possessions. There are other less tangible but highly important factors which must be taken into consideration—the type of government, schools, social organizations and the like. In the big-farm community there was no local government; in the small-farm community local government not only existed, but was a matter of widespread public interest.

In the small-farm community only 3 out of 22 teachers did not return for the following session. In the big-farm community 14 out of 22 did not return. Moreover, as pointed out above, the big-farm community did not even have its own high school, which in the small-farm community was the center of many healthful social activities.

In the other social aspects of community life—clubs, school events, picnics, and so on—through which friendships are formed and the spirit of neighborliness and good fellowship develops, the residents in the small-farm community held an average of 42 club memberships per 100 persons, whereas the citizens of the big-farm community held only 29 memberships per 100 persons. In the big-farm community there was little for the youth to do except go to the movies or the pool halls. In the small-farm community he could go to a dance, play either on the school grounds under supervision or at a park, participate in high-school activities, go to Scout meetings or to DeMolay (or Rainbow) meetings, spend his evenings in the recreation center, or participate with others under supervision in one or more hobbies. Here again, the opportunities for social contacts and personal development were far greater in the small than in the big-farm community.

The Social Costs of Monopoly

Admittedly, the evidence presented in these reports is fragmentary. In the last analysis, however, nothing is more important than the conditions in the community in which one lives and raises his children. To an incalculable extent it is these conditions which mold the society of the next generations and determine the kind of world in which they will live. It is unfortunate that the only studies available on the crucial issues involved are those described here. Sometimes I wonder if it is wholly accident that this pioneer work on the social costs of high industrial concentration ceased before it hardly began.

Some of the reasons are suggested in a provocative little book by William H. Whyte, Jr. published in the early 1950's.[8] Much of Whyte's fire is directed to what he calls "The Great Free Enterprise Campaign" in which the public is inundated with propaganda on the "free enterprise system." He remarks:

Never before have businessmen appeared so gripped with a single idea; there is scarcely a convention that is not exhorted with it, and of all the general speeches made by businessmen, by far the greatest single category is that in which the audience is warned to spread the gospel before it is too late. And so it goes, this message: We must cure misinformation with information; we must tell the business story; above all, we must *sell* Free Enterprise. . . .

All in all, the Free Enterprise campaign is shaping up as one of the most intensive "sales" jobs in the history of the industry—in fact, it is fast becoming very much of an industry in itself. At the current rate, it is accounting for at least $100,000,000

[8] William H. Whyte, Jr. and the editors of *Fortune* magazine, *Is Anybody Listening?* (New York: Simon and Schuster, 1952).

of industry's annual advertising, public relations and employee-relations expenditures. More to the point, it is absorbing more and more of the energies expended by the top men in U.S. management.[9]

Thus it would appear that at the very moment when objective assessment of the social consequences of increasing industrial concentration in our economy is most needed, the public is given an intensive selling campaign on the Free Enterprise theme.

Whyte also points out that much of this advertising portrays a mythical community life supposedly characteristic of our day. He says:

Look at many ads—particularly the Free Enterprise ones. What are they in terms of? When there is an identifiable "frame of reference," in the majority of cases the terms are those of Main Street: shady lawns, barbecue dinners in the back yard, mansarded roofs, the town firehouse, church suppers, and so on. . . .

But do most Americans live on Main Street? The greatest single proportion live in the dirty, smelly city. But this is something we do not like to face, for the problems that urban life has wrought are among the most disagreeable we have to meet. . . .[10]

What may really be at stake, then, is the continued vitality of a mythical community life so long pictured on the covers of the *Saturday Evening Post*. Its existence, even in the public imagination, could hardly withstand the pressures of such sober, objective accounts of community comparisons as are presented in these reports.

[9] *Op. cit.*, pp. 4–6.
[10] *Ibid.*, pp. 30–32.

Chapter 6

*

PUBLIC POLICY
AND PRIVATE MONOPOLY

The problems of public policy in the realm of private monopoly are acute. An increasing number of important industries in our economy have acquired—and are continuing to acquire—a built-in immunity to the forces of the market. In a variety of ways the dispossession of market controls by administered prices is taking place; in each case the effect is to insulate the industry against price competition with little or no resort to conspiratorial action. The problems posed by this economic transformation matter to more than the government agencies concerned with the maintenance of competition. They raise vital questions about the kind of industrial structure that is coming into being in this country and the ultimate effects it will have upon our democratic institutions.

As Professor Frank J. Kottke remarked:

The traditional threats to our competitive economic system have been conspiracies and unfair practices. These our laws can check. But in recent decades a new problem has emerged; results in some respects similar to those of monopoly (and in some ways worse) frequently appear in markets supplied by only a few firms. Prices are set high, sometimes with scant regard to the level of costs. These high prices are maintained with little change during business recessions because the rivals prefer deep cuts in production to substantial cuts in prices. The courts and the Federal Trade Commission have been slow to discern conspiracy in these actions of rival suppliers, and today our economy is nearly as defenseless against parallel-supplier policies in few-seller markets as in 1880 it was defenseless in single-seller markets.[1]

Other witnesses in the Subcommittee's policy hearings expressed similar views on the decline of the market as the instrument of control. Professor William Fellner put it this way:

In a highly concentrated industry each large corporation is aware of the fact that its individual pricing decisions have an influence on the profits of the other firms, and that the other firms are aware of the same interdependence. It is obviously not a reasonable policy objective to try to make corporate management act as if it were incapable of understanding this interdependence. However, it is important to remember that the coordination of pricing policies tends to become tighter in extremely concentrated oligopolistic markets, than in markets with somewhat more sellers none of whom has a dominant position.[2]

The theory of free enterprise rests entirely upon the automatic checks of the market which are assumed to exist. By each person's seeking his own maximum gain, the ends of society are served. Seller is pitted against seller in the eternal rivalry of the marketplace; in this competitive struggle, each offers the best of which he is capable in order to effect the greatest gain as well as to survive and prosper. In this economic order, any deviation from the competitive pattern is an assault upon the instrument of regulation; for the market, with its system of built-in checks and balances, reigns supreme. Society depends on the market to extinguish

[1] U.S. Senate Subcommittee on Antitrust and Monopoly, *Administered Prices: A Compendium on Public Policy*, 88th Cong., 1st. Sess., Committee Print. Frank J. Kottke, Prof. of Economics, Washington State University, "Four Industries with Administered Prices Investigated by the Senate Subcommittee on Antitrust and Monopoly: 1957–61," p. 182.

[2] William Fellner, Professor of Economics, Yale University, "Some Timely Problems of Antitrust Policy," *ibid.*, p. 135.

the unfit and to ensure the survival of the competent. Everyone prospers under an economic system which brings a flow of high-quality merchandise to market at reasonable prices.

The theory postulates the existence of a multiplicity of small, individually owned firms whose competitive vigor wanes with the life of the owner. It does not take into account the giant corporation which may lord it over an industry for generations. In its detail it stems from the work of Alfred Marshall who likened an industry to a forest with individual trees, sprouting, growing to maturity, and finally declining. In his later years, Marshall modified his views to accord with changing economic conditions. In his sixth edition, twenty years after his principles were formulated, Marshall changed the tree analogy to read "as with the growth of trees, so it was with the growth of businesses as a general rule *before the recent development of vast joint-stock companies.*" In pointing this out, Dr. Gardiner Means told the Subcommittee that "today the great bulk of traditional economic thinking, and so many of our economic texts, are built on the conception of enterprises very much like Marshall's representative firm."[3]

The concern of public policy is with results to be attained from competition, not the particular means employed. Our public policy came into being because of the strongly held belief that a competitive system would bring to the public a more varied assortment of goods, of higher quality, at the lowest possible prices. In this context it little matters whether price inflexibility is the result of outright collusion among sellers or the tacit understanding arising from trade practice. As Professor Fritz Machlup of Johns Hopkins University put it:

A covenant signed with blood, an agreement signed with ink, an understanding without written words, concerted acts approved with a wink or a nod, a common course of action followed with-

[3] U.S. Senate, Committee on the Judiciary, Subcommittee on Antitrust and Monopoly, 86th Cong., 1st Sess., *Hearings on Administered Prices*, (1959), Part 9, p. 4771.

out physical communication, these may be different methods of collusion, but the differences are irrelevant, if the effects are the same.[4]

And Professor Ben Lewis of Oberlin College added that the problem is not reduced where the industry maintains, for public relations purposes, a mere semblance of competitive behavior.

Nor is the presence or strength of competition convincingly shown by the fact that giant firms may upon occasion adopt and follow a competitive routine—may make competitive motions, may choose deliberately to stop short of monopoly, or as a matter of management policy may institute competition among their company branches or divisions. The test is whether the big firm is compelled to compete, whether it is driven by competition in its quest for maximum gain or survival.[5]

The Problem of Concentration

The core of the economic problem facing us today is the concentration of power in a few hands. A few figures will illustrate the point: In 1962 the 20 largest manufacturing corporations alone had $73.8 billion in assets, or about one-quarter of the total assets of United States manufacturing companies. In turn, the 50 largest companies held 36 per cent; the 100 largest, 46 per cent; the 200 largest, 56 per cent; and the 1000 largest, nearly 75 per cent. This left for all others—approximately 419,000 manufacturing concerns —the remaining one-quarter of the total assets.[6]

In terms of corporate profits after taxes, the comparison is equally startling. The 20 largest manufacturing corporations accounted for 38 per cent of all profits after taxes;

[4] *Ibid.*, p. 4782.

[5] *Ibid.*, p. 4714.

[6] U.S. Senate, Committee on the Judiciary, Subcommittee on Antitrust and Monopoly, 88th Cong., 2d Sess., *Hearings on Concentration of Economic Power* (1964). Testimony by Dr. Willard F. Mueller, Director of Bureau of Economics, Federal Trade Commission, Transcript, Vol. 2, p. 300.

the 50 largest for almost 48 per cent. And going farther down the line, the 100 largest accounted for over 57 per cent, and the 1000 largest for over 86 per cent.

Betwen 1947 and 1962 the share of total industrial output produced by the country's 200 largest corporations increased one-third.[7] In 1947 these companies accounted for 30 per cent of the value added by manufacture. By 1962 their proportion had risen to 40 per cent.

Studies of concentration in particular industries show a varied pattern. A real problem arises out of the fact that, in many of these calculations, broad product groupings are employed; each contains a miscellany of individual products, some of which are monopolized and others highly competitive. Obviously, their inclusion in a single product category blurs the picture, and makes realistic appraisal extremely difficult.

In addition, many of the largest firms are highly diversified in their operations, and concentration ratios for individual industries do not reflect this aspect of the problem. In 1958, for example, the 200 largest companies had nearly a quarter of their manufacturing employment in major industry groups other than the one in which they were principally engaged. And the figures show that, in those products which these large companies manufacture, they are frequently found among the four leading producers.[8]

It is not the mere fact of concentration which causes concern. It is what follows in its wake which is significant. In too many industries there has developed an essentially feudal economic structure—a small handful of dominant firms, with a medley of smaller producers who exist in the crevices of the monolithic structure and survive at the will of the

[7] *Ibid.*, p. 213. Testimony of Dr. John M. Blair, Chief Economist of Subcommittee on Antitrust and Monopoly. This measurement is in terms of value added by manufacture, that is, the value of shipments minus the cost of materials and lesser items. Unless these costs are eliminated from the calculations, they will be counted twice—once at the time of sale or interplant transfer by the supplier and again later by the recipient of the goods.

[8] *Ibid.*, p. 223.

major companies. Here and there, in favored spots, a small producer may dig in and develop for himself an entrenched position where he can wage effective economic war with his larger rivals. And in time, if the course of economic events is with him and he has the audacity and skill to seize the opportunities, there may be room for him at the top.

Yet such entry into the corporate elect appears to be increasingly difficult. Of the 50 largest companies in 1962, 38 had been in this group in 1954, and 29 were among the 50 largest in 1947. Even more revealing is the fact that, of the 50 largest in 1962, all but one was among the 200 largest in 1947.[9] While some shifts in position occurred among the biggest firms during these years, there appeared to be little opportunity for entry by growth of the medium or small-sized firms. Thus, for the great majority, a state of feudal bondage remains their lot.

This situation poses problems of the utmost magnitude insofar as the effectiveness of the market mechanisms is concerned. The issue is whether the presence of giant corporate complexes leaves room for the natural, self-generating forces of the market to discharge their function. For unless the automatic mechanisms of the market can subdue these vast private enterprises to the free play of competition, the whole system of automatic control, implicit in laissez-faire capitalism, breaks down. Big business takes over the job of the market; the instrument of regulation is seized and operated by those it is intended to regulate.

But is bigness more of a problem today than it has been in the past? In this country the latter half of the nineteenth century has frequently been referred to as the "era of the trusts"; the term "muckraker" was used to describe the economic writers of that day who inveighed against the "railroad trust," the "oil trust," the "steel trust," and other combinations of industrial power. Indeed, so great was the public outcry during this period that, in addition to the passage of the Sherman Act in 1890, Congress also concluded that

9 *Ibid.*, p. 229.

some industries, such as the railroads, could never be expected to meet competitive norms and that Government regulation of their activities was the only answer.

Two eminent economic writers have drawn a vivid comparison between then and now. In describing the industrial conditions which occasioned the passage of the Sherman Act, Walton Hamilton wrote:

The unruly times offered opportunity to the swashbuckling captains of industry, whose ways were direct, ruthless, and not yet covered over by the surface amenities of a later age. In sugar, nails, tobacco, copper, jute, cordage, borax, slate pencils, oilcloth, gutta percha, barbed fence wire, castor oil, they bluntly staked out their feudal domains. The little man caught in a squeeze play—the independent crowded to the wall by "the Octopus"— the farmer selling his wheat, corn, or tobacco under the tyranny of a market he did not understand—the craftsman stripped of his trade by the machine—the consumer forced to take the ware at an artificial price or go without—here were dramatic episodes. Industry was in the clutch of radical forces—and of inequity.[10]

Professor Lewis remarked to the Subcommittee:

A half century ago, bigness was a brash newcomer fighting its way doggedly into the economy, clawing, biting, slugging, stomping to gain power over the market. Its predatory practices were limited only by its unrestrained ambition and its fertile imagination; and it was on these practices that the public fastened its critical attention.[11]

Today, things are different. The giant firm in the concentrated industry has arrived, and it has become respectable. According to Walton Hamilton, "The Sherman Act has been the initial instrument of education, and the Government itself has supplied the stimulus." As the crude combinations were attacked in court, the leaders of these industries began to give conscious thought to their defenses.

[10] Temporary National Economic Committee, *Antitrust in Action*, Monograph No. 16, 1941, p. 5.
[11] U.S. Senate Subcommittee on Antitrust and Monopoly, *Hearings on Administered Prices*, Part 9, p. 4715.

As good citizens they were concerned to be lawabiding; as able business men they were loath to refrain from activities which were to their advantage. Where values clash, a formula must be found—one which will reconcile the pursuit of gain with the prohibition against monopoly. Old ends came to be served with modulated means; coercion was dissipated into a discipline of gentle reminders; crude restraint was subdued into a fine art. Once education was under way, lessons were eagerly learned; and those who in defense had forged nimble weapons taught their use to men of affairs not yet under attack. Thus as business has become civilized, its leaders have professed the amenities. They are now versed in propriety, indirection, circumlocution. They operate in an economy so intricate as to give full play to ingenuity and finesse.[12]

After remarking that bigness is far more impressive today, with its roots lodged deep in our economy, Professor Lewis said:

The behavior of bigness today is spotless, at least no spots remain unremoved for long; and its appearance and demeanor are attractive and ingratiating. Tutored by its attorneys, bathed, barbered and cosmeticized by Madison Avenue, nourished and sanctified by war and cold war, and enthroned by public opinion which sees only goodness in bigness that is well mannered and well behaved, bigness exhibits the supreme confidence and gracious assurance that bespeak stature, status, and a clear conscience. Bigness was once the bad boy in Sunday school; now it sits on the vestry.[13]

Some of the economic experts appearing before our Subcommittee expressed alarm that, with greater size and concentration, corporations have increasingly moved outside the economic arena into the political realm. As a result of court decisions, the rights granted to human beings under our Constitution have been extended to artificial corporate persons; thus they exercise the same rights of free speech, petition, and assembly guaranteed by the Constitution to

[12] *Antitrust in Action, op. cit.*, p. 13.
[13] *Hearings*, Part 9, p. 4715.

natural persons. Further, they have the financial resources continuously to make their views known, through all of the "popular mass media," to the most remote hamlet in the nation. Professor Horace M. Gray informed the Subcommittee that,

. . . corporations are no longer restricted to the mundane economic functions stipulated in their charters; they are now free to exercise political power in the larger arena of public opinion, social values, political action and public policy determination. Going farther we grant them the privilege of treating all outlays for such activities as legitimate *"costs of doing business"* for purposes of pricing and taxation. As a consequence, consumers and taxpayers are compelled to subsidize the propaganda of private monopolies—to pay for the deception practiced upon them.[14]

The sheer magnitude of the country's largest corporations is staggering. For some years General Motors has ranked first in *Fortune's* listing of the 500 largest industrial corporations. The 1963 report showed its assets to be in excess of 10 billion dollars, with sales of nearly 15 billion dollars and employees numbering over 600,000. Its rate of profit, based on invested capital, amounted to 22 per cent. Standard Oil of New Jersey, second on the list, had assets of 11.5 billion dollars, with sales amounting to nearly 10 billion dollars. Next in order came Ford, with sales exceeding 8 billion dollars, and General Electric with nearly 5 billion dollars of sales.

Is it any wonder, then, that some of our country's leading economists raised the question as to whether these industrial aggregates can properly be called "private enterprise"? Dr. Gardiner Means told the Subcommittee:

The first step is to get rid of the idea that the big corporations are "private enterprise." Just what is private about an enterprise

---

[14] Horace M. Gray, Prof. of Economics, Univ. of Illinois, "Supplemental Action to Reinforce Antitrust," *Administered Prices: A Compendium on Public Policy, op. cit.,* pp. 150–51.

that organizes a quarter of a million workers into a great productive unit using the capital of more than a quarter of a million
stockholders and serving millions of ultimate customers? Is it
any more private than, say, the government of New York State?[15]

It may be, as he suggested, that we need a new term for
these enterprises to give us a new focus in our thinking.
Obviously, when such massive segments of the country's
productive energy are closeted within a single corporate
domain, the word "private" is something of a misnomer.
The well-being of the entire economy is tied to the prosperity
of these industrial aggregates, and hard times for them spells
widespread unemployment, losses in public revenues, and
insecurity throughout the entire business structure. One
suggestion has been made that they be called "collective
enterprises." Others have used the terms "private socialism"
and "private economic government."

Market power is frequently described as being vertical,
horizontal, and conglomerate in character. Vertical power
enables a major firm to squeeze its competitors through
denial of critically needed supplies or in the manipulation
of prices for material at different stages of the production or
distribution process. Horizontal market power exists when
a company, by sheer size, lords it over its competitors. Professor Walter Adams of Michigan State University pointed
out that conglomerate power is exercised by a firm "when
its operations are so widely diversified that its survival no
longer depends on success in any given product market or
any given geographical area." It exists when, through sheer
size, it can "discipline or destroy its more specialized competitors." He continued:

I venture to say that if General Motors suddenly decided to enter
the ice cream industry and to capture 20, or 40, or 100 per cent
of the sales, it could easily do so and be assured of success. It
would matter little whether General Motors is an efficient ice
cream manufacturer, or whether its ice cream is indeed tastier

[15] *Hearings on Administered Prices,* Part 9, p. 4773.

than more established brands. By discreet price concessions, by saturation advertising, by attractive promotional deals, it could commit its gargantuan financial power to the battle until only so much competition as General Motors is prepared to tolerate would be left in the industry.[16]

Using a more homely analogy, he likened the situation to that of a poker game where one player is considerably more affluent than the others.

Put differently, in a poker game with unlimited stakes, the player who commands disproportionately large funds is likely to emerge victorious. If I have $100 while my opponents have no more than $5 each, I am likely to win regardless of my ability, my virtue, or my luck. I have the one asset the others lack, the power to bankrupt my rivals.

Some Policy Alternatives

The important question is: What are we going to do about it? A number of policy alternatives are available. We can simply sit tight, ride out the storm, and at the end of a few more decades assess the situation and make what adaptation we can. In the meantime, we can voice alarm on all suitable occasions, hoping that business will exercise restraint and moderation with respect to both further concentration and administered prices. To a surprising extent, this is exactly the policy that has been followed since World War II.

Another possibility is boldly to "face up to the economic facts." We begin with the premise that our economic thinking needs to be "modernized," that the pace of industrial events has outstripped our economic concepts, that it is time we cease living mentally in one economic climate and physically in quite another. On this hypothesis we can move readily and inevitably into a program of government regulation of industry. This follows from our recognition that his-

[16] *Ibid.*, Part 9, p. 4780.

torically the private exercise of monopoly has always meant abuse, and that sooner or later society steps in to impose restrictions upon the unbridled exercise of private power. In times past, efforts to impose such restraints have on occasion spelled civil war and bloodshed, fighting in the streets and revolution.

Another approach is use of the spotlight of publicity to acquaint our citizens with the realities of the economic world they live in. To a considerable extent this has been the function of many of our Congressional investigating committees which have sought to probe "soft spots" in our economy which needed correction. Of necessity, this approach involves governmental action; on many industrial fronts there is a marked unwillingness to disclose essential facts such as the extent of the corporate domain, pricing practices, and the web of trade usages which guide industrial behavior.

As the drug hearings showed, public examination of an industry's practices has marked usefulness. It presents an opportunity for the more moderate elements in the industry to take at least some of the corrective steps that need to be taken. Often, without pressure from some quarters, business executives tend to remain silent and eventually adopt the very trade practices they deplore. Publicity also has the effect of forcing a re-examination by the regulatory agency not only of the industry's practices but of its own role in the network of regulations that have been built up over the years. And, finally, public indignation can create a climate of opinion in the Congress that results in the passage of needed legislation.

Then there is the direct antithesis of price regulation and government control of industry. In a sense the struggle to create and maintain a competitive economy is a more far-reaching approach, because it would destroy monopoly rather than accept its existence and try to control it. Its wellsprings of support have traditionally been the independent entrepreneurial class—farmers and small businessmen—and that vast politically amorphous mass of our population that we call consumers.

THE POLICY OF INACTION

The first policy that has been mentioned with respect to concentration and administered prices is to do nothing at all. Though negative in character, this is truly a policy of action —or perhaps better, a policy of inaction. It means that industrial concentration will continue unabated, and that many of the industries which appear today to be in the early stages of merger development—paper and textiles are good examples—will become transformed in the next few decades. Here and there in an industry a technological innovation will upset the trend or a newcomer in the front ranks of corporate aristocracy will break ranks and for a time follow a competitive bent. In the main, however, the drift, if left unchecked, would appear to be a rapid intensification of concentration in those industries which have not already attained a high level of private corporate control.

This trend can be, and indeed already has been, rationalized as being socially beneficial and desirable. In years past the standard justification for the giant corporation was that its size was necessary in order to take advantage of the economies of large-scale production. This coincided with the era of primarily vertical and horizontal integration in industry. In the former case, the firm moved backward to bring raw material supplies within its control or it moved forward into distribution channels for the marketing of its products. In the second, it moved horizontally to acquire a miscellany of smaller firms, usually the more profitable enterprises, engaged in the same or a similar line of business. In either case there was some sacrifice of competitive vitality within the industry.

In recent years the defense that business must be large to enjoy economies of large-scale production has faded in importance. The argument lost force as it became increasingly apparent that the size of our modern corporate giants is far beyond any conceivable requirements of efficiency. Furthermore, there is evidence that, in some industries, the trend of technology has reversed itself and is now reducing the size of plant required for efficient operation. Interesting examples of these new technologies in the steel industry—direct reduction of ore, continuous casting of ingots, and small-scale planetary rolling mills—were presented before our Subcommittee during the steel hearings. In drugs, the evidence presented to the Subcommittee clearly indicates that the smaller companies not only match their larger competitors in plant efficiency, but, by eliminating certain traditional advertising costs arising out of the heavy promotion of brand names by the big companies, can undersell them as well.

Furthermore, a new factor has been added to reduce the effectiveness of the argument for bigness as a prerequisite for efficiency. This has been the mushrooming of the so-called conglomerate firm—the combining under a single corporate roof of a constellation of highly diverse enterprises which have little relation to each other. The survival of the conglomerate firm no longer depends upon its success in any given product market; success arises from its ability, through sheer size and economic power, to slug its more specialized competitors.

The new rationale for corporate size is now pinned to advances in technology. Big business, it is argued, means big research laboratories, big expenditures for the release of the inventive talents, big technological developments. Thus, whatever may be lost in the way of competitive activity among firms is more than compensated for by the steady flow of important inventions which enrich the lives of us all. Indeed, by implication the argument goes even farther: monopolistic practices, high prices, the bludgeoning of smaller competitors can be excused, if not condoned, because of the inventive benefactions bestowed by big business on society.

Like many theories, this particular doctrine arrived on the

economic scene unsupported by anything more than positive assertion. It was not based upon an examination of the significant developments in important industries to pinpoint their origins. Instead, as often happens, the idea was embraced by those who found it was to their benefit, and by dint of sheer repetition it has become accepted as fact. The modicum of available evidence on the subject gives little support to the doctrine; indeed, it suggests that exactly the opposite is true. A recent study by Professor John Jewkes of Oxford University, England, discloses that most of the world's creative discoveries are the product of individuals working in isolation or in small research laboratories.[17]

Who is the genuinely original and creative inventor, the man who makes a major breakthrough in man's conquest of the unknown? Few of these men appear to function satisfactorily in the large, highly organized corporate laboratory; there, too often, emphasis is placed primarily upon research work which will yield quick results in terms of commercial exploitation of the product. And in common with other organizations of any size, the big research laboratory tends to be infected with creeping bureaucracy. Its staff is frequently composed of competent researchers whose limited inventive gifts are more than compensated for by a willingness to work on projects that are dictated by business management and which promise immediate exploitative advantages.

In general, the highly gifted inventor prefers an intellectual environment where he is freer to follow his own leads in pursuit of more fundamental goals. It is not surprising, therefore, that most of the really significant developments in the field of medical research have occurred outside the research laboratories of the large corporations. More favorable environments appear to be provided by universities and similar nonprofit institutions.

During the course of the drug hearings, Dr. David Novick of the Rand Corporation presented a breakdown of expendi-

[17] Jewkes, J., D. Sawers and R. Stillerman, *The Sources of Invention,* (London: Macmillan, 1958).

tures for research and development. Only a small fraction of the large sums spent actually go into creative work because, he said, "For the most part this research involves one or a few highly qualified individuals, the equipment is paper and pencil, or blackboard and chalk, and *relatively small laboratories*. It is only when use or application is involved that expenditures jump sharply."[18] In consequence, he estimated that of the 10-billion-dollar expenditures for research and development in 1959, about 9.6 billion dollars went into "application." Almost all of this was spent in the development of new uses of established products or slight modifications of existing products and their applications.

Thus the functions performed by the large corporate research laboratory are not as decisively important as has been frequently claimed. The development of commercial products is a useful function. But the point is that this kind of work is not confined to the large corporate laboratory, nor is bigness an essential in its pursuit. It occurs in every research laboratory in the country, large or small. In most cases it does not require prohibitively costly equipment nor a vast body of technical skills.

An interesting illustration of this very point relates to antibiotics. In his prepared statement for the Subcommittee, Dr. Austin Smith, president of the Pharmaceutical Manufacturers Association, had a section entitled "The Parade of Discovery" which contains this remark:

Private industry played a major role in discovery and development of almost all these medicinals. All but one antibiotic discovered since World War II and produced commercially in the U.S. came from American research. And of these antibiotics, every one, including the four broad-spectrum antibiotics, resulted from efforts of private pharmaceutical manufacturers.[19]

An examination of the origin of the antibiotics discovery must, however, take account of events prior to World War

18 *Hearings on Administered Prices,* Part 18, p. 10513.
19 *Hearings,* Part 19, p. 10685.

II. As early as 1929, Sir Alexander Fleming discovered penicillin in England, and investigative work was carried on at Oxford University and English hospitals. The remarkable therapeutic properties of the drug were recognized in England; and in 1941 a small group of English physicians arrived in this country and conferred with officials in private industry and in the government. The Office of Scientific Research and Development, a wartime government agency, became interested in its possibilities for the treatment of war injuries.

The immediate problem was commercial production in adequate quantities. To this end the U.S. Government agency contributed large funds and enlisted the efforts of drug manufacturers, universities, and government research groups. The work of the large drug companies lagged. Perhaps the development was too revolutionary in character and the commercial possibilities not sufficiently apparent. Another factor was the uncertainty among corporate executives as to the patent rights they might be able to claim, with the Government acting as sponsor.

When the smoke cleared away, it was apparent that the significant contributions on commercial production had emanated from the Northern Regional Research Laboratory of the U.S. Department of Agriculture in Peoria, Illinois. In conformity with established patent policy in that agency, patents on these developments were dedicated to the public and thus made available to the twenty or more companies which had been financially aided by the government to enter production.

The next development was the discovery of streptomycin at Rutgers University. As recognition grew that nature provided a variety of molds, the research efforts of the private companies were redoubled, and within a short time a host of antibiotic specialities appeared on the market. These included chloramphenicol (Chloromycetin), oxytetracycline (Terramycin), chlortetracycline (Aureomycin), and tetracycline. Their importance cannot be minimized. It is only fair to state, however, that their appearance was made possible first by the basic discovery of the British and later by the creative solutions of the Government scientists in Peoria to the problems of large-scale production. The discovery of new molds in nature was undoubtedly time-consuming and costly to the companies in terms of laboratory work and clinical testing, but it hardly falls in the same creative category as the earlier work. It is of interest that all of the antibiotics, subsequent to penicillin and the streptomycins, were made subject to monopoly controls under patents. Until the start of the Subcommittee's hearings, they were all priced identically both to the druggist and the patient.

The economic experts who appeared before our Subcommittee were not satisfied that the available evidence supports the supposed correlation between giant size and advance in the technical arts. As Prof. Adams remarked:

How, for example, can they reconcile the relative stagnation in steel and meatpacking with the dynamism of chemicals and electronics, all industries with considerable concentration? How do they account for the fact that the automobile industry today is no more progressive technologically than it was 40 years ago when the industry was young and composed of many firms?

How do they explain the fact that the highly concentrated anthracite coal industry is no more progressive technologically than the competitive bituminous coal industry? How do they account for the fact that in a concentrated industry like steel, the medium-sized companies have been more progressive than the giant United States Steel Corporation?[20]

On the contrary, the very fact of competition is a spur to innovation. Where an industry lives under the shelter of monopolistic restraints, it has little real interest in the genuinely novel advance; too often such an event constitutes a hazard to the fixed investment in established modes of manufacture. Slight modifications, which give the appearance of newness but are not a threat to orthodox production methods,

[20] *Hearings*, Part 9, p. 4784.

are quite acceptable. Particularly in an oligarchic industrial structure, they provide a competitive outlet for firms barred, by tacit agreement, from engaging in price competition. It is only when there is vigorous industrial rivalry that important technological advances which threaten the old order have their chance; for each firm is keenly aware that his competitor is breathing hotly down his neck. Even here it is often the smaller companies which have the temerity and flexibility of operation to take the plunge into the unknown.

ADMONITION—AN ADVENTURE IN SERMONIZING

The basic purpose of government regulation of economic behavior is to correct rather than to punish. The aim is to amend an offending trade practice, to bring the industrial mores once more in line with public policy. Even the punitive sections of the Sherman Act, proving for fines and imprisonment, are essentially designed to make one offender a warning to the many; it is hoped that a few examples will be enough to discourage all industries from entering into arrangements designed to mitigate the forces of competition. Thus every antitrust case brought by the Government is in the nature of a sermon, pointing up a moral and exhorting every businessman to live within all four corners of the law.

As business has grown bigger, and as an increasing number of industries have fallen outside of the net of the antitrust laws through various forms of price-administered arrangements, it has become clear that something else is required. Why not employ the sermon direct, the admonition that big business—unrestrained by the automatic controls of the market—engage in self-restraint? To this end, there has been a flow of utterances from the White House on down through Cabinet officials and heads of agencies calling upon the country's largest corporations to bring their social consciences to bear in the conduct of business affairs. In time, this practice of invoking admonition as a guide was elevated to a theoretical rationale.

The idea has an engaging simplicity and the added virtue

of ease of administration. All that needs to be done, where a highly concentrated industry is characterized by an inflexible price structure and an idle productive capacity, is to call upon business leaders to act as statesmen rather than businessmen. If to this situation there is added the problem of a generally sluggish economy, these business executives—now metamorphized into statesmen—will take statesmanlike action. Presumably, they will initiate steps to amend the private trade restrictions, permit some modified play of competitive forces, perhaps reduce prices to utilize excess capacity and stimulate sales.

Unfortunately, the problem is not quite so simple. It is true that on particular occasions admonition has been strikingly effective. In the still-remembered steel crisis of April 1962, for example, a strong Presidential admonition had the effect of changing the industry's announced course of raising steel prices in the face of reduced sales of steel products, heavy excess capacity, and high profits of the major producers. But this device is, by its very nature, an *ad hoc* procedure. It can be invoked for a particular crisis of major importance to the economy; it cannot be used as an everyday instrument of regulation. A constant stream of admonitory remarks from high Government officials on a wide range of industrial problems cannot continue to capture the interest of the public—a factor of critical importance in making admonition a potent device. In time such admonitions will, as indeed has happened in the past, fall upon deaf ears of industrial leaders; for, in the absence of public concern, the spur to action is absent.

There are also other problems. It is unrealistic to believe that business leaders in a single industry, even with the best will in the world, can take on the burden they are asked to assume. As big business has grown, a multitude of feudal industrial estates have come into being. Often, no one group can completely impose its will on the others. Thus, what is asked for is a number of independent judgments by business leaders on the steps needed to set matters straight; in some unexplained fashion, all of these decisions will automatically mesh to form a coherent, intelligent public policy. In essence this is an abdication of the Government's role to guide and direct the multifold activities of society in the public welfare.

But even if this form of governmental abdication of its functions were practicable, the executives of the country's largest corporations are hardly the likely choice as substitute statesmen. Their entire training and experience have been attuned to the acquisitive arts; they have devoted decades of time and talent to the art of advancing the fortunes of their corporations over those of others. They may be knowledgeable in the manufacturing processes and technological developments in their own industries—though increasingly in these large corporations, production men have given way to lawyers and sales experts in guidance of industrial policy. Even where such knowledge exists, it is limited to a particular industry or group of industries. In short, what is required is the mentality and broad view of the statesman; what is available is the narrowly oriented knowledge and experience of the business executive.

The difficulty is exemplified in the wage-price spiral which has been an important factor in our inflationary economy. In price-administered industries, sustained demand for the products invites price increases. Both a powerful motive and an easy rationale are provided for the use of this price discretion when wages are raised; and usually the price increase is a little in excess of the added wage costs. The very business executives who see little cause for concern in this upward spiral are the first to use the argument of inflation to discourage the Government's exercise of its rightful powers in the public welfare. As Kenneth Galbraith remarked:

The danger of inflation can be made a powerful argument against things which are opposed on generally conservative grounds. This is now happening. The price of more spending on education, health, defense, foreign aid, or conservation, is, it will be said, more inflation. So to the man who opposes the expansion or improvement in these activities, the person who favors some or all, becomes automatically a spender and an inflationist.[21]

Actually, Professor Galbraith was a participant in an experiment where admonition really worked. During the early 1940's, prior to the establishment of the OPA, the Government relied upon admonition to businessmen to fight inflationary price increases. But the situation then was quite unusual. Not only had the country recently emerged from a devastating economic depression; it was about to embark, as a major participant, on World War II. Further, as Galbraith pointed out, these were not the kind of

. . . open-end or . . . unstructured admonitions which have been emanating from the administration these last several years. These were instructions not to raise prices for any reason without prior consultation with the Government, and with a rather specific promise that if this were done it would be reported to the Congress, and it would become a subject of criticism. So there were both standards and in some degree there were sanctions.[22]

Under a system of free enterprise, it is basically illogical to expect businessmen to subdue the acquisitive urge to social ends. Profit-seeking is the accepted purpose of their undertakings; self-interest is the motivating force that drives them. Does it make sense to admonish business leaders to pursue courses of conduct that may endanger the security of their own corporate domains? Can we really expect executives, steeped in the tradition of "protecting the interests of their stockholders," voluntarily to relinquish opportunities for profit in order to serve the public welfare?

GOVERNMENT REGULATION

Another approach to the problem is Government regulation of price-administered industries. Clearly, society cannot tolerate for long an era in which large industrial aggregates are freed from the automatic restraints imposed by the

[21] *Hearings*, Part 10, p. 4933.
[22] *Ibid.*, p. 4935.

market and no longer subject to the forces that make for competitive behavior. Just as in the days of the monopolistic excesses practiced by the railroads, there will be a public call for action by the Government. And the very existence of a highly concentrated structure in the industry will seem to make this proposal a practicable solution. Professor Lewis told the Subcommittee:

Our giant firms are sitting like fat, delectable ducks, virtually inviting the Government to open fire with something more effective than antitrust. The invitation will be accepted. One cannot even guess at the occasions which will prompt the firing, or the pattern which the firing will take. It will not be laid down in a single, all-embracing, finely articulated barrage. . . . But, the conviction that great power over the economy must reside only in a government of the people will be acted on relentlessly, bluntly, and with force. Events will count more heavily than fine logic in determining the action; but events will surely occur, and public action to repossess the power to economize will surely follow.[23]

Professor Walter Adams said the real question is: "Do you believe that private power should be allowed to have a stranglehold on the public without any supervision, or do you believe that the public should have some supervision over private power?"[24] and added:

My preference is not for Government regulation or Government ownership. My preference is the old-fashioned preference for the competitive marketplace, and I say let's have competition to do as much of the world's work as it possibly can. . . . But if given the choice between absolute power in private hands or in public hands, I must choose the latter, simply because the people at least have the opportunity to elect their representatives. They have no such opportunity to elect the managers of private concentrated economic power.[25]

There is good reason for harboring doubts about the

23 *Iibd.*, p. 4719.
24 *Ibid.*, p. 4797.
25 *Ibid.*, pp. 4797–98.

effectiveness of Government regulation. In setting up the important regulatory agencies that exist today, Congress hoped that their overriding function would be the protection of the public interest in industries where competition was absent. Over the years, however, it has become apparent that, in the press of daily problems, this function has often been obscured or forgotten. Too often the regulatory agencies see themselves as arbiters of intra- or inter-industry disputes; their major concern is to reach a compromise settlement which will be acceptable to the parties directly concerned. Frequently, the issue of whether a decision accords with the interests of the public may never even get raised.

Partly, the problem has been one of the kinds of appointments that have been made to the regulatory commissions. Obviously, the industry subject to regulation is concerned that the commissioners be aware of the complexity of their problems, and have a sympathetic understanding of the difficulties under which they are laboring. Often this has resulted in appointments of individuals with ties in the industry, direct or indirect. Such individuals usually seem to have the technical competence required, and they command strong industry support.

Thus, it is not surprising that the records of the regulatory agencies have sometimes been disappointing. Instead of developing policies making the industry more responsive to public needs, they too often spend their energies protecting fixed investments, freezing obsolete modes of doing business, excluding new entrants from the industry, and perpetuating the existence of high-cost operators. In a word, the regulated take over the regulators, and for all practical purposes, monopoly comes to be elevated to the position of high public policy.

The classic example is the case of the railroads. In recent decades they have been subject to intensive competition both in the passenger and freight fields, and the efforts of the regulatory agency have been primarily directed to softening the impact of this competition. To this end a host of restrictions have been imposed upon the trucking industry. Professor Walter Adams remarked that the ICC "does not protect the public against the industry but protects the industry against the bargaining power of the public." He suggested that the Commission "deregulate such industries as trucking, where competition can do more to protect the public interest than a monopoly-minded commission."[26]

The situation has been graphically illustrated in the proceedings involving railroad merger proposals before the Interstate Commerce Commission. Decisions affecting directly the economic growth of communities, the adequacy of freight and passenger transit, the national defense, and other issues of concern to the public have been made solely on the basis of what evidence may find its way into the legal record. Railroad merger petitioners, represented by highly paid and skillful lawyers, have poured into the cases thousands of pages of complicated testimony and exhibits which were subjected to little critical examination. Other railroads capable of challenging petitioners' cases have either failed to appear or have given token opposition for fear of upsetting their own merger plans and rocking the industry's boat. Other participants such as rail labor, states and municipalities, stockholders, and smaller railroads have struggled to fill the void in these "public interest" records, but their funds and manpower have been so limited and their efforts so disorganized that their presentation, except on briefs, has hardly been effective. As a result of this situation, a special staff group from the Interstate Commerce Commission was moved to state in an official report: ". . . no voice speaks before the Commission for the public as a whole in rail consolidation cases. Thus the question arises as to whether the Commission receives all of the evidence it requires respecting the over-all public interest as differentiated from the various private interests."[27]

[26] *Ibid.*, p. 4785.
[27] *Railroad Consolidations and the Public Interest*, Staff Study by Bureau of Transport Economics and Statistics, ICC, March 1962.

Faced with overburdened records and virtually no effective "public interest" presentation, the Commission at the last minute called into a few cases its enforcement lawyers, largely unschooled in economics and merger issues. But these counsels have remained generally silent during cross-examination and have presented little if any effective evidence to assist the record.

Congress has empowered the Federal Communications Commission among other things to regulate telephone, telegraph, and radio and television communications in this country, the lion's share of which involve the public directly. Here, as in the case of the ICC, vital decisions have been made upon reports or records developed by private vested interests with no coordinated voice of public concern, except that which might be rendered by Commission Counsel in their efforts to get the laws and regulations clarified and enforced. As in the case of the ICC, the existence of "house counsel" within the FCC framework and guided by the agency's policies has not assured adequate legal protection for the public.

The Federal Power Commission—gas and utility rates—and the Civil Aeronautics Board—airline fares and service—have special staff members assigned to test petitioners' cases and to take independent views on issues of public interest. However, the closeness of these staff members to established Commission policies does not make for any assurance that a full record for the public will be made. Certainly in the area of airline travel, there is a great need to preserve the benefits of competition among carriers on as many routes as possible. Such benefits go directly to the consumer in lower rates, better service, and technological innovation.

These are not isolated cases. The same criticism has been leveled at virtually all of the regulatory agencies of the Government. In part, the Congress itself must take some responsibility for their failure to live up to expectations. The independent administrative agencies were set up as arms of the legislative branch of the Government to over-see matters too detailed, technical, and continuous for the deliberative body directly to attend. But someone must also oversee the regulators, and too often this task has received only the most casual attention of the Congress.

In fact, the attention given has on occasion resulted in the defeat of genuine efforts within the administrative agency to protect the interests of the public. In recent years, as the importance of economic decisions by the administrative agencies has become increasingly manifest, real effort has been made to recruit top-flight commissioners. A number of the appointees to the agencies have taken their jobs seriously, and have sought to direct the industries under their supervision in the paths of public interest. But these industries learned long ago that the protection of special interests could be most effectively served when their spokesmen came from Capitol Hill.

THE SPOTLIGHT OF PUBLICITY

In the long run the response of our industrial system to public welfare must depend upon an informed electorate. This task of keeping the public informed is becoming increasingly difficult. The reason does not lie alone in the complexities wrought by the great advances in technology in many industrial areas. It is also due to the fact that, as economic power has become more concentrated in a few hands, secrecy with respect to primary industry and corporate data has increased. The apparent purpose is to preserve the fiction of a multitude of independent firms engaged in competition, even though the reality in many industries has disappeared.

The antitrust actions brought by the Federal Trade Commission and the Department of Justice do not serve the educative function they should. The occasional case of great significance—such as FTC's action on tetracycline or the DuPont case in the Department of Justice—wins the wide public attention it deserves. But the litigative approach to industrial problems, with all the paraphernalia of cross motions, rules of evidence, and the like, tends to obscure the basic economic issues involved. Except for the trade press, there is little newspaper or magazine coverage of most antitrust cases which may involve problems of great economic importance. The result is an ever-widening rift between industrial structure and public understanding.

The antitrust agencies could attempt to fill this gap with economic reports on each of the industries that has been subjected to their critical examination. Had this policy been followed from the beginning, there would now be available a large number of industry analyses which would provide valuable clues, not only on the economic transformations occurring within individual industries, but also on the general drift in the whole economy. Instead, when a case is completed, the data lie untouched in agency files and after a time get carted off to a Government warehouse. The most that can be garnered from the vast effort expended on the case is what shows up in court decisions. And where the case is settled by consent among the parties, all of the economic facts that have been gathered are locked in secrecy within the agency.

The Federal Trade Commission was specifically given the function by Congress to educate the public with a flow of reports on our changing economic structure. As Professor Heinrich Kronstein of Georgetown Law School remarked, the principal purpose of the Federal Trade Commission Act was to extend the work of the Bureau of Corporations established during the administration of Theodore Roosevelt.

Theodore Roosevelt and his friends were deeply convinced that publicity on corporate organization and activities, especially on technological deficiencies in production or distribution, would be a sufficient method of business policing. The Bureau of Corporations was only secondarily interested in the activities of any particular corporation or in prosecuting any criminal, civil, or administrative case against any particular entity or its officers. The Bureau's goal was a structural study of vital industrial fields.

Congress, the executive, and the public should learn to know the economic structure with which they have to deal. Industry itself, however, was considered one of the most interested recipients of information on its own structure.[28]

Thus, Section 6 (a) of the Federal Trade Commission Act of 1914 gives the agency the power

To gather and compile information concerning, and to investigate from time to time the organization, business, conduct, practices, and management of any corporation engaged in commerce, excepting banks and common carriers subject to the Act to regulate commerce, and its relation to other corporations and to individuals, associations, and partnerships.

In the early days of the FTC this function was performed with outstanding success, and the reports to Congress and the public resulted in important legislative action. But, over the years, the legal-case approach has taken precedence in the work of the agency, and there has been a drying-up of the educative function which the Commission was originally designed to serve.

Obviously, any solutions to the complex problems of private restraint and monopoly must be grounded upon factual knowledge of the industrial structure. Yet the Subcommittee on Antitrust and Monopoly had merely to initiate inquiry into a particular industry to discover how scattered and incomplete are the available published data. Ordinarily, cases in the antitrust agencies are instituted only after months of painstaking preparation. Indeed, such cases can rarely be brought without resort, at some point, to the compulsory processes of Government.

Until the last few years this was a serious problem in the Antitrust Division of the Department of Justice. The agency's lack of subpoena power in civil actions necessitated use of criminal grand jury proceedings in order to secure access to essential economic data. This resulted in the institution of criminal actions providing for punitive treatment

[28] *Reporting on Corporate Activities,* 38 U. Det. L. J. 591.

in the event of guilt. Yet the real purpose was to correct trade practices that had gone astray; and often the agency had to institute a second civil action to achieve this result. For decades Justice officials have called this problem to the attention of Congress. In 1961 the Subcommittee held hearings on S. 167, "A bill to authorize the Attorney General to compel the production of documentary evidence required in civil investigations for the enforcement of the antitrust laws." The proposed legislation won the affirmative vote of the Subcommittee and the full Judiciary Committee, and in 1962 was enacted into law by the Congress.

A number of the economic experts testifying before our Subcommittee stressed the urgent need for industrial information. Professor Corwin Edwards, speaking from the vantage point of service in top positions in both of the antitrust agencies, remarked that "We need to have basic facts clear before we can even begin to make sense in developing policy." Even on such an important matter as the extent of concentration existing today in industry, he pointed out that we are operating on bits and pieces of inadequate knowledge.

It is noteworthy that everything done thus far has been *ad hoc* —somebody, somehow, scraped some money together and made a study. There has not been any continuous responsibility, any certainty that there would be recurrent studies at regular intervals on a common plan, and hence there has not been a well-worked-out plan to deal with all the very difficult conceptual and statistical problems that underlie such studies and to deal with them in a way that will win the support and assent of the people who have a legitimate concern with them. Now this means that we still are in the absurd position of having people argue as to whether concentration is increasing or decreasing, and how much.[29]

Professor Edwards also emphasized the need for fuller knowledge of the large corporate entities in this country. We need, as he put it, to know how these companies "hang

[29] *Hearings*, Part 9, p. 4808.

together." The most recent published list of the corporate empires of the thousand largest companies was made by the Federal Trade Commission in 1951. Enormous changes have taken place since that time; firms have merged, subsidiaries have multiplied, corporate reorganizations have taken place. Yet this compilation remains our single, most up-to-date source of information on this subject. Speaking of this problem, Corwin Edwards remarked:

A corporation is, in a sense, a false face behind which there are some real people. People operating in different corporations may constitute a single community of interest. We cannot follow a very sensible policy toward them unless we know that they are really the same people. Now I am not suggesting that business enterprises generally should operate in a goldfish bowl or anything of that sort. I am just saying that the question of who controls or owns a great concern, and to what extent the ownerships and controls interlock, is a part of the question of how concentrated the economy is. And we ought to be able to get intelligible answers to those questions.[30]

One of the most serious attempts to stem the trend toward concentration in this country was the passage of the amendment to Section 7 of the Clayton Act in 1950. This legislation, which I sponsored in the Senate along with Emanuel Celler in the House of Representatives, forbids the acquisition of one firm by another where the effect may be substantially to lessen competition, or to tend to create a monopoly. A number of actions by both antitrust agencies have been instituted under this provision, and several have been successful in halting mergers that would have been harmful to competition. In addition, it must be remembered that, in the area of antitrust enforcement, the full impact of the law is never entirely discernible. In this respect, the effectiveness of the antitrust laws has frequently been likened to a floating iceberg; only a tiny portion protrudes above the surface and is visible to the human eye. No one

[30] *Ibid.*, p. 4811.

can guess how many potential mergers reached the discussion stage and were finally abandoned by the parties because of the Clayton Act amendment, nor how many were summarily dismissed on this ground before negotiations had entered the preliminary stages.

But even in mergers there is a surprising void in essential information. Up to the present no machinery exists in either Government agency concerned with antitrust for the regular reporting of mergers among firms. Instead, there is a studied combing of the trade press and other similar sources for clues and hints of the industrial marriages that are in negotiation or have taken place. No doubt a large number are picked up in this fashion; how many are handled in such a secretive way as never to reach the public press is a matter of speculation. In either event, it would seem that this information is of such moment in the enforcement of the merger provision of the law that a routine Government report program should be inaugurated. It would also offer the advantage of prompt apprisement to the enforcement agencies. Where the properties have been combined and plants disassembled before news of the merger has reached the street, there is often difficulty in restoring the parts to independence.

THE MAINTENANCE OF A COMPETITIVE ORDER

At least up to now no better system has been devised to protect the public than the competitive system. I am not speaking of the mere superficial appurtenances of competition—of the occasions when firms, for public relations purposes, use the rhetoric of competition in rationalizing their conduct, or engage in a little theatrical by-play to prove its existence, or even reach a management decision that some competitive behavior is in order. Nor am I speaking of a competition that is carefully channeled into certain forms such as advertising claims and ornate packaging displays, but which is rigidly barred from the field of price.

The distinct advantage of the market as the instrument

of control is that, in its way, it constitutes a form of representative government. It allows the massive aggregate of the country's consumers to vote their preferences by extending or withholding their custom. And where there is a multitude of independent producers each vying for business, there need be no cause for concern; the market will issue its decree of survival or downfall with utmost impartiality. For the fortunate few who find price a minor factor in the decision to purchase, the luxuries and extra services can be supplied at extravagant charges. For the great mass of people to whom the price tag is of vital importance, the genuinely competitive market will best answer their needs.

The competitive market will also respond more quickly to the industrial revolution which is still proceeding at a headlong pace. The economic transformation that has occurred in the last century has shown us some of the possibilities it can provide for a more abundant life. And, along with the headaches which inevitably accompany change, there is more to come. Fullest and quickest realization of the potentialities of industry can best be achieved in a competitive economy.

It is true that some of our newer technologies require a physical plant of great size. But many of them move in the opposite direction, and are a stimulus to small-plant operations. Furthermore, much of the concentration that exists today is not plant-oriented but relates to corporate control. For example, the 50 largest companies in 1958 accounted for 23 per cent of the total value added by manufacture. In terms of plants, it took the 500 largest plants to reach 20 per cent.[31] This would seem to indicate that corporate size has already far exceeded technological demands regarding plant size. The outstanding example is, of course, the conglomerate firm, in which the corporate empire envelops a

[31] Concentration Ratios in Manufacturing Industry, 1958, Report prepared by the Bureau of Census for the Subcommittee on Antitrust and Monopoly, 87th Cong., 2d Sess. (1962), Part I, p. 8 and pp. 290–91.

host of widely different industrial activities. Here, clearly, there are no technological advantages arising from single-ness of control; the productive unit, know-how in manu-facture, markets to be captured, are all quite distinctive in character.

Current discussions on industrial structure frequently ob-scure the fact that there are real hazards in the fact of size. Yet this aspect of the problem is never ignored in con-nection with Big Business and Big Government. Great emphasis is placed upon the immobility and inflexibility that arise from a huge, sprawling bureaucracy, the inertia that gradually sets in, the inability of the organization to accommodate itself readily to the changing needs of the people who called it into being.

Indeed, this was precisely the problem that worried Adam Smith about industrial bigness in the eighteenth century. Much of his fire was directed against such corporations as the old East India Company and the private joint-stock companies that were just coming into vogue. Except for his manner of speaking and his choice of illustrations, he might easily be talking about administered prices today in highly concentrated industries. Monopoly, as he describes it, con-stitutes a double tax upon the people: "first, by the high price of goods, which, in the case of a free trade, they could buy much cheaper; and, secondly, by their total exclusion from a branch of business, which it might be both con-venient and profitable for many of them to carry on." Because of problems of mismanagement and bureaucratic inflexibility, they could hardly continue to exist except under the sheltered protection of monopoly. So alarmed was Adam Smith about this latter aspect that he set up a few simple rules under which big business could survive where com-petitive conditions prevailed. In essence, industrial opera-tions had to be "capable of being reduced to what is called a routine, or to such a uniformity of method as admits of little or no variation."

Something of the same point in modern dress was made by economic experts before the Antitrust Subcommittee. Professor Machlup remarked that:

. . . these monopolistic restraints of competition eliminate the penalty which competition imposes for inefficiency and inertia, and they thus maintain inefficient management and operation. This we see in many industries where firms are sheltered from the competition of more vigorous firms, or from the competition of newcomers; inefficiency creeps up and the whole economy pays the price.[82]

For many years the aluminum industry in this country was an unchallenged monopoly under the dominion of the Aluminum Company of America. Remedy of the situation involved not only a prolonged antitrust suit that ran on for many years, but during World War II the Federal Government actually financed the development of rival firms to insure adequate supplies. During the hearings this exchange between the chairman and Dr. Walter Adams occurred:

Senator Kefauver: What has been the result of the diffusion of some competition into the aluminum industry? Has it hurt efficiency and raised prices or what has been the tendency?

Dr. Adams: I do not think it has. . . .
As a matter of fact, I would argue that the increase in competition resulting from that diffusion of power has served as a stimulus for firms to be on the constant lookout for ways of increasing efficiency.[83]

Government Encouragement of Monopoly

The passage of the Sherman Act in 1890 was the first formal recognition that economic theory and industrial fact were going their separate ways. It affirmed our national policy that a competitive economy best serves the public

[82] *Hearings on Administered Prices,* Part 10, p. 4953.
[83] *Hearings on Adminstered Prices,* Part 9, p. 4793.

welfare. The government, acting on behalf of the public, was empowered to step in to remove monopolistic roadblocks and restore the competitive play of the market. It could proceed punitively through invocation of fines or imprisonment for offenders; it could also seek correction of offending trade practices through the courts. In addition, the private party injured by the restraints could, under the triple-damage provision, sue the offender and recover threefold the losses he had suffered. The subsequent legislation contained in the Federal Trade Commission Act was designed to supplement and strengthen this basic approach to the monopoly problem.

Why then have monopoly practices continued to flourish? Professor Horace M. Gray provided the answer to the Subcommittee.

Antitrust, when unsupported or nullified by other public policies which shape the economic structure, is a limited and ineffective weapon against the concentration of economic power. In the American institutional system there are many diverse and often contradictory public policies which exercise varying degrees of control over the evolving economic structure. Some of these policies operate to facilitate the concentration of economic power and the development of monopolies; others operate in a contrary direction to inhibit concentration and preserve the free market. Thus, in the total institutional context, there is no simple, unidirectional orientation of institutions toward either monopoly or competition; rather, there is a conflict among institutional forces, some pulling one way, some another.[34]

Professor Corwin Edwards had the same problem in mind when he remarked that the maintenance of competition is "the only major policy of the Federal Government which has no high-level centralized responsibility." He explained:

When you get to questions of the bearing of tax policy, public resource policy, foreign policy, or any other aspect of Government action upon the competitive policy and its effectiveness,

[34] *Administered Prices: A Compendium on Public Policy, op. cit.,* p. 140.

there is no one whose major job it is to look at that problem and make decisions.

Phrasing the whole problem in terms of his own personal experience, he added:

While I was in the Antitrust Division, we found ourselves from time to time thinking that some action of the Secretary of Agriculture, or the Interstate Commerce Commission, or the Department of State, raised problems for competition. We were in the position of trying to negotiate, as staff people with staff people, or via the Government's law office, in matters which were of primary concern to someone else, and there was no one in the cabinet whose function it was to view the entire policy of competition in its various aspects and seek to determine what was best in the light of it.[35]

Dr. Edwin G. Nourse, the Council of Economic Advisors' first chairman in 1946, was concerned with government practice in this area.

Consistent antitrust action, like charity, should begin at home. There is glaring inconsistency when a government pledged to free-competitive enterprise, harbors within itself a great variety of structures and programs which grant immunities or extend disproportionate privileges to special classes or groups. And yet the roster of such discrepancies in our economy is long. It runs from our ancient (but now somewhat moderated) system of protective tariffs to the modern (and growing) array of import quotas and export subsidies. It runs from a patent system originated in the eighteenth century to today's marketing controls and the powers exercised by the Atomic Energy Commission, and Civil Aeronautics Commission, the Interstate Commerce Commission, and the Federal Power Commission in their respective fields of technology. These limitations on industrial competition are implemented by bureaucratic control over the awarding of many and massive Government contracts.[36]

[35] *Hearings*, Part 9, p. 4806–4807.
[36] *Administered Prices: A Compendium on Public Policy, op. cit.*, "Government Discipline of Private Economic Power," p. 249.

Professor Fritz Machlup of Johns Hopkins University said:

I believe the antitrust laws are excellent, and they should be used to the greatest extent possible. But I believe that it is not enough merely to use our antitrust laws. It happens that our Government has done much more to create monopoly than to destroy monopoly. I need refer only to the tariff laws, to the corporation laws, to the patent laws, to the large numbers of franchises and licensing laws in the States and in municipalities. There are features in our tax law which foster concentration.

We have been doing much more to create monopoly than to destroy or reduce monopoly. We are still going on doing it, day after day.[37]

In fact, he suggested, "we go ahead and eliminate a little monopoly here, or a little there, but on the other hand we create monopolistic restraints all the time through restricting imports through raising tariffs, through reducing quotas, through enforcing support prices, through making it more difficult for newcomers to enter industries."

To this current state of affairs, Professor Gray applied the term "the new mercantilism of the late twentieth century." Stimulated by the passage of the Sherman Act, new ways were sought for the achievement of monopoly power; what better method could be found than special grants from the government itself?

Thus, year after year aspirants to monopoly power exerted unrelenting pressure on government for grants of privilege; and year after year government yielded to this pressure, slowly and grudgingly at first, out of deference to the tradition and public hostility, then at an accelerated pace as new and more sophisticated rationalizations were perfected. This movement has resulted in an enormous proliferation and accretion of privilege until today privilege permeates the whole economy and has become the keystone of modern monopoly. Purely private monopoly has, for all practical purposes, ceased to exist except in

[37] *Hearings*, Part 10, pp. 4955–4956.

the backwashes of our society; all monopolies of major significance today rest squarely on some special privilege granted by government.[38]

Dr. Edwin Nourse told the Subcommittee:

Business enterprise in 1962 is free in its competitive discretion in only a highly Pickwickian sense, and the greatest single concentration of economic power over the competitive process rests in the hands of the Federal Government. Every one of these restrictive expedients has been designed to cope with some special problem of the times out of which it grew. But each was engineered by some special group, working through the political process. Many a "joker" or *ex parte* provision was slipped into the original legislation or subsequent administrative rulings. Likewise, many features of our tax system are inimical to fair and effective competition.[39]

Thus it would appear that our national public policy has been greatly weakened by a combination of forces within the Government itself. It is too much to expect a couple of small antitrust agencies, ill-equipped with staff and funds, to carry on the gigantic task of maintaining a competitive system in our economy. And how can this be accomplished when, against a small guerilla corps of enforcement officials, there is arrayed virtually the whole massive machinery of Government?

SOME ILLUSTRATIVE EXAMPLES

Our historical economic literature abounds with references to "the tariff as the mother of trusts," and this charge was frequently heard in the Subcommittee's hearings on public policy. Professor Machlup remarked that if automobile prices appear too high in this country, there is a simple remedy—get rid of the duties. Faced with vigorous competition from abroad, the domestic industry would have to abandon its current emphasis on styling and other non-price forms of

[38] *Administered Prices: A Compendium on Public Policy, op. cit.,* p. 142.
[39] *Ibid.,* pp. 249-250

— 224 —

competition; it would be forced to plunge into price competition. When a protest was made that a reduction in tariff barriers would put high-cost producers out of business and create unemployment, Professor Machlup rejoined that stagecoaches—once the center of a thriving industry—have long since perished.

Indeed, he suggested, this is precisely what is happening in farming. In 1830, about 70 per cent of the labor force was used in agriculture to feed the population of the country. By 1880 it had dropped to 50 per cent and by 1930 to 20 per cent. Today, it is 8 per cent or less. Would anyone propose that in the interest of maintaining jobs the agricultural labor force should have been frozen as of 1830 or 1930?

There are also inescapable consequences of preferential treatment of industry by the Government. A protectionist tariff on lead and zinc does more than permit the high-cost operators to remain in operation and cause a price structure which yields high profits to a few. It is a perpetual invitation to retaliation by other countries. A tariff hike on lead and zinc is met with a ban by Germany on coal imports. So the price of protection of lead and zinc miners is the destruction of jobs in the coal-mining industry. In this connection Professor Machlup cited the famous candlemakers' petition—a clever parody by the French writer Bastiat of the protectionists' arguments. The candlemakers, it seemed, were seeking a ban on the free importation of sunshine, a commodity which seriously injured their operations:

This sunshine is produced abroad entirely free, and dumped into our country without cost. There isn't even a cent charged for it. Now if we follow the principle of cost equalization, we feel that we are justified in asking for a tariff on sunshine, so that everybody who uses sunshine has to pay for it. This would help us candlemakers, we would have a fairer opportunity to compete, people would buy many more candles, and imagine the employment that this would create in our industry, and think of the wages received by our workers. They would energize the whole economy. Our workers would buy textiles, and they would buy food, and thus the farmer would have a better market and the textile industry would be more prosperous, and all the others, too.[40]

Conservation measures constitute another Government sanction used to promote monopoly. The oil industry not only enjoys the protection of mandatory and increasingly stringent quotas on the importation of foreign oil; it has a system built into the governmental structure for controlling the amount of domestic oil produced. At this moment an oil expert employed in the Department of Interior is calculating the demand for oil in this country on a monthly basis, and he makes allocation of the "needed production" among the oil-producing states. Obviously, these predictions are based upon demand *at a given price,* for price is an essential element in the demand equation. Upon this simple structure is built a scheme of control by the producing states; they, in turn, allocate "allowable production" among the wells inside their borders. To enforce this dual program of control, the Federal Government prohibits the shipment of "hot oil" in interstate commerce. Outspoken critics of this scheme charge that here, in the name of conservation, the government lends its vast powers to promote private monopoly. This kind of program is frequently defended on the ground of need for protecting the small units in the industry. But the contribution of the small producers to the country's oil supply is insignificant. The net effect is to provide Government sanction for a structure of high prices under which the few large oil companies become increasingly more affluent.

Even the Government's tax policies are invoked to enhance their positions of power. Whatever may have been the original justification for the favorable treatment of the oil companies under the existing oil depletion allowances, none

[40] *Hearings on Administered Prices,* Part 10, p. 4964.

exists today. Indeed, the tax treatment of the oil companies is now regarded as the prime example of the inequities which have been accorded a virtually sacrosanct status under our jerry-built tax system. The large oil companies are further helped by the American taxpayer through tax reductions on their foreign developments. As one expert ironically remarked to the Subcommittee, "First we help them with tax reductions to develop their foreign production abroad, and then we impose import quotas so that our consumers cannot get the oil they helped to finance. The inconsistency of our policy is appalling."[41]

GOVERNMENT PROCUREMENT

Another area fraught with hazard respecting the maintenance of competition lies in the procurement policies of the Government. Federal purchases of goods and services have, over the years, been rising steadily; in the future they may be expected to constitute about a quarter of the Gross National Product. Obviously the buying policies represented by this segment can have both immediate and long-range impacts upon our whole economy. Indeed, this fact has been apparent to some of our state governments, which have become alarmed at the flight of sizable blocks of procurement contracts from their areas to other states. The industrial activity arising from these contracts can spell the difference between financial solvency and state deficits, as well as minimal or serious unemployment problems in the affected states. It is no wonder, then, that states have sent representatives to Washington to discover how to effect shifts from the production of conventional military hardware, which is rapidly becoming obsolete, to the newer types of procurement contracts.

The military mind, of course, has little interest in the effect of its procurement policies upon the industrial structure of this country. Some critics have suggested that, in

[41] Professor Machlup in *Hearings on Administered Prices*, Part 10, p. 4958.

the name of saving democracy, the military appears often ready to sacrifice the very institutions that give it reality. In any event, the predisposition to award military procurement contracts to the country's largest corporations is of long standing and has been a source of perpetual concern to the Congress. To correct this inequity, Congress created the Small Business Administration, and officials of the important agencies of procurement have pledged their efforts to see to it that smaller corporations will have opportunity to secure government contracts.

On the whole the results have been disappointing. Despite the efforts that have been made, only a small fraction of the contracts go to small business. In the fiscal year 1961, for example, the Department of Defense awarded $23 billion dollars in contracts for work in the U.S.; about 16 per cent went to small business in the country, and most of this was concentrated in transactions of less than $10,000.[42]

The situation with respect to the Government's research and development contracts is even more alarming. Obviously, companies that grasp control of the new technologies will sit in the driver's seat in their industries for some years to come. Until recently research fell primarily within the domain of private enterprise. Today the scene is dominated by the Federal Government. Roughly, of the $15 billion dollars spent for research and development by all sources in 1961, the Federal Government alone contributed about two-thirds. In simple terms, this means that every person in the country has made substantial contributions to Federal funds allocated to research. Surely, this fact gives the public a vital stake in how these funds are handled and their effect upon the whole economy. This is particularly true because, though the military is the largest spender, much of the research work involved has, or will have, direct application to civilian use.

[42] Hearings before the Joint Economic Committee, 87th Cong., 2d Sess., *State of the Economy and Policies for Full Employment* (1962), Testimony of Dr. Richard J. Barber, Professor of Law, Southern Methodist University, p. 860.

The current handling of Government funds for research provides serious hazards to the maintenance of a competitive economy. The bulk of the funds spent by the military goes, of course, to private industry; in 1959, 100 large corporations received about 80 per cent. Yet these same firms accounted for only 41 per cent of total sales within their respective industrial categories.[43] In a word, though these companies are today dominant in their fields, there is every promise that they will be more dominant tomorrow.

This fact arises from the manner in which inventions based on Government-financed research are currently handled. It would seem only common sense that, if the public contributes the funds for research, it is entitled to the benefits. If discoveries culminate in the issuance of patents, title should reside in the hands of those who paid for the work. This policy is accepted practice in private industry. A research scientist who joins the employ of General Electric or Boeing or Bell Telephone must assign his discoveries to his employer. He performs the work and is paid for his services, but his employer takes title to the inventions. The agencies of the Federal Government, for the most part, follow a different policy. The private corporate contractees receive the funds for the research work; they are paid a fee for their services; and then they are allowed to retain title to the research discoveries.

Speaking of this problem, Professor Alfred E. Kahn of Cornell University remarked:

Where the public interest in the area of technology in question is sufficiently great, taxpayer-supported research is superior to private, patent-oriented and patent-rewarded research as a method of achieving technological progress consistent with competition. It obviously follows that patents ought not to accrue to the private contractors who conduct such research, except where it can be demonstrated that the innovations would not be forthcoming without this incentive. The general policy of the Department of Defense, of permitting private businesses as a matter of

[43] *Ibid.*, p. 861.

course to take out patents on the results of taxpayer-financed research, would certainly seem to conflict with the basic rationale of public financing—one fundamental reason for which is the desirability of making the fruits of such efforts freely available to all comers.[44]

The situation would be less serious if the Government's research contracts were equitably distributed among large and small companies. This would at least establish the possibility that, in the crucial issue of access to the new technologies, the smaller firms would have a fighting chance to gain entry. As the situation now stands, however, they are increasingly being pushed aside to make room for their bigger rivals. It is impossible at this moment to assess the ultimate cost of this policy upon our economy; certainly it cannot help but have very vital consequences in terms of alterations of our entire economic structure.

The argument, of course, is that the present external threat does not permit of time for the niceties in maintaining balance among competitive forces in our industrial system. But does not this argument really beg the question? If we are concerned with maintaining a free competitive economy, can we—in the name of preserving that economy—surrender its existence without even a struggle? Can we afford to take a public stand on the need for preserving a free competitive system, and yet use the enormous powers of the Government establishment to chip away at its very foundations?

The antitrust agencies are, of course, powerless in this area. As Professor Gray remarked:

If government procurement operates in disregard of antitrust policy there is not much that the antitrust agencies can do about it. They cannot challenge the procurement authorities; nor can they challenge a procurement contract, however monopolistic its character, when the Government is a party to the contract. The right of Congress to authorize programs and to appropriate

[44] "Public Policies Affecting Market Power," *Administered Prices: A Compendium on Public Policy, op. cit.,* pp. 173–74.

money therefor, and the right of the Executive to spend the money so authorized and appropriated, are sovereign powers superior to police statutes, such as the antitrust laws. If the two powers are to be coordinated and directed toward the common goal of preserving free competition then Congress must change the laws governing procurement to compel the procurement agencies to operate on competitive principles. This would contribute mightily to shifting the institutional balance away from monopoly and toward competition.[45]

THE PATENT GRANT

No discussion of Government restraints on competition can omit reference to patents as an instrument of private monopoly. Interestingly enough, our Constitution makes no reference to the word "patent"; it simply endows Congress with the power "to promote the progress of science and useful arts by securing for limited times to authors and inventors the exclusive rights to their respective writings and discoveries." The form these "exclusive rights" are to take is left to Congress, and the Congress may redefine them at any time. Thus there is nothing sacrosanct in the present statutory term of seventeen years for a patent to run; nor is there anything to prevent re-examination and modification of other provisions if the Congress determines that such changes are in the public interest.

At the time of the writing of the Constitution, considerable doubt was expressed concerning the social desirability of granting exclusive rights under patents. A number of early inventors of eminence actually refused to take out patents. Speaking of an invention of his stove, Benjamin Franklin wrote:

Gov'r Thomas was so pleas'd with the construction of this stove, as described . . . that he offered to give me a patent for the sole vending of them for a term of years; but I declined it from a principle which has ever weighed with me on such occasions, viz., That, as we enjoy great advantages from the inventions of

[45] *Administered Prices: A Compendium on Public Policy, op. cit.,* p. 149.

others, we should be glad of an opportunity to serve others by any inventions of ours; and this we should do freely and generously.[46]

Thomas Jefferson, at the time of his invention of the hemp-break, took positive steps to prevent the issuance of a patent. He wrote a friend:

Something of this kind has been so long wanted by cultivators of hemp, that as soon as I can speak of its effect with certainty, I shall probably describe it anonymously in the public papers in order to forestall the prevention of its use by some interloping patentee.[47]

Jefferson himself entertained grave doubts as to the basic premise inherent in the patent grant. On one occasion he remarked that "other nations have thought that these monopolies produce more embarrassment than advantage to society; and it may be observed that the nations which refuse monopolies of invention are as fruitful as England in new and useful devices.[48]

This basic question received much attention in the Subcommittee's drug hearings. Officials of the major companies placed great stress, in their testimony, on the importance of patents in the development of new drug products. Dr. W. G. Malcolm, president of American Cyanamid Company, aptly reflected their views when he told the Subcommittee:

Progress in our industry is dependent on patents. The availability of patent protection for new drugs provides the incentive to invest in research and development that has given the public the enormous benefits of drugs developed under the lash of intense rivalry. In our own case, the possibility of patent protection has been essential in inducing us to invest heavily in research.[49]

During the Subcommittee's hearings, staff exhibits were presented showing the country of origin for many of the

[46] *Writings of Benjamin Franklin,* Albert H. Smith, ed., 1907, p. 370.
[47] *Writings of Thomas Jefferson,* Vol. 6 (H. A. Washington ed., 1854), p. 506.
[48] *Ibid.,* p. 181.
[49] *Hearings,* Part 24, p. 13649.

world's most important drug contributions. A very substantial number were of foreign origin. Dr. Chauncey D. Leake professor of pharmacology at Ohio State University, testified:

Up to World War I, we were dependent almost entirely upon foreign drugs. The interrelations of the drugs, dye and explosives industry were important factors in the preparation of Germany for its aggressive action in World War I. After World War I, we found it possible to develop an independent American drug industry.[50]

Dr. Austin Smith, speaking on behalf of the Pharmaceutical Drug Manufacturers Association, had also spoken of "American drug progress which has been great only in the last twenty years."[51]

This fact raises some interesting questions. The United States has had on its statute books since 1793 the most stringent patent law of any country in the world. The European countries have generally taken the position that public health is of such paramount concern to the national welfare that patents in the pharmaceutical field fall in a special category and warrant exceptions from the usual treatment accorded to patent grants. To this end, patents in most European countries are permitted on processes of manufacture but not on drug products, and provision is made for compulsory licensing if the process is not "worked" or if such licensing would serve "the public interest" or enhance the "public health."

In contrast, the United States has, for the last 170 years, permitted the patenting not only of drug processes but also drug products. It has never adopted the compulsory licensing provision, prevalent in Europe, which is designed to protect the public health from the abuses of monopoly. But if patents granting exclusive rights of exploitation are the key to the unlocking of important drug discoveries, why has

50 *Hearings,* Part 18, p. 10415.
51 *Hearings,* Part 19, p. 10836.

it functioned effectively in this country only for the twenty years? Can it be that there are other factors of far greater significance, such as the state of the industrial arts, the particular form of economic development occurring within the country?

The fact is that, in the present state of technological advance in our society, the private monopoly created by patents constitutes one of the most formidable obstacles to competition. If exclusive rights were limited, as was the original intent of the framers of the Constitution, to the novel and brilliant insight of a highly creative mind, that would be one thing. Ordinarily such inventions are the result of efforts by a multitude of minds—often located in different countries— working on the frontier of the particular technology. Speaking of radar, the eminent British scientist C. P. Snow remarked that by 1940 "English, American and German scientists had all begun developing radar at about the same time —which incidentally tells one something of the nature of 'secret' discoveries."[52]

Where an important invention is the product of a number of minds working in different research laboratories, too often the reward of a patent goes to the individual or corporation most alert in the acquisitive arts. The effect is to penalize all others who make a contribution, and sometimes to stifle the continuance of their work. The ultimate result is to deprive society of the benefits of developments that would have occurred had these others had freedom to continue. In cases where a technology takes years to perfect, with the accretion of knowledge supplied by a multitude of research workers, the patent reward often goes to the perfector of the final step in the discovery. Thus the effect is to give him a monopoly on a product or process which is the end result of many contributions from diverse sources.

Private privilege, in whatever form it manifests itself,

[52] C. P. Snow, *Science and Government* (New York: Mentor Books, 1962), p. 44.

tends to dig in and broaden its base of operations. The Congress which enacted the first patent statute in 1793 could hardly have envisioned the present corporate practice of "portfolios of patents" blanketing an entire technology. Patents are secured on minor changes in the art; they are carefully spaced so that corporate control is never lost; they can, with ingenuity, be used to exclude competition indefinitely. Many of the patents may be completely worthless and would be declared invalid in the courts. Indeed, those that have been tested in litigation have, on the whole, fared badly. But defense of an infringement suit by a small firm is a costly undertaking; one may emerge a victor in the legal fray but be vanquished financially.

A primary statutory requirement is that the patent fully disclose the new art. The Commissioner of Patents informed the Subcommittee that "Even during the monopoly, the disclosure—the knowledge—is public; and serves as a basis and a spur for further invention."[53] However, the U. S. Patent Office lacks the resources to police this provision, and, more often than not, in the array of technical steps listed in the patent, a key step is lacking. This failure to disclose fully is a common complaint of the smaller producers, for even when the patent finally expires great difficulties are encountered in unraveling the technical steps, and considerable expense may be involved. During the Subcommittee's administered-price hearings, Professor Kahn proposed a number of patent reforms to protect the public interest more fully. The first on his list was that patents should be promptly rescinded "when they fail to disclose sufficient technical information to permit the working of the invention by qualified persons."[54] Others provided for the issuance of patents of varying terms, particularly "petty patents" involving minor innovations, and compulsory licensing at reasonable royalties "if not worked after some period of time." He also suggested:

[53] *Hearings on S. 1552*, Part 3, p. 1198.
[54] *Administered Prices: A Compendium on Public Policy, op. cit.,* p. 173.

If patent licenses are offered to one firm they should have to be offered to all applicants at reasonable royalties, and free of price, output or territorial restrictions. The same should be true of all patents acquired by purchase. This means also that membership in all patent pools should in effect be open to all applicants. These various provisions might be made to apply only in instances where the patents, licenses or pools in question confer dominance in some relevant market.

Years ago the Congress provided the machinery for settlement of arguments among contestants as to who is entitled to the patent. The Patent Office declares an interference; all of the evidence is presented to the patent examiner who acts as a judge in the dispute. His judgment, subject to appeal, settles the issue as to which applicant was first in the discovery. In the course of the drug hearings, the Subcommittee was surprised to discover that this procedure is often bypassed. Instead, the practice has developed under which the parties to the contest meet privately and arrive at their own determination. One applicant is chosen to secure the patent; all others withdraw their applications; and, lacking a controversy, the Patent Office proceeds automatically to issue the patent to the one remaining party. Invariably the private arrangement includes an agreement that all parties to the controversy are to be licensed, often on a royalty-free basis and with the additional proviso that outsiders are to be denied licenses.

Obviously, this kind of procedure provides opportunity for real abuse. The private parties have everything to gain by stretching the monopoly grant as far as possible. It is to their interest to work out as tight a market control as possible. Yet under these circumstances the Government, which grants this exception to our national policy respecting competition, does not participate in the negotiations; the public is unrepresented and is not even informed of the terms of the private settlement.

This problem was so flagrantly evident in the drug hearings that the original bill contained a provision that all interference settlement agreements in this industry were to be placed in the public record of the Patent Office. The provision was referred to the Patents Subcommittee and the subsequent legislation passed by the Congress required such agreements in all industries to be filed with the Patent Office. Restrictions were, however, placed upon public access to these documents, which may nullify the usefulness of the provision.

In many industries it has become common practice for monopolistic conditions to be established even before the patent has issued. The defense usually presented to justify such agreements based on patent applications is that an exchange of technology and know-how is involved, and that the presence or absence of a patent is irrelevant. In fact, however, these agreements go far beyond the fixing of compensation for access to technology; they establish the commercial pattern for monopoly exploitation of the product. When the patent finally is issued by the Patent Office, it provides the ultimate sanction for a tight marketing structure that is already in operation.

In this kind of situation, the seventeen-year limitation on the patent grant becomes meaningless. The statutory term does not begin to run until the issuance of the patent; the monopoly conditions built upon agreements based on patent applications do not count in the calculations.

The Future of the Economy

We can drift with the tide, or we can attempt to steer a course. Our industrial advancement occurred during a period of relative economic freedom when a whole continent was steadily being opened up for conquest. The open market played a dominant role in providing opportunity for talent, for novel ideas in production and merchandising, for new ways of doing things. Without this kind of industrial viability, a kind of rigor mortis sets in. For society, like the members that make it up, cannot for long maintain a state of equilibrium; in a complex industrial world such as ours, failure to move forward means—for all practical purposes —a few steps backward. The tremendous industrial vitality currently being manifested in some countries abroad suggests their recognition of this fact. They are profiting from our preachments of the values of a competitive economy just at the moment when, in many areas, we appear to be turning our backs on it.

As Professor Lewis remarked, "The economic system in operation in any country at any time represents the way in which the people of that country, at that time and as they are then persuaded, want the economizing function in their society to be performed." He explained:

. . . Any economic system—market, Marxist, or mixed—involves control by society over the behavior of individuals. Its weapons and sanctions may be direct or indirect, sharp or blunt, but their function is clear: to make individuals behave as society wants them to behave and as they would be quite unlikely to behave in the absence of society's economic controls. It is the function of controls to control, to be unpleasant and even to hurt; and so to affect the actions of individuals. This is true both of the directives and legal penalties of authoritarian systems and the price-cost directives and coercion by competition that characterize free enterprise. Whatever the arrangements and forces, they represent the application of socially sanctioned power to behavior of individuals: they can properly express no will or purpose other than the will and purpose of society.[55]

It is difficult to believe that this country will, for long, tolerate an industrial organization in which control over basic economic policy is lodged in the hands of officials of a few private corporations. Our traditions of a free, democratic society are too deep-rooted; the strain of Populist philosophy, too widely disseminated; the values involved, too great. We have an historical antagonism toward living our lives within the metes and bounds of the benefactions be-

[55] *Hearings,* Part 9, p. 4710.

stowed on the many by the select few. If mistakes are to be made—and they will be made—let them be made in the context of democratically organized society in which we all have a voice. Just as there is no end to the task of making our social institutions responsive to the needs of the people, so it is with the equally arduous job of maintaining a competitive economy.

NOTE

The footnotes in the book refer to the following documents:

Hearings on Administered Prices before the Subcommittee on Antitrust and Monopoly of the Committee on the Judiciary, U.S. Senate:

Opening Phase: Economists' Views, Part 1, 1957
Steel, Parts 2-4, 1957
Asphalt Roofing, Part 5, 1958
Automobiles, Parts 6-7, 1958
1958 Steel Price Increase, Part 8, 1958
Administered Price Inflation: Alternative Public Policies
    Parts 9-10, 1959
Price Notification Legislation, Part 11, 1959
Bread Industry, Part 12, 1959
Identical Bidding (TVA), Part 13, 1959
Drugs, Parts 14-26, 1959-1961
Drug Industry Antitrust Act, S. 1552, Parts 1-7, 1961-1962.

Hearings before the Committee of the Judiciary, U.S. Senate on Refusal of Certain Steel Companies to Respond to Subpenas, 1962.

Economic Reports, Senate Subcommittee on Antitrust and Monopoly:

Concentration in American Industry, 1957
Administered Prices, Steel, 1958
Administered Prices, Automobiles, 1958
Administered Prices, Bread, 1960
Administered Prices, Drugs, 1961
Concentration Ratios in Manufacturing Industry, 1958,
    Parts 1-2, 1962

All documents available from Superintendent of Documents, U.S. Government Printing Office, Washington 25, D.C.

INDEX

Achromycin, 26, 30

Adams, Walter, 46, 195-196, 203, 208, 210, 220

AFL-CIO, 141

Agriculture, Dept. of, 202

Agriculture, Sec'y of, 222

Alien Property Custodian, 47

Allen & Co., 43

Aluminum Co. of America, 220

American Bakeries Corp., 148, 149, 155

American Cyanamid Co., 26, 29, 232

American Economic Assoc., 95

American Heart Assoc., 61

American Home Products Corp., 24 n., 25, 41, 45, 47

American Iron & Steel Institute, 107 n.

American Medical Assoc., 72-77

AMA *Journal,* 60, 62, 73-76

American Motors Corp., 83, 90, 101-102

Antitrust Division (Justice Dept.), 87, 119, 156, 214, 222

Armco Steel Corp., 109, 110

Arvin, Calif., 179-183

Arvin and Dinuba Study, 178-183

Atomic Energy Commission, 222

Aureomycin, 26, 202

Automobile Manufacturers Assoc., 97

Bakery and Confectionery Workers union, 141-142

Barber, Richard J., 228 n.

Bastiat, Claude, 225-226

Bean, William, 49, 51

Bell Telephone Co., 229

Bethlehem Steel Corp., 109-113, 119-121, 126, 132-134

Bethlehem-Youngstown merger, 134

Blackman, Seymour, 16-18, 38

Blair, John M., 190 n.

Blough, Roger, 121-123, 125-126, 131-132

Boeing Co., 229

Bowes, James E., 48-49, 50

Bristol Co., 26, 29

Brown, Francis, 13-16

Brush, Alvin G., 25

Campbell-Taggart Associated Bakeries, 144, 145, 150, 157, 158

Carroll, Sen. John A., 46

Carter Products Co., 24 n., 24-25, 31-32, 41, 45, 47

Celler, Rep. Emanuel, 216

Census, Bureau of, 218 n.

Chase Chemical Co., 20

Checker Co., 83

Chemical Fund *Newsletter,* 36

Chevrolet, 87, 90, 102

chloramphenicol, 66, 202

Chloromycetin, 66-68, 202

chlortetracycline, 202

Chrysler Corp., 83, 88, 90, 92, 93, 95, 98-99, 100

CIBA Pharmaceutical Products, Inc., 19, 21-23, 35, 42, 69

Civil Aeronautics Board, 211, 222

Clayton Act, 113, 216-217

Community Chest, 165

Compazine, 23, 35, 44

Connor, John T., 37, 39, 42-43

Console, A. Dale, 49-50, 65-66

Consumers, Office of, 105, 160

Consumers Union, 94

Continental Baking Co., 140, 142, 144, 145, 147, 148, 155, 157, 158

Corporations, Bureau of, 213

cortisone, 11, 13

Decadron, 16

Defense, Dept. of, 228, 229

Deronil, 16

DeWind, Loren T., 53-55

Dexedrine, 18

Estes Kefauver was born in Madisonville, Tennessee, in 1903. After graduating from the University of Tennessee and the Yale Law School, he practiced law in Chattanooga. In 1939 he was elected as a Democrat to the U. S. House of Representatives where he served until his election to the U. S. Senate in 1948. In 1956 he was the Democratic nominee for Vice-President.

During his career in the Congress he won widespread recognition for his conduct of investigations in the public interest. In 1950, as chairman of a special committee of the Senate, he conducted the famous "crime hearings"; in 1957, as chairman of the Senate Subcommittee on Antitrust and Monopoly, he embarked on hearings on administered prices in industry. These were still in process when he died on August 10, 1963.

At the time of his death, Senator Kefauver had largely completed the first draft of this book; it was finished by Dr. Irene Till, an economist and teacher who worked actively with the Senator in the preparation and conduct of the administered price hearings.

PELICAN BOOK
A760
IN A FEW HANDS:
MONOPOLY POWER IN AMERICA
ESTES KEFAUVER

Estes Kefauver was born in Madisonville,
Tennessee, in 1903. After graduating from the
University of Tennessee and the Yale Law
School, he practiced law in Chattanooga. In
1939 he was elected as a Democrat to the U. S.
House of Representatives where he served
until his election to the U. S. Senate in 1948.
In 1956 he was the Democratic nominee
for Vice-President.

During his career in the Congress he won
widespread recognition for his conduct of
investigations in the public interest. In 1950,
as chairman of a special committee of the
Senate, he conducted the famous "crime
hearings"; in 1957, as chairman of the Senate
Subcommittee on Antitrust and Monopoly,
he embarked on hearings on administered prices
in industry. These were still in process
when he died on August 10, 1963.

At the time of his death, Senator Kefauver had
largely completed the first draft of this book;
it was finished by Dr. Irene Till, an economist
and teacher who worked actively with the
Senator in the preparation and conduct of the
administered price hearings.